Public participation in sustainability science.

This book discusses how citizens can participate more effectively in sustainability science and environmental policy debates. It discusses designs for participatory procedures, and experiences of their application to issues of global change. While the focus is on citizen participation, the involvement of specific stakeholders – including water managers and venture capitalists – is also addressed. The book describes how focus group methods were combined with the interactive use of computer models into new forms of participation, tested with six hundred citizens. The results are discussed in relation to important sustainability topics, including greenhouse gas and water management. By combining this with an examination of issues of interactive governance and developing country participation, the book provides state-of-the-art, practical insights for students, researchers and policy-makers alike.

BERND KASEMIR is a research fellow at the John F. Kennedy School of Government at Harvard University. He is also a Director of SustainServ Consulting, Zurich, and of the Sustainable Mobility Intelligence Group, Boston.

JILL JÄGER is the former Executive Director of the International Human Dimensions Programme on Global Environmental Change (IHDP), Bonn.

CARLO JAEGER is Head of the Social Systems Department at the Potsdam Institute for Climate Impact Research (PIK), and Professor of Modelling Social Systems at the University of Potsdam.

MATTHEW GARDNER is Program Administrator of the Earth System Initiative at the Massachusetts Institute of Technology (MIT). He is also a Director of the Sustainable Mobility Intelligence Group, Boston.

Public Participation in Sustainability Science.

A Handbook

Edited by

Bernd Kasemir, Jill Jäger, Carlo C. Jaeger,
and Matthew T. Gardner

CAMBRIDGE
UNIVERSITY PRESS

PUBLISHED BY THE PRESS SYNDICATE OF THE UNIVERSITY OF CAMBRIDGE
The Pitt Building, Trumpington Street, Cambridge CB2 1RP, United Kingdom

CAMBRIDGE UNIVERSITY PRESS
The Edinburgh Building, Cambridge CB2 2RU, UK
40 West 20th Street, New York, NY 10011-4211, USA
477 Williamstown Road, Port Melbourne, VIC 3207, Australia
Ruiz de Alarcón 13, 28014 Madrid, Spain
Dock House, The Waterfront, Cape Town 8001, South Africa

http://www.cambridge.org

© Cambridge University Press 2003

This book is in copyright. Subject to statutory exception
and to the provisions of relevant collective licensing agreements,
no reproduction of any part may take place without
the written permission of Cambridge University Press.

First published

Printed in the United Kingdom at the University Press, Cambridge

Typeface Plantin 10/12 pt   *System* LaTeX 2_ε [TB]

A catalogue record for this book is available from the British Library

ISBN 0 521 81818 4 hardback
ISBN 0 521 52144 0 paperback

Contents

Notes on contributors

CHRIS ANASTASI currently holds a visiting professorship at the University of Maastricht, and is Senior Environmental Advisor for British Energy plc. He was educated at the Universities of London and Cambridge before joining Shell Research Ltd in 1977 where he led a number of energy and environment related projects. In 1985, he set up and ran an environmental research group at the University of York, and worked in Strategic Planning in Shell International in 1993 and 1995, first as consultant and subsequently as Senior Advisor on Environment and Technology. He returned to the University of York in 1996.

KAREN BAKKER is currently a Research Fellow in Water and Environmental Management at Jesus College and the Oxford Centre for Water Research at the University of Oxford, and formerly a post-doctoral Research Fellow at the Environmental Change Institute, University of Oxford. Her research interests include water privatization, water and development, the impact of climate change on water resources, and public participation in water management.

TOM R. BURNS is Professor of Sociology at the University of Uppsala, Sweden. He is the founder of the Uppsala Theory Circle at the Department of Sociology in Uppsala. Burns has published several books and numerous articles in the areas of social and institutional theory, a new theory of games, and evolutionary theory. His empirical research is in the areas of the comparative analysis of organizations, the sociology of technology and environment, and political sociology. His current research concerns the evolution of democracy as well as lobbying and policy-making in the EU, and the legal and ethical impacts resulting from the development of biotechnologies.

URS DAHINDEN holds a Ph.D. in Sociology and is currently a lecturer at the Institute of Mass Communication and Media Research (IPMZ), University of Zurich, Switzerland. His research interests include risk and science communication, the methodology of public participation, and new information and communication technologies such as the Internet. At the time of the research discussed here, he was a research associate at the Swiss Federal Institute for Environmental Science and Technology (EAWAG) and, in 1997, a Visiting Research Fellow at the Center for the Integrated Study of the Human Dimensions of Global Change, Carnegie Mellon University, Pittsburgh, PA, USA.

ÉRIC DARIER is currently working for Greenpeace Canada. At the time of this research, he was working at the Centre for the Study of Environmental Change at Lancaster University (England). His scholarly work has been published in various journals, and he has edited a book on the impacts of Michel Foucault on the studies of environment (*Discourses of the Environment*, 1999). His most recent publication is a chapter in William Leiss *et al.* (ed.) (*In the Chamber of Risks: Understanding Risk Controversies*, 2001).

BRUNA DE MARCHI is the head of the Mass Emergencies Program (PEM) at the Institute of International Sociology of Gorizia (ISIG), Italy. She also teaches a course in Environmental Risk at the University of Trieste and is a consultant to many state and regional agencies, in Italy and elsewhere. Her main research interests are in the sociology of disasters, human dimensions of environmental change, risk perception, risk communication, governance, and public participation, and she has published widely in these areas. She has great experience in fieldwork and expertise in different research techniques including surveys, in-depth interviews, and focus groups, also in combination with ICT.

THOMAS DOWNING (Stockholm Environment Institute, Oxford office) focuses on topics related to the impact of climatic variations: extreme events and climate change; drought and food security in developing countries; and vulnerability and the human dimensions of global change. He is a Director of the UK Climate Impacts Programme and Chair of the International Geographical Union's Commission on Vulnerable Food Systems. He edited *Climate Change and World Food Security* (1996) and *Coping with Drought in Kenya* (1989).

SILVIO FUNTOWICZ taught mathematics, logic and research methodology in Buenos Aires, Argentina. During the 1980s he was a Research Fellow at the University of Leeds, England. He is now Head of the Knowledge Assessment Methodologies Sector at the European Commission Joint Research Center. He is the author of *Uncertainty and Quality in Science for Policy* (1990) in collaboration with Jerry Ravetz, and numerous papers in the field of environmental and technological risks and policy-related research. He is a member of the editorial board of several publications, is on the scientific committee of many international conferences, and has lectured extensively.

MATTHEW GARDNER served as Education Program Coordinator at the Laboratory for Energy and the Environment at the Massachusetts Institute of Technology (MIT). In that role, he helped to establish an education, outreach and training program that helps disseminate the knowledge and results from MIT's cutting edge environmental research programs to the most appropriate audiences. He also served as a founding member of the Task Force on Environmental Education of the Alliance for Global Sustainability, a research alliance of MIT, The Swiss Federal Institute of Technology, Zurich, the University of Tokyo, and Chalmers University of Technology.

ÅSA GERGER SWARTLING is Research Associate at the Stockholm Environment Institute (SEI), Sweden. She holds a M.Phil. in Sociology at the University of York. Her main research interests include sociology of science and participatory research in the field of environmental policy and management.

CONSUELO GIANSANTE is currently a consultant in water and natural resources management. Her background is in biology (BSc Biology, University of Milan, Italy; DEA, Université Paris VII, France) and natural resources management (MSc Conservation, University College London, United Kingdom). She has been research assistant at University College London and the University of Seville and has been involved in several projects on integrated river basin management and drought management practices. She is currently finalizing her Ph.D. thesis at the University of Barcelona (UAB) on the application of multicriteria analysis to water management options in the Lower Guadalquivir Basin.

CLAIR GOUGH is a Research Associate at Manchester School of Management, UMIST and at the Tyndall Centre for Climate Change Research, UK. Her involvement in the research described in this volume was during her time at the EC Joint Research Center, Ispra, Italy. She has worked on developing indicators for social aspects of sustainability, scenario development, participatory integrated assessment and integrated assessment modeling for acidification. She is a member of the European Forum for Integrated Assessment.

ROBIN GROVE-WHITE is Professor at the Institute for Environment, Philosophy and Public Policy at Furness College, Lancaster University, UK, and is also the Chair of Lancaster University's Centre for the Study of Environmental Change (CSEC). Previously, he has held positions as Senior Research Fellow in Environmental Research Policy at Lancaster University and as Research Fellow at the Centre for Environmental Technology at Imperial College, London. From 1981 to 1987 he was Director of the Council for the Protection of Rural England, London. His research interests include the development and implementation of new and original social science-based approaches to 'environmental' research.

ÂNGELA GUIMARÃES PEREIRA obtained a Ph.D. in Environmental Engineering at the New University of Lisbon (Portugal) in collaboration with the European Commission's Joint Research Centre (EC-JRC) in Italy. Since January 1998 she has held the position of Scientific Officer of the EC-JRC at the Institute for the Protection and Security of the Citizen. Her activities relate to research, design, and implementation of ICT for public involvement in decision processes, participating in European research projects within the framework of Integrated and Knowledge Assessment and Science and Governance.

MATTHIJS HISSCHEMÖLLER has a background in political science. He worked as a research associate at the University of Amsterdam, Leiden University, and Erasmus University Rotterdam. He was a visiting Fulbright scholar at the University of Pittsburgh (1990) where he did his Ph.D. research. Since 1992 he has been affiliated with the Institute for Environmental Studies (Vrije Univesiteit Amsterdam). His main research interests are problem structuring in environmental policy, the utilization of scientific knowledge by policy actors and the effectiveness of International Environmental Agreements. He was project leader of the National Dialogue of the Dutch Climate OptiOns for the Long term (COOL)-project.

CARLO C. JAEGER is Head of the Social Systems department at the Potsdam Institute for Climate Impact Research (PIK), and Professor of Modeling Social Systems at the University of Potsdam, Germany. He holds a Ph.D. in economics and an MA in sociology. He was the co-ordinator of the ULYSSES project, and at that time both Research Director of the Human Ecology Division at the Swiss Federal Institute for Environmental Science and Technology (EAWAG) and Professor of Sociology at Darmstadt University, Germany. His main research interests are the integrated assessment of climatic risks and water problems, and issues of modeling socioeconomic systems.

JILL JÄGER is the former Executive Director of the International Human Dimensions Programme on Global Environmental Change (IHDP). She received her Ph.D. in climatology from the University of Colorado, and has been a consultant on energy, environment, and climate for numerous national and international organizations. From 1991 to 1994 she was Director of the Climate Policy Division of the Wuppertal Institute for Climate, Environment and Energy. From 1994 to 1998, she was Deputy Director for Programs, and then Deputy Director, of the International Institute for Applied Systems Analysis (IIASA), Laxenburg, Austria. She participated in the ULYSSES project while she was at IIASA, and subsequently as a consultant to IIASA.

BERND KASEMIR holds a Ph.D. in theoretical physics, has worked extensively on socioeconomic research of global change, and received management education at the International Institute for Management Development (IMD), Lausanne, Switzerland. His main research interest is the role of business in sustainable development, with a focus on the financial industry. He was responsible as project manager for the ULYSSES project. At that time, he was a research associate at the Swiss Federal Institute for Environmental Science and Technology (EAWAG). Currently, he is a Founding Director of SustainServ, a sustainability consulting group, and a research fellow at the John F. Kennedy School of Government, Harvard University.

KATE LONSDALE (Ph.D., Sheffield Hallam University, 1994, MSc Manchester University, 1990; BA, Oxford University, 1989) works on vulnerability and stakeholder participation issues at the Stockholm Environment Institute (Oxford office). Her research currently focuses on global climate change and livelihood security. She coordinates the International Geographical Union's Task Force on Vulnerability. She is also an active member of the Local Agenda 21 team of Oxford City Council, through which she has helped to organize and run several community participation events.

VANESSA MASING studied Economics at the European Business School in Oestrich-Winkel, Germany. Prior to joining the Potsdam Institute for Climate Impact Research (PIK) as a research assistant for the ULYSSES project during 1997 and 1998, she worked at KPMG and Mees Pierson Bank. She continued her career as a consultant at Deloitte & Touche, and is currently working for a small venture capital company.

ARTHUR MOL is Professor in Environmental Policy at the Department of Social Sciences, Wageningen University, the Netherlands. His research interests are in environmental reform in Asia, Europe and the USA and he has published extensively on (international) environmental policy and sociology. His last book is *Globalisation and environmental reform. The ecological modernization of the global economy* (2001). He was

European sub-project leader of the Climate OptiOns for the Long Term (COOL)-project.

MÅNS NILSSON, M.Sc., is a Research Fellow at the Stockholm Environment Institute (SEI). His main research interests are in environmental policy analysis, institutional development, and strategic environmental assessments. He is leading the SEI research group on Policy and Institutions, and is currently (2001–02) a Fellow with the Carnegie Council for Ethics and International Affairs.

TIM O'RIORDAN is a Professor of Environmental Sciences at the University of East Anglia. He is associated with the three centres of excellence that are linked in the School of Environmental Sciences. These are the Tyndall Centre for Climate Change Research, the Leverhulme Program on Understanding Risk, and the Center for Social and Economic Research on the Global Environment. His work encompasses sustainability policy and practice in Europe and South Africa. He has edited a dozen books on these topics. He is a member of the UK Commission on Sustainable Development, and of the Prince of Wales' Business and Environment Program.

CRISTINA QUEROL has been analyst in the 'governance and sustainable development' area at the International Institute on Governance (IIG), Barcelona, Spain. While carrying out the research described here she was consultant for the Stockholm Environment Institute and worked at the Spanish Council for Scientific Research. Trained as a sociologist and holding a MA in Public Environment Management, her interests include institutional adjustments in response to unsustainability and, particularly, support initiatives for LA 21.

KILAPARTI RAMAKRISHNA is Deputy Director of the Woods Hole Research Center (Woods Hole, MA, USA) and Director of its program on science in public affairs. He obtained his Ph.D. in International Environmental Law from Jawaharlal Nehru University, New Delhi, India. He attended Harvard Law School in 1985 as a Fulbright Visiting Scholar, and has held many teaching and research positions, most recently at Yale University (1999–2000) and Harvard Law School (2000–01). He served as a Special Advisor to the United Nations in drafting the Framework Convention on Climate Change, and was the Coordinator of the World Commission on Forests and Sustainable Development from 1992 to 1995.

JERRY RAVETZ was for many years Reader in the History and Philosophy of Science at the University of Leeds, England. He is the author of

Scientific Knowledge and its Social Problems (1991, 1996) and *The Merger of Knowledge with Power* (1990). He is the co-author (with Silvio Funtowicz) of *Uncertainty and Quality in Science for Policy* (1990). With him he has developed the NUSAP notation for scientific information, and also the theory of Post-Normal Science.

JAN ROTMANS is a Professor at Maastricht University, the Netherlands, as chair of "Integrated Assessment." He is Director of the International Center for Integrative Studies (ICIS), Maastricht, and co-director of ICIS-BV, a consulting firm that has been developed as a spin-off from the ICIS research activities. He is one of the founders of Integrated Assessment (IA), has (co-)developed the IMAGE, ESCAPE, and the TARGETS models, and was coordinator of the European VISIONS project in which challenging scenarios for a sustainable Europe have been developed. He has been involved in numerous international assessments, including the Climate Change Assessment of the Intergovernmental Panel on Climate Change, where he was a lead author.

DANIELA SCHIBLI holds an MA in sociology and is currently a research assistant at the Institute for Social Planning and Social Management (ISS), University of Applied Sciences, Bern, Switzerland. There she conducts research on addiction and "social time." At the time of the research described in this volume, she was a research assistant in human ecology at the Swiss Federal Institute for Environmental Science and Technology (EAWAG), working on sociology of science. Daniela Schibli has published in *Environment* and *Abhängigkeiten*, and is a member of the Swiss Sociological Association.

RALF SCHÜLE worked as researcher and project manager at the Darmstadt University of Technology (Department of Sociology), Darmstadt, Germany, from 1995 to 1999. Within the ULYSSES project, he was responsible for the assessment process in the Frankfurt area. He has published this research as *Public Perceptions of Global Climate Change – A Case Study from the Frankfurt Area* (2001). Since 2000 he is senior researcher at the ifeu-Institute of Energy and Environmental Research (Department of Energy), Heidelberg, Germany. His main fields of research are environmental sociology, integrated environmental assessment, global climate policy, and local sustainability initiatives.

SIMON SHACKLEY is Lecturer in Environmental Management and Policy at the Manchester School of Management, UMIST; his involvement on the ULYSSES project was during his time at the *Centre for the Study of Environmental Change* at Lancaster University. His main research interests are in stakeholder responses to present and future environmental change, especially climate change impacts and adaptation. His research aims to combine insights from environmental science, economics and management science. He is a Research Program Manager of the recently established Tyndall Center for Climate Change Research, leading the research program on "decarbonisation," combining engineering and social science approaches.

SUSANNE STOLL-KLEEMANN is senior researcher and project leader at the Potsdam Institute for Climate Impact Research (PIK). She won The Chorafas Foundation's 1998 prize in Environment and Sociology for her Ph.D. on protected areas management. She is coeditor with Tim O'Riordan on *Biodiversity, Sustainability and Human Communities* (Cambridge 2002). She has written other articles based on her research on partnerships in biodiversity protection and social perspectives of climate change e.g., in the *Journal of Environmental Psychology, Society and Natural Resources, Environment* and *Global Environmental Change*. She is continuing her analysis of biodiversity management strategies in South Africa and Germany.

NEIL SUMMERTON was appointed Director of OCEES, the Oxford Centre for the Environment, Ethics and Society, in April 1997 and is a Fellow of Mansfield College. He is also Director of the Oxford Centre for Water Research in the Environmental Change Institute in the School of Geography and the Environment, Oxford University. Previously, he was Under-Secretary in the UK Government's Department of the Environment, where he successively led policy directorates advising on land-use planning and development control (1985–88), local government finance (1988–91), water (1991–96), and water and land (1996–97). At OCEES his focus is on environmental policy and environmental ethics.

ERIK SWYNGEDOUW is University Reader in Geography and Fellow of St. Peter's College, Oxford University. His main interests are in political economy and political ecology. Recent research includes work on technological change and industrial restructuring, urban–regional development in the European Union, the structure of the international financial system, and the political ecology of water. In addition, he is interested in sociospatial theory, in particular from a critical perspective. He is currently working on a book on the political ecology of urban water.

DAVID TÀBARA is associated lecturer in Environmental Management at the Pompeu Fabra University of Barcelona, and in Environmental Sociology at the Autonomous University of Barcelona (UAB), where he carries out research at its Center of Environmental Studies. He formerly worked for the Institute of Advanced Social Research of the Spanish Council for Scientific Research. His interests deal with questions of public perception, communication and action regarding socioenvironmental change and sustainability. He has published articles in *International Sociology, Global Environmental Change*, and in *Revista Internacional de Sociología* among other journals.

FERENC L. TOTH was an economist and policy analyst at the Potsdam Institute for Climate Impact Research (PIK) on leave from the Budapest University of Economic Sciences and State Administration at the time of the research reported here. Over the past twenty years, Dr. Toth's research activities have covered socioeconomic and policy aspects of global environmental change. He has published numerous papers in learned journals, edited several books and journal special issues. Dr. Toth served as coordinating lead author of Chapter 10 in Working Group III and lead author of Chapter 2 in Working Group II of the *Third Assessment Report of the Intergovernmental Panel on Climate Change*.

WILLEMIJN TUINSTRA is currently researcher at the National Institute for Public Health and the Environment (RIVM) in Bilthoven, the Netherlands. Her research interests include the role of science and integrated assessment modeling in environmental policy and the co-production of knowledge between science and different groups in society. Based at Wageningen University she was involved in the Climate OptiOns for the Long term (COOL) project as a project coordinator. Before that she was involved in the ULYSSES work at IIASA, Austria.

MARJOLEIN B.A. VAN ASSELT is senior researcher on Integrated Assessment methodology at the International Center for Integrative Studies (ICIS), Maastricht, the Netherlands, and co-director of ICIS-BV, a consulting spin-off from the ICIS research activities. Her Ph.D. research has been published as *Perspectives on Uncertainty and Risk: The PRIMA approach to decision support* (2000). Together with Jan Rotmans she developed the concept of perspective-based model routes as an approach to highlight inherent uncertainty and subjectivity in Integrated Assessment Models. She took part in the ULYSSES project when she worked at the Swiss Federal Institute for Environmental Science and Technology (EAWAG) in 1996/1997.

MARLEEN VAN DE KERKHOF received her masters degree in environmental policy sciences at Nijmegen University in the Netherlands in 1998 and currently works as a Ph.D. student at the Institute for Environmental Studies at the Vrije Universiteit of Amsterdam, the Netherlands. She conducts research on the methodology of stakeholder participation in complex environmental issues.

BRIAN WYNNE is Professor of Science Studies at the Institute for Environment, Philosophy and Public Policy at Furness College, Lancaster University, UK. His current interests include research that looks at ways to raise awareness of sustainable development through increasing the understanding of the links between socioeconomic and environmental processes. His many publications include *Risk Management and Hazardous Wastes: Implementation and the Dialectics of Credibility* (1987), and *Rationality and Ritual: The Windscale Inquiry and nuclear decisions in Britain* (1982).

Science, participation, and sustainability

This book reports the results of a grand experiment in how lay publics might be more effectively engaged in linking science and technology to the quest for sustainable development.

The experiment integrates three long-established but usually isolated lines of thought. The first concerns the appropriate role of science and technology in a transition toward sustainability. Early thinking on sustainability – such as that articulated in the World Conservation Strategy of 1980 – relied heavily on scientific studies of renewable resource management, carrying capacities, and environmental limits. The Brundtland Commission's 1987 report "Our Common Future" properly stressed the importance for any sustainable development strategy of targeted investments in knowledge creation and application. Over the subsequent decade, however, such investments generally lagged far behind needs. It has only been in the context of discussions surrounding the 2002 World Summit on Sustainable Development that widespread attention has begun to return to securing the scientific and technological foundations for a transition toward sustainability. One of the exceptions to this general trend has been in the relatively well-supported problem of climate change addressed in the study reported here. Climate change is, of course, only one aspect of the overall sustainability challenge. It none the less incorporates many of the most formidable elements of that challenge: tight coupling between social and environmental systems across multiple spatial scales; complexity in the resulting interactions that makes counterintuitive surprise the norm; and sufficiently long time lags between interventions and consequences to make wait-and-see management an option only for ostriches. This study's critical reflection on our experience with harnessing knowledge to meet the challenge of climate change therefore is important not only for its particular results, but also for the pathfinder role it serves in illuminating larger questions of how science and technology can be harnessed to support a sustainability transition.

The second big issue engaged in this study is how to ensure that the resource constituted by specialized knowledge is equitably available to all stakeholders in development. This, again, is a topic that has been grappled with for decades, with some of the contributors to this volume playing seminal roles in the debate. It was initially framed in the 1960s in terms of the challenge of imposing democratic control over new technologies. Subsequent work focused on problems of communicating expert knowledge to lay publics in order that they could make more informed decisions on complex issues involving risks to health and environment. More recently, it has become increasingly clear that the sorts of science and technology assessments used to address climate change and related sustainability issues are necessarily shaped by value-laden choices regarding which questions to ask, who to treat as an expert, and how to deal with disagreements. Democratic societies must therefore find means of assuring appropriate participation of affected citizens in the process of negotiating such value judgments. Where the scale of issue is small – for example, a choice involving facility siting within a community – the design of such participative assessment processes may be politically difficult, but the challenge may not be qualitatively different from challenges local governing bodies have grappled with for years. Where the scale of the issue is large – as with climate change or biotechnology – there is much less precedent to draw on. The resultant difficulties are compounded for many sustainability issues by the practical need for assessments that will be useful at local scales to integrate universal knowledge with knowledge particular to the social, ecological and historical circumstances of particular places. Trial and error experiments in how to incorporate citizen participation in ways that make scientific assessments both more equitable and more effective are now being pursued in many arenas around the world. What makes the work presented here so valuable is its systematic approach to those experiments, and its reflexive, self-critical treatment of the results.

Finally, the third line of work explored in this volume concerns the role of systematic modeling approaches in helping to link science, citizens and decision-makers in the exploration of complex social problems. Many of the approaches reported here are not new. I, for one, spent a very distant graduate career in C. S. Holling's lab at the University of British Columbia helping to develop simulation modeling approaches that integrated academic research and practitioner experience in problem-driven assessments of local resource management issues. And a number of institutions – including the International Institute for Applied Systems Analysis at which several of the contributors to this volume have worked – have been involved in applying interactive modeling approaches for sustainability problems since the mid-1980s. What is special about the experiment reported here is the range of formal and informal approaches it explores.

Encompassing collage approaches, scenario development, focus group discussions and reports, and the use of some of the most advanced computer models for understanding the interactions between humans and nature, this study provides a sophisticated and systematic exploration of the strengths and weaknesses of the various approaches across a range of national and issue contexts that is unparalleled in the literature. These approaches and the methodology that binds them together will be important in the further development of integrated studies that examine the democratic, scientific, and multiscale challenges posed by the transition to sustainability.

Those of us who work in parts of the world that have been slower in stepping up to the challenge of exploring how lay publics might more effectively harness science and technology to the quest for sustainable development have much to learn from this pathbreaking European study, even as we puzzle over and debate its conclusions. In a time when so little research squarely addresses the messy issues of sustainability, and when so much of what research there is confines itself to the relative safety of narrow academic disciplines, we owe a collective vote of thanks to the innovative research programs, program managers, and researchers who have brought us this fine body of work.

John F. Kennedy School of Government   WILLIAM C. CLARK
Harvard University

Sustainability, energy use, and public participation

Sometimes I am astonished when taking a "sustainability" look at energy relevant news. The continued operation of smaller hydroelectric power plants, which are producing electricity with extremely low life-cycle carbon dioxide emissions, is questioned due to the availability of cheap electricity from fossil fuels. Heat insulation of buildings is progressing, yet the energy management of new buildings is considered clearly less important than aesthetic design and other factors. Small, light-weight fuel efficient vehicles are available on the market, yet the trend of current sales favors heavier and ever more powerful cars. Energy efficient appliances stay on the shelf as less efficient devices are offered at lower prices.

These facts show that ecologically favorable technical solutions are presently not being chosen, as sustainability arguments are not ranked high within the set of preferences of public and individual actors. This is why *Public Participation in Sustainability Science*, the subject of this book, is of utmost importance. Unless we succeed in engaging those stakeholders who ultimately decide on energy relevant investments and purchases better in sustainability debates, the market penetration of energy efficient or ecologically benign technology will be impeded or severely delayed. Such delays could have far-reaching consequences for our planet. Hence, it is necessary that not only Sustainability Policy but also *Sustainability Science* starts to involve the public in its discussions.

The approach of Integrated Assessment Focus Groups presented in this book combines two important aspects. The first is to get to know the perspectives or "mental maps" of average citizens on sustainability issues. These citizens will play a major role in the decisions that are ultimately taken. It is not possible to talk about lifestyle changes without knowing the current perceptions of problems and values. In this context the free expression of thoughts on a specific question (here, the global climate change issue) is highly valuable; in the focus groups described in this book, the creation of collages by the participants provided such an opportunity. Second, to advance beyond the level of round table discussions, the stakeholders must be given access to state-of-the-art scientific knowledge in the field. Computer models have been used for this purpose: they were made available to the participants by an expert, the model moderator, and were termed *metaphors* rather than decision support tools. This explicit acknowledgment of uncertainties aimed at guaranteeing that this form of public participation would indeed create additional information, rather than just confirming those conclusions that the modelers themselves would have derived from their scenario runs.

For scientists and engineers who are active in research and development of technologies aimed at advancing a more sustainable energy system, the conclusions derived from this first Integrated Assessment Focus Group project are highly relevant. They show that there is fairly wide agreement among the general European public that climate change induced by our present use of fossil fuels is indeed a problem, and also that there is a willingness to act based on ethical/ecological considerations above and beyond pure economic ones. At the same time, there are high expectations that science and industry will find cost-effective solutions that can provide the energy services we are accustomed to in a more sustainable way. Policy is expected to pave the way for ecologically benign technologies through incentives and subsidies, rather than by making conventional energy use more expensive.

The big challenge, therefore, is to design eco-efficient products in such a way that they provide comparable customer value, while at the same time reducing resource consumption and environmental burdens due to waste and emissions. It is often claimed that ultimately the most ecological solution is also the least expensive one. Taking the example of a car, the specification of standards for expected fuel efficiency and maximum permissible emissions would certainly advance this aim, as it would automatically favor the most economic solution within the acceptable range of operating conditions, without *a priori* giving preference to one technology over the other. At the same time, it is important to take customer wishes explicitly into consideration. As mentioned above, fuel thrifty cars have often seen limited demand, but recent market studies show that the product became quite successful as soon as the highly ranked attributes of sporty image and driving pleasure were taken into account. Hence, the challenge to the engineer – as unaccustomed as it may be – is to design the ecologically efficient car not as the expensive austerity object, but as the lifestyle product that is capable of achieving the strongly required consumption and emission performance at the same time.

Finally, the book provides a subtle answer to the apparent schism between sustainability awareness on the one hand, and personal action on the other hand. Citizens are obviously quite ready to support public policies aimed at advancing sustainability and mitigating climate change issues, yet in everyday life their purchase decisions are guided by economic principles, and their activity choices are governed by lifestyle and current trends. Hence, it appears that the setting of standards and regulations, which eliminate or penalize ecologically inefficient products, is more promising than relying purely on the voluntary decision of pioneers to go for (in the short run) more expensive ecological solutions. A policy with the effect that the most sustainable energy service is also the most attractive one for the customer, will enable citizens to choose the latter by applying those same criteria that they have been accustomed to throughout their lives. This thought suggests that a transition toward a more sustainable lifestyle of society might indeed be possible, not so much by voluntary behavioral changes of individuals, but by society agreeing on standards that would make sustainability the mainstream of everyday choices.

Head of General Energy Research   ALEXANDER WOKAUN
Paul Scherrer Institute (PSI)
Villigen, Switzerland

Preface

This book is the result of collaborations by a network of researchers across Europe and beyond. As a group, we share the conviction that sustainability science needs public participation to be successful. We also think that in order to really work, such public participation requires not only an open mind on all sides, but also improved tools. How did we reach this conviction?

Sustainability is an elusive concept. One of the few things that can be said with certainty is that sustainable (as well as unsustainable) development depends on an intricate web of interactions in linked systems, both natural and social. This web cannot be steered by any simple action into a premeditated direction. There is no easy way to open this Gordian knot, and trying to do so with the proverbial sword would damage rather than enhance our chances of a sustainable future.

This situation implies two things. First, sustainability cannot be approached by a grand master plan with a precise mapping of the end point and the trajectory to get there. Rather, it is 'our common journey' as humankind; it consists of one tentative step after the other, with the need for continuous feedback about whether we are going roughly in the right direction or not (National Research Council 1999). Given the complex systems involved, there is not much hope of achieving such meaningful feedback without using the potential of modern information technology, especially computer modeling.

Second, restricting sustainability science (for a discussion of sustainability science concepts see, for example, Kates *et al.* 2001) to a modeling exercise of deterministic systems would be inadequate. It would contradict the complexity of the social systems involved – especially in democratic societies, which fortunately are gaining ground around the globe. The Earth System includes gases, plants, and humans, and at least the latter have some degree of intentionality and freedom of will. Ignoring this dimension would not only be scientifically wrong, but also practically misleading. We need non-deterministic models – stochastic and otherwise. And we need to develop these models in a meaningful dialogue with stakeholders and the public, both to learn about them and to make scientific arguments accessible to different actors. Such a dialogue can then help to shape the direction of our journey in a democratic process.

Taking these two arguments together, we conclude that computer modeling and public participation processes have to be combined for sustainability science to be successful. It is well known that bridging technical expertise in general with democratic decision-making processes is no easy feat. Formal processes for doing this have been developed, especially in the US policy process. Here procedures by which experts advise public policy-makers have been codified, at least in part opened to the participation of different interest groups within society, and monitored by courts regarding the balancing of voices in this process. Both strong and weak points of such a system have been discussed in depth (Jasanoff 1990). Such procedures for integrating technical expertise with democratic decision-making traditionally involve panels or committees of experts. In such a system, 'extended peer review' (Funtowicz and Ravetz 1992) is possible by having experts questioned by different stakeholders in a hearing format. But how can one conduct a hearing process with computer models?

For this question the earlier work of a number of groups, most notably Holling and his team (1978), on communicating environmental models to various stakeholder groups is a highly relevant starting point. The research discussed in this volume faced the challenge of extending this tradition in two dimensions. First, these earlier approaches often concerned local or regional ecological problems, while the work described here addressed much broader sustainability issues up to the level of global change. Second, in earlier work linking expert assessments with stakeholders, the latter were usually policy-makers or professional groups with some previous specialized knowledge of the environmental issue under discussion. In the research discussed in this volume, however, a main goal was to design participatory processes suitable for ordinary citizens. Thus, this approach aimed to bridge an unusually large gap, from global change to local citizens' perspectives. We saw bridging this gap as essential for effective public participation in sustainability science, but were faced with the need for new tools to make this feasible.

We decided to tackle this challenge in the particular branch of sustainability science dealing with Integrated Assessment (IA). When we embarked on this journey around 1995, Integrated Assessment was just in the process of becoming an established interdisciplinary research field. Early experiences had been made with integrated models on large-scale environmental issues like acid rain. The quest of IA was to provide information to policy-makers in a more integrated and useful form than is possible with purely disciplinary methods (Weyant *et al.* 1996). This fitted well with the need in sustainability science to integrate across complex systems. Integrated models, focused on but not limited to climate change issues, were available. We took this situation as our starting point for designing participatory processes that could facilitate between such expert models on the one side, and citizens on the other.

Our journey into the largely uncharted terrain between integrated computer models with global scope, and participation by ordinary citizens in different local contexts, was like an expedition exploring the coastline of an unknown continent. Sometimes you see what seems like a viable passageway between the cliffs, only to recognize that you have been mistaken and need to change course in order to save the vessel. Sometimes you unexpectedly find a beautiful beach or the mouth of a river providing sweet water. During our search, we have been fortunate to meet many thoughtful people, modelers and citizens alike, who have made our voyage a very rewarding one. And despite all difficulties along the way, our expedition was great fun for those aboard. We hope that the reader will be able to share this sense of excitement and fun in our account that follows. What we have brought back from our voyage is a rough map, the description of procedures for public participation in sustainability science that we have found to work even if they are not perfect. The purpose of this sketch of the coastline we explored is to support others in embarking on their own voyage, drawing better maps as they go along.

Acknowledgments

Much of the research discussed in this volume was conducted within the European ULYSSES project (Urban Lifestyles, Sustainability, and Integrated Environmental Assessment). This project was sponsored by the European Commission, DG XII (Fourth RTD Framework Program, Environment and Climate, Human Dimensions of Climate Change; contract no. ENV4-CT96-0212). The Swiss Federal Office for Education and Science supported the Swiss part of the project. Furthermore, a close collaboration with the Center for Interdisciplinary Studies in Technology of Darmstadt University of Technology, and substantial synergies with the Swiss CLEAR project (supported by the Swiss National Science Foundation, grant no. 5001–44598) were important as well.

The ULYSSES research team consisted of around thirty researchers in ten countries. In their work, the ULYSSES researchers profited very much from discussions with many colleagues, including Chris Anastasi, Ulrich Beck, Tom Burns, Mike Chadwick, Bill Clark, Bruno Dente, Tom Dietz, Hadi Dowlatabadi, Chris Hope, Tim O'Riordan, Steve Rayner, and Jan Rotmans. More people have helped them than can possibly be named here. Fortunately, many of them can be thanked as a group by acknowledging the very fruitful exchange within EFIEA, the European Forum for Integrated Environmental Assessment, coordinated by Pier Vellinga. The close contact with Angela Liberatore and Andrew Sors, who were responsible for the project from the side of the European Commission, was extremely helpful. And the ULYSSES team wants especially to thank the citizens, policy-makers and business representatives who participated in the group discussions conducted within the study. It was their commitment to the process that made this project possible. Finally, the editors want to acknowledge the technical support by Raphael Schaub with putting this manuscript together. His help was invaluable in producing the present volume.

The authors of Chapter 1 particularly want to thank all their colleagues from the ULYSSES project and also from the closely related CLEAR project for sharing their empirical material and for many fruitful and enjoyable discussions. They are also very grateful to William Clark, Hadi Dowlatabadi, Ortwin Renn, Timothy O'Riordan, Jan Rotmans, and Pier Vellinga for discussions that were essential in preparing this chapter. The usual disclaimers apply. Finally, the authors want especially to thank the citizens who took part in the focus groups discussed in this chapter.

The authors of Chapter 2 will be eternally grateful to those members of the public without whom this research would not have been possible. In the case of St. Helens, the active involvement of Richard Sharland (Groundwork Trust St. Helens, Knowsley and Sefton) and Tom Ferguson (Planning Department of the St. Helens Metropolitan Borough Council) is gratefully acknowledged. The Italian team would like to thank Eli Rota for the key role that she played in the development and running of the Venice groups. Chapter 2 closely follows the paper "Between Democracy and Expertise? Citizens' Participation and Environmental Integrated Assessment in Venice (Italy) and St. Helens (UK)" by the same authors, which appeared in the *Journal of Environmental Policy and Planning*, vol. 1(2), September 1999, 103–121, and is reproduced here with permission from the publishers, John Wiley & Sons Limited.

The author of Chapter 3 wants to acknowledge his debt to colleagues on the ULYSSES project, particularly Carlo Jaeger, Bernd Kasemir, Cristina Querol, and David Tàbara, for their stimulus and criticisms. Also, the provocations of Simon Shackley and Éric Darier have been a source of enjoyment and illumination. The author is also indebted to Nuria Castells, Jill Jäger, and two referees of an earlier draft, for their important comments. An earlier version of this chapter was published with Inderscience Enterprises Ltd. under the title: "Developing Principles of Good Practice in Integrated Environmental Assessment," *International Journal of Environment and Pollution*, vol. 11(3), 1999, 243–265. Reproduction with kind permission of Inderscience Enterprises Ltd.

The authors of Chapter 4 are grateful for discussions with U. Beck, H.-R. Böhm, E. David, D. M. Imboden, P. Raskin, E. A. Rosa and to the collaborators of the ULYSSES and CLEAR projects. They also want to thank Cristina Querol and Meritxell Costejà for their help in interpreting the collages discussed in this chapter. The usual disclaimers apply. Finally, the authors are most grateful to the citizens participating in our IA Focus Groups. Their first names have been changed in this volume to secure anonymity. The findings discussed in Chapter 4 were first presented at the 1999 Annual Meeting of the American Association for the Advancement of Science (Anaheim, California, 21–26 January). A previous version of this chapter was published as Bernd Kasemir, Urs Dahinden, Åsa Gerger, Ralf Schüle, David Tàbara and Carlo C. Jaeger (2000). "Citizens' Perspectives on Climate Change and Energy Use," *Global Environmental*

Change, 10(3), 169–184. We are grateful for the permission of the publisher, Elsevier Science Ltd., to reproduce this revised version here.

Chapter 5 is mainly based on research performed in the ULYSSES project. Further research was supported by the Swiss National Science Foundation within the CLEAR project (Climate and Environment in Alpine Regions). The partner project from Pittsburgh was sponsored by the Center for the Integrated Study of the Human Dimensions of Global Change, Carnegie Mellon University, Pittsburgh, which is supported by the US National Science Foundation. The opinions expressed in this paper are those of the authors. The authors of Chapter 5 are very grateful to all their colleagues working in the project for sharing their thoughts and data with them. Special thanks go to Janet Stocks and Ralf Schüle, who specifically prepared input for this chapter (Stocks 1998; Schüle, Haffner, and Jordan 1998) and to Éric Darier, Åsa Gerger Swartling, Hadi Dowlatabadi, Paul Raskin, and Christoph Schlumpf for their comments on earlier versions of this chapter. Jerry Ravetz and Chris Hope reviewed an earlier version of the chapter and provided invaluable comments and criticism. The responsibility for any remaining errors is with the chapter's authors. Last but not least, they want to express their gratitude to the participants in the focus groups for their insights and contributions. An earlier version of this chapter has been published with Kluwer Academic Publishers: Urs Dahinden, Cristina Querol, Jill Jäger, Måns Nilsson (2001), "Exploring the Use of Computer Models in Participatory Integrated Assessment – Experiences and Recommendations for Further Steps," *Integrated Assessment*, vol. 1, 2000, 253–266. Reproduction with kind permission of Kluwer Academic Publishers.

Chapter 6 is based on research performed in the ULYSSES and also the CLEAR project. The authors are grateful to all their colleagues from these projects for sharing their thoughts and data with them. They are especially grateful to Jill Jäger, Éric Darier, and Ralf Schüle for fruitful suggestions at an early stage of this chapter. They would also like to thank three reviewers of an earlier draft for their helpful comments. Finally, they are also most grateful to the citizens participating in the IA Focus Groups.

The authors of Chapter 7 want to thank the workshop participants from venture capital and young technology firms, and their interview partners from the European Commission, for making the study described in this chapter possible. They are grateful to the collaborators of the ULYSSES project, especially to Carlo Jaeger, for fruitful discussions. Contributions to this study made by Eva Hizsnyik, Jens Heydecke, Marco Jansen, and Carsten Helm are gratefully acknowledged. The usual disclaimers apply. A previous version of this chapter was published in the *Journal of Common Market Studies*, vol. 38(5), 2000, 891–903. The authors are grateful for the permission of the publisher, Blackwell Publishers Ltd., to reproduce this revised version here.

The authors of Chapter 8 want to acknowledge that the COOL project was financed by the National Research Program on Global Air Pollution and Climate Change in the Netherlands. They wish to thank especially the participants in the COOL Dialogue for their time investment and their contributions.

The authors of Chapter 9 acknowledge the support of the EU and the major contributions of the entire SIRCH team. They also wish to thank their colleagues in the FIRMA project, particularly Claudia Pahl-Wostl, Matt Hare, and Scott Moss, for insightful discussions on participatory integrated assessment (PIA). Of course, the greater PIA community, including the editors of this book, have stimulated their research.

The author of Chapter 10 wishes to acknowledge the many colleagues he has worked with on scenario development over the years who have helped shape the views expressed in this chapter. In particular, Roger Rainbow, Ged Davis, and Georges Dupont-Roc of Strategic Planning at Shell International, Dominique van der Mensbrugghe at the Development Department of the OECD, Veerle Vanderweerd at UNEP, and most recently, Jan Rotmans and Marjolein van Asselt of the International Centre for Integrative Studies at the University of Maastricht. He would also like to thank Bernd Kasemir of Harvard University for suggesting this chapter, and his help and patience in delivering it.

The authors of Chapter 11 want to acknowledge that this chapter substantially benefited from discussions with Bernd Kasemir. Furthermore, comments of Dale Rothman, Sandra Greeuw, Nicole Rijkens-Klomp, Joerg Krywkow, and Susan van 't Klooster on earlier drafts were very helpful. Finally, they would like to thank Joanne Mellors for her support.

The author of Chapter 12 wishes to thank the editors of this volume, and particularly Bernd Kasemir for his patience and critical comments. The author wants to thank Jan Martinez, Irving Mintzer, William Moomaw, Atiq Rahman, Pinguelli Rosa, Youba Sokona, and Larry Susskind for conversations over the past several years on issues touched on in this chapter. The author also wishes to thank his research assistant, Linda Jacobsen, for her close reading of the manuscript and help with references.

The authors of Chapter 13 want to thank Carlo Jaeger and Bernd Kasemir for fruitful discussions. They are also grateful to the European Working Group on the Quality of Legislation chaired by Luciano Violante, President of the Italian Chamber of Deputies. Within this group they are in particular grateful to Alessandro Pallanza, Giovanni Rizzoni, Angela Liberatore, and Yves Meny.

PART ONE

Concepts and insights

INTRODUCTION

This first part summarizes underlying concepts and major insights of the research on public participation in sustainability science discussed in this book. In Chapter 1, Kasemir *et al.* argue that currently decision-making on sustainability issues in general, and climate policy in particular, is in a transition from taking first careful steps of analysis to preparing major shifts in socio-economic activities. This transition needs an improved integration of citizens' and stakeholders' views into policy making to be successful. Documented and tested participatory procedures, which integrate expert knowledge with views held by the public, are necessary. The IA Focus Group methodology, developed to address this need, is discussed, and major results concerning citizen views on climate change and energy use are summarized. In Chapter 2, Gough *et al.* then focus specifically on conditions for meaningful participation in such procedures. Their findings include that open-ended settings, in which both participants and moderation team steer the process together, may initially even increase scepticism, but in the longer run support the establishment of mutual trust and understanding. Also, the medium of interaction between lay publics and expertise in participatory procedures was found to be crucial. In most IA Focus Groups conducted in the research discussed in this book, computer models were an essential medium of this interaction. In Chapter 3, Jerry Ravetz suggests that such integrated models on global change issues face such high uncertainties that they can be understood to have a metaphorical rather than a predictive function. These models can never be 'true' in the classic scientific sense, but as metaphors they can support insights and teach us about ourselves and our perspectives. With this, Ravetz continues the argument begun in Chapter 1, that for complex issues like global change and sustainability, science cannot settle but should support debates within society. This was the rationale behind the research discussed in this book, combining model use with public participation in sustainability science.

CHAPTER ONE

Citizen participation in sustainability assessments

Bernd Kasemir, Carlo C. Jaeger, and Jill Jäger

The challenge

Perhaps the biggest challenge of our times is the task of achieving a transition to sustainability, a transition that will enable people around the world to live free from want and fear without compromising the ability of future generations to do so as well (Annan 2000). Research that supports such a transition can build upon first steps toward understanding nature–society interactions from two converging areas of study. The first area is work in environmental science, that has not only made substantial contributions toward our understanding of the natural world, but also has begun to include human causes and impacts of environmental change. The second area is work in economic, social, and development studies, that has started to go beyond purely societal issues and to incorporate environmental factors as well.

The emerging field of 'sustainability science' combines these two areas of study and uses these foundations for a better understanding of complex dynamic interactions between social, environmental, and economic issues. In order to be successful and robust, sustainability science needs to include methods and procedures for increasing public participation in its discussions and debates. In the current volume, we discuss why this is the case, and what such procedures for public participation in sustainability science could look like. We have used the issue of climate change and its relation to urban lifestyles as a case study to examine the possible roles of public participation in sustainability science.

While the beginnings of global climate policy were shaped by research results from the natural sciences, another phase has started with the development of the Kyoto Protocol to the UN Framework Convention on Climate Change (UNFCCC). Before Kyoto, results from the natural sciences were crucial in initiating a worldwide awareness of the problem of climate change as well as in encouraging the negotiation of the UNFCCC and Protocol. As discussions of the Kyoto Protocol have shown, the process of reducing greenhouse gas emissions will be slow and difficult.

In response to this situation, it will be necessary to design further institutions and mechanisms to respond to the climate change issue, the implications of which are gradually being explored. This phase is essential to build up the know-how and the trust relationships that are required to develop effective environmental policies on a global scale (Jaeger *et al.* 1997a; Social Learning Group 2001). However, this alone is clearly insufficient, if the problem of climate change is to be effectively addressed on a global scale. If an effective climate policy is to emerge, actions taking place at the level of international environmental diplomacy must be combined with actions involving various kinds of stakeholders. These stakeholders range from peasants to forest managers, from tourism operators to inhabitants of coastal zones, and from financial investors to ordinary citizens. Involving such a wide variety of the world's citizenry in debates on an issue as complex as climate change is a difficult challenge, and needs innovative participatory procedures.

This chapter discusses the overall approach of a major research initiative to address this challenge and to develop procedures that facilitate the participation of stakeholders – especially citizens – in integrated sustainability assessments. The special focus was on processes that allow interfaces between expert models of sustainability issues on the one hand, and lay participants in focus group discussions on the other hand. The procedures were tested in seven urban regions throughout Europe. Approximately 600 citizens participated in this process. The design of these 'IA Focus Groups' is discussed in detail in this chapter, together with an overview of main results.

To prepare this discussion, we will address briefly three topics in the remainder of this introductory section. First, the history of climate change debates. Second, the need for public participation in taking these debates further. And, finally, knowledge claims advanced by various scientific communities about the orders of magnitude involved in debates on climate change and sustainability.

A brief history of climate change debates

While individual scientists and groups had discussed the issue of climate change earlier, broader scientific interest as well as public attention concerning this issue increased in the late 1970s.[1] In 1970, the first Earth Day was held in the US, one of the largest demonstrations in human history. In the same year, the US Congress passed the Clean Air Act, and the

[1] We have used the excellent web-site www.puc.state.oh.us/consumer/gcc/chron.html as our main source for the following overview.

Environmental Protection Agency was created. Three years later, oil prices surged and worldwide fear of energy shortages emerged. The oil crisis of the time was a trigger for the largest global recession for many decades. Nuclear energy was proposed as the key energy source for the future by some, but met fierce opposition because of fear of the risks involved. In this setting, the risks of climate change were emphasized by proponents of nuclear energy – like Helmut Schmidt, the German chancellor at that time – as a key argument against further reliance on fossil fuels. Environmentalists countered not by denying the risks of climate change, but by stressing the need for a different energy future, based on increased energy efficiency and the use of solar and other renewable sources of commercial energy. While disagreement about energy policy loomed large, agreement about the seriousness of climatic risks was rapidly established. In 1979, the United Nations' World Meteorological Organization (WMO) sponsored the First World Climate Change Conference in Geneva. In the same year, the British scientific journal *Nature* claimed: "The release of carbon dioxide to the atmosphere by the burning of fossil fuels is, conceivably, the most important environmental issue in the world today."

At that time, there was no direct evidence of human-induced climate change. Rather, a long-lasting scientific effort had made humankind aware of an unprecedented global risk. That effort started nearly 200 years ago. In 1827, the French mathematician Jean-Baptiste Fourier outlined a process by which solar energy is captured by the Earth's atmosphere, thus raising the planet's temperature. He suggested the term 'greenhouse effect' for this phenomenon as an imperfect, but graphic analogy to the way glass windows allow for the warming of the inside of a greenhouse. In the 1890s, Svante Arrhenius, a Swedish chemist, predicted that a doubling of atmospheric carbon dioxide due to burning of fossil fuels would lead to a worldwide warming on the order of 5° Celsius. Complex as the fast dynamics of weather events and the slower dynamics of climatic processes are, he could only make a very coarse model. In the 1950s, computers could be used to start modeling the climate system in much greater detail. Up to the present day, these models have shown that Arrhenius' basic finding is remarkably robust.

In 1957 Charles Keeling, a postdoctoral student at the California Institute of Technology, initiated the longest continuous series of detailed atmospheric measurements in modern history. He established monitoring stations on Mauna Loa in Hawaii and at the South Pole to sample the concentration of carbon dioxide in the atmosphere. Meanwhile, the steady increase of that concentration has been established beyond doubt. Sophisticated measurement networks have been established, many of them over the past decades, to measure temperature, precipitation, and other meteorological variables worldwide at regular intervals. In 1987 a team of Soviet and French scientists took an ice core 2,000 meters deep at Vostok in the Antarctic. Other teams probed the ice in the Arctic. By analyzing air bubbles trapped in the ice, they were able to estimate atmospheric composition and temperature over a period of about 160,000 years. By 1990, it was clear that in the 1980s the Earth's annual average temperature was higher than for any decade in the twentieth century, and as far as one can tell for any decade since at least 1,000 years. The 1990s were warmer still: the seven globally warmest years recorded in modern history have occurred in the 1990s, including the year 2000.

In 1988, the Governing Council of the United Nations Environment Program (UNEP) established, together with the WMO, an intergovernmental body to review ongoing studies of climate change. This organization, the Intergovernmental Panel on Climate Change (IPCC), is now the most important single agency dealing with climate change on an international level (www.ipcc.ch). The huge number of findings collected by IPCC clearly indicate that climate change involves serious risks. Global warming is likely to raise sea level through thermal expansion of ocean water and melting glaciers and portions of the Greenland Ice Sheet. It is also likely to change precipitation patterns, leading to more severe and more frequent extreme weather events – including floods and droughts – in many regions. How likely these and other events will be is hard to tell, and assessing their severity in economic, aesthetic, and moral terms is even harder.

To decide which actions to take, and which actions to stop, in the face of such risks is impossible without a wealth of scientific findings. However, to take these decisions, scientific information must be combined with arguments and judgments that draw on other sources, ranging from common sense to the experience of different cultural traditions as well as different human individuals. Designing ways to foster such integration is the focus of the present book.

Public participation is essential

The main goal of the research discussed in this book, much of which was based on work conducted in the ULYSSES project (see Acknowledgements), was to explore procedures for citizen participation (see Kasemir *et al.* 2000; Schüle 2001). Involving citizens in climate policy debates is necessary, because successful implementation of climate mitigation measures will require consumer, worker, and citizen consent (see Kempton 1991; and also Löfstedt 1992). Without integrating the points of view of citizens, environmental policy runs the risk of getting stalled early in the implementation phase. Climate policies that are consistent with the visions, beliefs, and aspirations of citizens will have more chance of success in the twenty-first century than policies imposed without consideration of citizen opinion.

However, the role of the public in decision-making on sustainability issues depends very much on whether, in principle, science can articulate a comprehensive, complete and unique description of the issues at stake. If this were the case, the main question about the public would be whether it had understood the scientific information properly, and if not, how it could be educated. But if such a complete and unique overview of the problems themselves and their interrelations with other issues on the decision-makers' agendas is not possible, then the public can and should play a more active role. The way that the public understands and defines the issues then becomes a complementary input to the scientific assessment and ultimately the policy-making process. In such cases of multiple legitimate descriptions of the decision-making issues at stake, the role of science changes. Scientists are then expected to provide a variety of plausible assessments regarding different courses of action, and thus to support rather than to settle an informed and pluralistic public debate.

Global change and sustainability are complex issues. While the term 'complexity' has been used with many different connotations (Shackley, Wynne, and Waterton 1996), we will use it here specifically to denote systems or situations for which there are inherently multiple legitimate descriptions. This has been described as the essence of complexity e.g. by Rosen (1977) and Casti (1986). Along these lines, it has been argued, for example, that the climate problem cannot be adequately understood on the basis of any one unique description (Pahl-Wostl et al. 1998). Funtowicz and Ravetz (1994a) have distinguished between ordinary and emergent complexity. In emergent complex systems "at least some of the elements of the system possess individuality, along with some degree of intentionality, consciousness, foresight, purpose, symbolic representations and morality." Global change, where people in different situations and different cultures are a central part of the equation, is certainly an emergent complex system in this sense.

Given the complex nature of democratic decision-making, together with the complex nature of global change, the simple pattern of science supporting policy-making in the mode described by the familiar aphorism of "speaking truth to power" would not be fruitful here. While a continuing dialogue between science and policy will remain essential (Moss 1995), it will have to be complemented by the involvement of wider stakeholder groups. A lot of research has been carried out discussing the relationships between science, decision-makers, and the public at large (see, for example, Jasanoff 1990; Jasanoff *et al.* 1995). Especially regarding assessments of global change from a regional perspective, the need to integrate stakeholder views has been stressed in recent research (see, for example, the discussions by Yin and Cohen 1994, concerning the Mackenzie Basin; by Magalhaes 1998, concerning Northeast Brazil; and by Cebon *et al.* 1998, concerning the Alps). The increased need for enhanced stakeholder interactions implies a growing need for integrating social science research (see Shackley and Skodvin 1995), and, in particular, participatory techniques, into research on sustainability.

The input that social science can provide is needed to gain knowledge about stakeholders and their ways of opinion formation, and also to create opportunities for including the knowledge of stakeholders and their judgments about controversial issues in the policy-making process. Integrating participatory techniques from the social sciences is especially promising for sustainability research that uses methods of Integrated Assessment (IA). IA research is characterized by focusing on integrated pictures of complex decision situations, rather than on highly detailed but not integrated pieces of knowledge (for more on Integrated Assessment concepts, see Weyant *et al.* 1996; Rotmans and van Asselt 1996; Tol and Vellinga 1998). Traditionally, IA research has mainly focused on the development of integrated computer models. But as IA aims to provide more comprehensive decision support to policy-makers than can be achieved with traditional disciplinary research, participatory procedures from the social sciences would fit well into this overall approach. Indeed, while the participatory dimension of IA – especially with regard to citizen involvement – is still somewhat underresearched, there is great interest on the part of the IA research community in developing techniques of participatory IA (Jäger 1998; Toth and Hizsnyik 1998; Schneider 1997).

What are the implications for IAs if the aim is to provide decision support in the context of democratic decision-making, where there is a network of interacting decision-makers who are accountable to the public at large? This question is especially pertinent for issues of sustainability, which may well be what Gallie (1956) called an "essentially contested concept" (see Kasemir *et al.* 1999b). Essentially contested concepts enable different parties to engage in a shared conversation about some controversial issue by providing adequate focus as well as sufficient ambiguity to fuel interesting and fruitful debates. While it may be important to acknowledge the creative potential of ambiguity, however, no debate about sustainability will make much sense without taking into account the knowledge claims advanced by various scientific communities. We will consider briefly some of these claims in the context of climate change in order to prepare our discussion of procedures for involving stakeholders in IAs of complex sustainability issues.

Science suggests major challenges for climate policy

Currently, humankind is using commercially supplied energy at a rate of about 2,000 watts per capita (see Imboden and Jaeger 1999, for a more detailed discussion).[2] The burning of fossil fuel, coal, oil, and natural gas, contributes to more than 90 per cent of the total energy used today. Presently, this leads to annual emissions worldwide of on average about 4 tons of carbon dioxide per capita. This is much more than the oceans and terrestrial systems can absorb from the atmosphere. Therefore, atmospheric carbon dioxide concentrations are rising. This rise in carbon dioxide in the atmosphere is a major contributor to increasing risks of potentially catastrophic changes in the world's climate. Energy use per capita varies from about 500 watts in Africa to approximately 1,000 watts in Asia, 5,000 watts in Europe and about 10,000 watts in North America. Energy use may or may not increase further in industrialized countries in the coming decades, but as developing countries strive to overcome misery and to emulate the lifestyles of industrialized countries, the global average of energy consumption per capita could potentially double in the next five decades. In the same period, global human population might increase by 50 per cent as well. As a result, global energy use would increase by a factor of three between now and 2050.

These figures are important because they convey the orders of magnitude involved in the sustainability debate. If one wants to substantially reduce carbon emissions, even combinations of several measures must involve truly massive efforts. Suppose four options are combined so that each one of them could reduce today's global carbon emissions by 50 per cent. Such a scenario could include the dedication of one quarter of today's total agricultural land to crop fuel production, the complete sequestration of carbon from half of today's fossil fuel production, and two more options of similar size. If total energy use increases by a factor of three, these options would stabilize today's emission level, but would not reduce it! It is quite obvious, then, that reducing emissions will have to include strategies to limit overall energy consumption, and will have to involve very substantial changes in the global energy system and infrastructure.

---

[2] One watt corresponds to using 1 joule of energy per second. Watt measures the rate of energy use much like an indication of kilometers per hour measures the speed of some movement.

Central to the debate is that these changes will certainly affect technologies, as well as lifestyles and the economic welfare of various parties. However, if emissions are not reduced, we must face the potential of severe risks of climate change such as sea level rise, desertification, or changes in the functioning of the Gulf Stream. Neither options for emissions reductions nor the risks of climate change or measures to adapt to such change can be identified without the expertise of the scientific community. Like debates on other issues of sustainability as, for example, increasing water scarcity or loss of biodiversity, meaningful debates on climate strategies require major inputs from scientific research.

Of course, any serious discussion of climate policy options requires some assessment of the potential costs and benefits involved for different parties. The qualification "for different parties" is essential here, and immediately points to a further difficulty. The ways in which sustainability issues affect a multitude of different parties cannot be dealt with adequately by any decision framework involving just one decision-maker (Jaeger *et al.* 1998). Nor can the relevant interactions of many decision-makers be handled simply by market mechanisms, as one of the basic problems in sustainability issues is whether and how existing markets should be modified or new ones brought into existence. Not even the well-known formula that markets should be supplemented by government measures in such a way as to internalize external effects offers a simple solution. The options that should be considered are often characterized by bifurcation points at which their development may take one of several very different trajectories (Hourcade 1993). As a result, at critical junctures external effects do not have well-defined magnitudes that could be used as obvious yardsticks for policy-making.

Under such conditions, the success of long-term strategies to deal with sustainability issues depends on multilateral negotiations between different stakeholder groups. In this process, "policy-makers" will not so much make decisions in splendid isolation but rather take on the role of facilitators between different interest groups (Beck 1994). This is part of a larger process of the changing roles of actors within today's societies, involving increasingly informal networks based on trust (for these changing roles of actors in society see, for example, the work by Fukuyama (1996; 1999), concerning the importance of informal networks based on trust, and the work by Beck (1994), on the changing role of state representatives). In relation to complex environmental problems, policy-makers especially need to find ways to deal with the extremes of a "technocratic" policy design, based on scientific results gained independently of wider public debates, and a "populist" policy design, enforcing policy choices without trying to legitimate them with rational arguments. Public participation in sustainability science can help to overcome this impasse by combining the rationality of expert models with the rationality of social discourses.

A procedure for stakeholder participation

In order to facilitate stakeholder participation in integrated assessments of sustainability issues, the researchers engaged in the ULYSSES project developed a methodology based on informed group discussions. While many terms (including Citizen Panels, IA Focus Groups, and In-depth Groups) can be used to describe this methodology and to emphasize specific facets of it, in the present chapter we use the label "IA Focus Groups" to designate an approach that comes in many variants, and which can be tailored to novel circumstances and applications. The point of our research was to show that citizen participation in assessments of complex sustainability issues is feasible, and to outline a procedure for achieving this.

While IA has become a common methodology in climate change re-search and other environmental studies (Jaeger 1998), up to now the tools used have usually been restricted to computer models and expert panels. In IA Focus groups, these tools are complemented with group discussions with various stakeholders, including ordinary citizens. The participatory techniques used in this procedure build on the focus group method (see Morgan and Krueger 1998a). Doble (1995) described a re-lated process that draws upon elements of focus group methods and of opinion polling on complex environmental issues. Kasemir *et al.* (1999b) have discussed the concept of IA Focus Groups, which combine focus group techniques with the use of IA computer models, and first results from IA Focus Groups in connection with the hypothesis of "reflexive modernization" are given by Jaeger *et al.* (1999).

In the following we first give an overview of some major traditions in understanding the foundations of stakeholder dialogues. We then discuss why we have chosen focus group methods, in particular, as the basis of participatory procedures with citizens presented in this volume. And finally, we discuss the general format of these 'IA Focus Groups', as well as an example for a detailed process design.

Is there a theory of stakeholder dialogues?

In many quarters, there is an increasing need for stakeholder dialogues in-volving both laypersons and scientific experts. The present book develops know-how for such dialogues. What are key theoretical ingredients of that know-how? This question allows for more than one answer – as is perhaps appropriate for a reflection on dialogues (for an in-depth discussion of the theoretical issues involved in deliberations between experts and layper-sons, see Jaeger *et al.* 2001). Here, we will discuss four possible answers to the question about the theoretical background for understanding such dialogues.

Dialogue as bargaining

First, stakeholder dialogues are often looked at as negotiations along the lines of game theory (Osborne and Rubinstein 1994). A powerful ap-proach along these lines has been proposed by Susskind and Field (1996). The theoretical framework of this kind of approach can be sketched as follows. Different agents with different interests, beliefs, values, and knowledge meet and try to reach their goals in the setting of a shared con-versation. They may hide or disclose information, provide incentives for or against certain actions, and perform speech acts – promises, offenses, reconciliations, etc. – in line with whatever strategies they pursue.

The conversation then may or may not reach some equilibrium between the different interests in play. In this setting, an equilibrium is defined as a Nash equilibrium, i.e. a situation where no player can improve her or his situation unilaterally. Of course, even if the system is in equilibrium, some individual may prefer a different state, but that individual has no means of reaching it. What is worse, there may even be reason to collectively prefer a state that is no equilibrium at all – but by definition this state cannot be stabilized. Such is the well-known situation of a social dilemma, to which we will return below.

If there is a unique obvious equilibrium, there is little point in running a conversation. The different agents will quickly realize that there is one best way for all of them. Some may not be particularly happy about it, but they will know that there is no better option. Unlikely as such a situation may be, it is still worth exploring. A unique equilibrium can be framed in terms of a cost-benefit analysis for the different agents: For each one of them, the advantages of moving away from equilibrium are offset by the disadvantages of the same move. Advantages and disadvantages need not be expressed in monetary terms, it suffices to use some index that relates them to the preferences of the various agents. The larger the move away from equilibrium, the larger the net cost of the move. These circum-stances allow the aggregation of the individual cost-benefit schedules with some arbitrary set of weights – the situation can be analyzed as if a single collective agent were maximizing its overall utility. The straightforward rhetoric of the common good is perfectly appropriate here.

If there is a unique equilibrium that is far from obvious, a conversa-tion may be an effective procedure to discover it. Often, there may be a need to feed expert knowledge into the conversation so as to make sure important information is not ignored. The rhetoric of the common good is still appropriate, and cost-benefit analysis provides a useful scheme of analysis. This is probably the situation most often taken for granted by decision-makers, at least in the way they justify their decisions. There is a single best choice for the collectivity on whose behalf the decision-maker is taking decisions, and of course she or he is striving for precisely that choice. However, in such situations a stakeholder dialogue has its drawbacks, too. It is cumbersome, may cost a lot of time, attention, and other resources, and it may be distorted by group thinking and irrational mechanisms. Therefore, some combination of expert knowledge with leadership by decision-makers may well be a superior procedure, not just from the point of view of the decision-makers themselves, but also from the point of view of the collectivity – a political community, a business firm, or whatever – involved.

The most important case, however, is the situation where more than one equilibrium is accessible. Now the question is not only how to reach an equilibrium, but what equilibrium to select. The famous issue of cooperation versus defection is a case in point. A married couple may be able to each earn $50,000 a year if they coordinate their professional lives. If one of them is reckless in pursuing his or her career while the other partner tries to adjust, they may earn $60,000 and $30,000, respectively. If both are reckless, however, they may end up with each earning $40,000. If individual greed is their main motive, they will end with the last situation and miss the superior outcome of the first one. And clearly things may be more complicated due to asymmetries, further options, additional players, etc. In a social dilemma of this sort – with preferences of different actors untainted by any form of solidarity – cooperation is not feasible, and all that remains is the urge to reflect on this sad state of affairs, much as in the face of a Greek tragedy.

But then even tragedies may inspire one to discover options that might have saved the characters in the play had they not ignored them. A social dilemma may turn out to be part of a larger game that was hidden in the beginning. There may be moves to avoid the weird equilibrium of the prisoners of self-interest and to form the trust required for a cooperative solution. Conversation then may work as a mechanism for equilibrium selection. Of course, one could also cast a dice or choose some other mechanism, and sometimes this will in fact be quite reasonable. Nevertheless, conversations provide opportunities to develop trust and mutual understanding. This in turn may be needed to embark on the journey from a given equilibrium toward another one with more attractive features.

Dialogue as understanding

The emphasis on trust and understanding actually marks the transition to the second answer concerning theoretical knowledge about stakeholder dialogues. In fact, one may see a conversation not only as a negotiation process but also as an exchange of arguments that enables people to reach a consensus both on factual and normative issues. Such is the ambitious program of Habermas (1981); for a recent application to public participation see Palerm (2000). In stakeholder dialogues, the weights between the two poles of factual and normative issues may vary, but there is little doubt that both are present.

The debate about global warming, for example, has led not only to shaky compromises about a couple of political issues, but also to a remarkable consensus shared by large scientific communities, networks of policy-makers, media operators, and larger publics. Of course, there are important open questions, and moreover, consensus need not protect from error. Nevertheless, this debate is an interesting example of a complex process of social learning in a rich fabric of oral and written conversations. And keep in mind that there is a consensus not only on some key facts and mechanisms, but also on important normative issues, like the responsibility of present generations for damage they may be causing in the future. Clearly, a normative consensus cannot be based on scientific insights alone, but then it is also often impossible without taking such insights into account. That is exactly the point of a conversation involving both scientific experts and laypersons.

Stakeholder dialogues can hardly produce compelling proof of any specific claim. Consensus emerges, if at all, through a subtle interaction between received views and specific criticisms based on new evidence or concepts. And while there is no recipe for managing a conversation that will lead to consensus, let alone to "truth," guidelines that have proved useful in practice can be indicated. The present book certainly proposes some such guidelines, for example, with the method of IA Focus Groups. But while the purists of rational debate may look for guidelines of idealized conversations so as to have a yardstick for assessing the much less perfect conversations of real life, here we are interested in procedures that are operational even under the often quite unsatisfactory conditions of practical problem solving. Such procedures might even be able to mitigate some of the imperfect conditions.

This pragmatic approach represents a compromise – or perhaps a problem-focused synthesis – not only between the two approaches discussed so far, but also between these and the two next ones. Just as the view of conversation as a shared search for reasonable consensus implies a criticism of the representation of conversations as pure bargaining, so the next approach is highly critical of the "idealistic" flavor of images presenting conversations as a rational pursuit of truth. This image is taken to task for neglecting and even hiding the role of power and domination in actual conversations between scientific experts and laypersons.

Dialogue as domination

The third answer to our question, then, is based on a critical analysis of the authority of science in modern society. For a philosophical discussion of related issues see Kelly (1994); for an example of how to use a critical awareness of power relations in empirical studies dealing with public participation see De Marchi *et al.* (2000).

According to this kind of analysis, the authority of science is geared to an alliance between scientific communities and nation states, an alliance that displaced the one between religions and empires in earlier times. Science, as we know it, is financed mainly from taxes, while giving amazing autonomy to the scientific community in allocating these resoures. From the point of view of the most powerful governments actually running world-class scientific systems, a main return on this investment is military technology. A second return is the existence of a body of professionals with sophisticated training in fields ranging from engineering to medicine, the law, and many others. Governments expect a third return in the form of competitive advantages for their national economies.

Since the development of the atomic bomb, the alliance between governments and science has been increasingly exposed to critical scrutiny. The debate about nuclear energy has made all parties involved much more sensitive to issues of trust that cannot be handled simply by invoking the authority of science and backing it with the authority of the state. Meanwhile, these trust issues have become prominent in a wide array of controversies about various kinds of risks, ranging from toxic waste to genetically modified organisms, from medical treatments to economic policy in a globalized setting. It is precisely these issues that have generated the increasing need for stakeholder dialogues involving both scientific experts and laypersons, ranging from powerful decision-makers to ordinary citizens.

When engaging with such a critical view of the science–state relation, we are faced with an ocean of problems that is extremely difficult to navigate. The attempt to disentangle the intricate and sometimes questionable links between science and power has led more than one author to assume a pretty irrational stance, sometimes tempered by a Socratian sense of irony and compassion, sometimes rather less so. If one were to wait for a satisfactory analysis of the relations between science and power in order to design workable schemes of public participation, one might have to wait for a long time.

Fortunately, another approach is feasible. Exercises in public participation, stakeholder dialogues, etc., may well be essential tools for an inquiry into the actual relations between science and power as well as into their possible future evolution. Therefore, it is not only justifiable, but even necessary, to engage in such exercises well before the theoretical issues involved have been fully clarified. By so doing, stakeholder dialogues become a form of scientific inquiry in their own right, and one that promises discoveries concerning some of the most fascinating unresolved issues in social theory, like the relations between arguments and incentives, knowledge and power, facts and values. This is the approach that we advocate here, and if the proof of this pudding lies in the eating, then we can say that we have eaten it and found it to be tasty.

Dialogue as common sense

As for the fourth answer, one may make a case for the view that there is simply no need for scientific theories here. Wittgenstein (1958) still provides one of the most inspiring warnings against the belief that human knowledge – and especially knowledge about humans – becomes truly reliable only when it takes the shape of a scientific theory. Perhaps this warning provides good guidance when looking at the huge body of practical experience synthesized in the management literature dealing with the importance of discourse for organizations (a case in point is Senge 1990).

In many ways, stakeholder dialogue is more an art than a technology. To be a great playwright takes many capabilities and a lot of training, but hardly a scientific theory. And even technologies sometimes are based more on experience and singular creative insights than on theories. Actually, a stakeholder dialogue between scientists and laypersons may suffer if it is shaped by scientific theories because equality between these two parties may then be tilted in favor of the former.

It seems odd to engage in a sophisticated technical argument in favor of such a view. To the extent to which it is appropriate, this must show in the fruitfulness of using common sense and ordinary language in running stakeholder dialogues, not in developing some arcane metalanguage to justify such use. And yes, a careful look at most, perhaps all stakeholder dialogues confirms what is known from human life in any case: wisdom, character, humor, and compassion matter, and so does a rich record of personal experiences with various dialogues. It would be foolish to expect any scientific theory to substitute for these, and even if it were feasible, that might well be a huge loss rather than a gain. The real question is whether in practice such virtues are impaired or enhanced by scientific theories.

While the fourth answer has not just its merits, but actually an indispensable and vital role to play in any serious attempt to think about stakeholder dialogues, it can be overstated in two ways. On the one hand, there are various attempts to top the sophistication of existing scientific languages with a jargon that is accessible only to the "cognoscenti." This is rarely helpful, as it tends to aggravate the lack of understanding between various parties involved in a stakeholder dialogue. The limits of specialized reasoning by scientific disciplines can be drawn in ordinary language rooted in real-life situations, but not in a specialized language designed for the business of criticizing specialization, scientific or otherwise. On the other hand, drawing such limits makes sense only if enough space is left within the fences for the wonderful gardens of scientific inquiry. Claims that stakeholder dialogue is just something for practitioners, with no need or scope for scientific inquiry and theoretical arguments, miss the potential of professional support in the face of a challenging task.

Dialogue
The three theory-driven answers that we have discussed above provide more than general philosophical framings for thinking about stakeholder dialogues. Even if their lineage goes back to thinkers such as Hobbes (for the game-theoretical approach), Kant (for the role of arguments in discourse), and through a critical turn even Plato (for the relation between truth and power), each approach has generated empirical research of considerable practical relevance. Anybody running stakeholder dialogues ignores the know-how generated by such research at her or his own peril, just as does anybody who ignores the indispensability of a know-how rooted in everyday life rather than in scientific studies. While Wittgenstein's restoration of common sense is indispensable for handling tensions between these traditions, it must not be misconstrued as the refusal of scientific insights in the dynamics of human conversations.

Therefore, we advocate a careful combination of approaches that have developed by criticizing each other. We propose a practice of stakeholder dialogue embedded in a larger inquiry, taking advantage of existing knowledge and addressing open questions so as to generate new knowledge. How do arguments about the appropriateness of norms work in a culture that tends to treat rationality as dealing with facts, not norms? How do science and power interact in a historical situation where their alliance is increasingly questioned? How does human reason deal with uncertainties generated by scientific inquiries that promised certainties in the first place? These are examples of research questions that can be fruitfully addressed by designing, implementing, and analyzing stake-holder dialogues.

One more example: how does a dialogue between two juxtaposed voices differ from a polylogue that is open toward a potentially infinite variety of voices (Kristeva 1977)? The philosopher and the king, science and policy, Romeo and Juliet, Faust and Mephisto are reminiscent of the dualistic mode. The interplay between aesthetic patterns in Giotto's "Campanile," the polyphony of voices in Bach's "Musical Offering," the interlinkage of events and personalities in Tolstoi's *War and Peace*, the interactions be-tween the "founding brothers" shaping the foundations of the American republic (Ellis 2000) transcend it. We do not propose a shallow com-promise that ignores the contradictions between incompatible theoretical outlooks. We advocate a debate that gives space to the various approaches so as to enable them to learn from each other – much as a well-designed stakeholder dialogue is supposed to do.

Why use focus groups in participatory IA?

In the stakeholder dialogues discussed in this volume, participatory tech-niques for IA were mainly based on further refinements of the focus group methodology. Why have we chosen focus groups as a starting point for participatory procedures in IA?

Focus groups are a research tool that has been used for more than fifty years (Merton and Kendall 1946; Merton 1987). They have been widely used in marketing research and applied social sciences, including evaluation research (Krueger 1988), communications and organizational research (Byers and Wilcox 1991), media research (Conner, Richardson, and Fenton 1991) and decision research (Stewart and Shamdasani 1990). However, it is only recently that focus groups are receiving increasing attention as a means to obtain qualitative data in an interactive context (Goss and Leinbach 1996).

The term 'focus group' derives its roots from a combination of two standard social scientific research methods.[3] First, the focused interview, in which an interviewer elicits information on a topic without the use of a fixed questionnaire guide. And second, the group discussion, in which a possibly heterogeneous, but carefully selected group of people discuss a series of particular questions raised by a skilled moderator. A focus group can meet once or several times. The group is provided with a common input and the reaction of the group to this input is explored. A focus

---

[3] The discussion of the focus group methodology in this section is based on the method-ology review given by Dürrenberger *et al.* (1997).

group can thus be described as a guided group discussion where a limited number of persons focus their attention on a specific topic.

Results of a single focus group may be biased, for example due to the specific people involved, perhaps some dominant individuals, or the moderation style. This implies that a series of focus groups should always be conducted in order to get reliable results. Data gathering is generally done by means of written notes, video taping, questionnaires and different types of output produced by the group. Data analysis techniques range from brief summaries with selected quotes to detailed coding of full transcripts. As qualitative data are subject to hermeneutic interpretations, more than one researcher should iteratively analyze the focus group output in order to produce robust results.

Why are focus groups an interesting basis for participatory methods in IA? The advantage of focus groups compared to individual interviews is that focus groups intrinsically exhibit social dynamics that allow for interactions between multiple perspectives, instead of just compiling different perspectives by individual questionnaires or interviews. Furthermore, an interesting feature of focus groups, in contrast to ordinary group discussions, is that purposive information on a focal issue (e.g., written documents and/or product demonstrations in the case of marketing applications) is given as stimulus to the participants. The aim of focus group discussions is then to elucidate relevant perceptions, attitudes, values, and behaviors of both the individual participants and of the group as a whole.

However, conventional focus group techniques are not sufficient to provide input for IAs of the complex issues related to sustainability. For this reason, the ULYSSES researchers adapted these techniques in several ways. The adaptations include the use of a longer and more structured discussion process than in conventional focus groups. This allows the participants to express their spontaneous associations (e.g., in collage work), and to access current research findings (usually by the use of computer models in the focus groups), before the group summarizes their views on the focal topic. The resulting focus groups were called IA Focus Groups to distinguish them from other types.

Because the principal purpose of the research discussed here was to study views that emerged in discussions between different types of participants (thought to be more indicative of public opinion dynamics than a study of the views of isolated segments of the population), it was important that the IA Focus Groups were diverse with respect to age, gender, income, educational level, and attitudes toward the environment. To that end, the potential participants were carefully screened, with quotas established for manual workers and college graduates; those who felt that

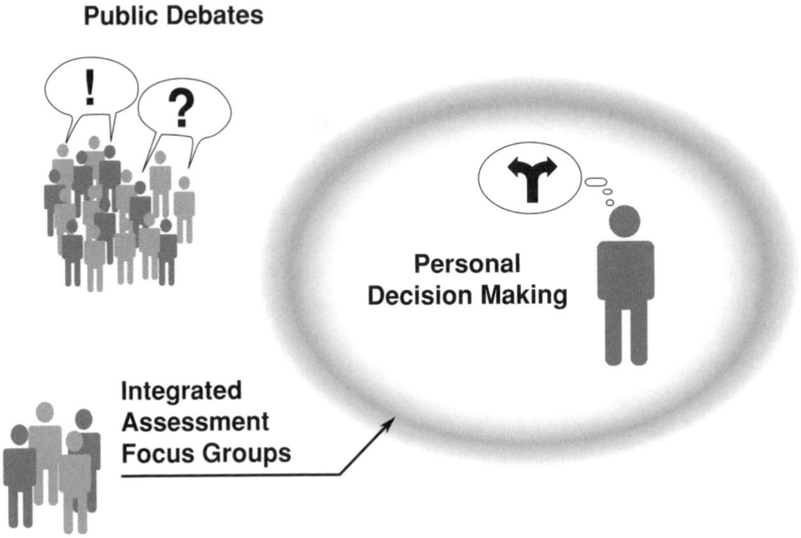

Public Debates

Figure 1.1 IA Focus Groups at the border between private decision-making and public debates

environmental problems were important and those who did not; and those who favored environmental regulation and those who did not.

A crucial feature of IA Focus Groups is that they explore the border between private decision-making and public debates (Figure 1.1). While the physical setting is more typical of a private conversation (a small group of people sit around a table and respond to each other's remarks), the topics introduced by the moderator and the overall group situation (people who have not met before and who may or may not produce common conclusions) belongs more to the realm of public debate. Because ordinary people tend to make up their minds about climate change (and, in fact, on most environmental issues) at the interface between their private lives and public debates, such participatory procedures that are built upon focus group techniques may be especially promising here. Understanding the private/public interface is essential for interpreting the results of IA Focus Groups. In decision theory as in micro-economics, the standard assumption is that any decision-maker, be it an individual, a household, or an organization, can be characterized by a set of stable preferences (Kreps 1988; Kleindorfer, Kunreuther, and Schoemaker 1993). These preferences cover the range of possible options in such a way as to enable the decision maker to order all of them so that any two alternatives are either indifferent or ranked according to preference. Useful as this default assumption turns out to be in many cases, it is insufficient to deal with the specific human ability to reflect on one's preferences and to try to change them – as may be the case with somebody who decides to change her or his eating habits. Moreover, it is also insufficient to deal with the case where a person or organization displays different preferences in different situations – as when different social roles come with different preference orderings. Both problems are highly relevant for sustainability issues. The lifestyles of people may be at stake, and a need to critically examine one's present preferences may well arise. Moreover, the role of citizens, which is relevant for policy decisions, may involve other preferences than the role, say, of consumers, which is obviously relevant for sustainability issues too.

IA Focus Groups are not designed to elicit consumer preferences – these are studied much more fruitfully by observing actual consumer behavior. Where new products are to be investigated, conventional focus groups may be a useful complement to the investigation of such behavior. IA Focus Groups, however, are designed to observe citizen preferences in a dynamic setting. This means that preferences may be expressed, criticized, and/or revised in the course of the conversation. It also means that the relevant preferences do not necessarily apply to individual consumption decisions, but rather to collective policy decisions. Such collective decisions can be understood to be at the heart of climate and sustainability problems:

Reducing carbon dioxide and taking further steps to curtail global warming will require collective action and institutional change (both intra- and internationally) and are unlikely to result primarily from people changing their consumption patterns on an individual basis. Indeed, one could argue that public support for environmental regulation and incentives, and for politicians who will implement them, is far more essential than voluntary change in individual consumer behaviors when it comes to achieving a global-level "public good" like a (reasonably) stable climate.   (Dunlap 1998)

Given a certain infrastructure and a certain pattern of monetary and other incentives, individual consumers may currently choose to use energy at a rate of 5,000 watts and more. As citizens, the same individuals may support policies that would enable them to consume much less energy in the future. Such behavior is not a sign of irrationality, it is an expression of human reflexivity in a complex society. IA Focus Groups are designed to stimulate this reflexivity.

A subtle understanding of preferences and their dynamics is especially relevant when it comes to decision-making under uncertainty. IA Focus Groups enable stakeholders to make up their minds about major choices that will have to be made on uncertain issues like global change in the light of scientific information. They also enable researchers to learn what preferences, including subjective probabilities, come into play in this process, and how such preferences are shaped by social interactions with scientific expertise and with other stakeholders.

General format of IA Focus Groups

IA Focus Groups are further developments of focus group techniques that allow lay participants to interact with expert inputs, for example, information on environmental change. This input is usually in the form of computer models. However, there is a fine line to be aware of in designing such procedures. On the one hand, if the process is dominated too heavily by expert input, participation becomes more symbolic than real. On the other hand, if expert input is not adequately integrated, the point of facilitating interfaces between expert and lay perspectives is missed and the result is more of a usual focus group process that assesses, for example, environmental attitudes. In order to keep a balance between these two extremes, for any issue to be debated, participants should be given the opportunity to express and share their initial knowledge and views before any expert input is provided. The debates should not be limited to the information provided by the facilitators, but discussions of diverse viewpoints should enable a shared learning experience.

In the IA Focus Group procedure discussed here, this concept of allowing for more open discussion before providing expert input was followed in the overall design. Indeed, there were three distinct phases to these focus groups (see Box 1.1).

Each group consisted of approximately six to eight citizens (while overall approximately 600 citizens participated in the study reported here). The citizens were invited to the meetings on the basis of recruitment criteria. The recruitment procedure ensured a heterogeneous mix of participants not only with regard to social stratification but also with regard to different environmental attitudes, and furthermore prevented the participating citizens from holding an unusually high level of expert/scientific knowledge about the issue before participating in the group debates. Most groups met for five sessions of approximately 2.5 hours per session, or for an equivalent amount of discussion time organized in fewer sessions. A moderator facilitated the group discussions, which focused on climate and energy issues and on possible or desirable urban developments in

Box 1.1: The three phases of IA Focus Group procedures

In order to allow for the free expression of the participants' feelings and opinions, as well as their reflection on expert input on the topic under discussion, the IA Focus Group procedures discussed here were structured into three phases (see Figure 1.2).

The first phase was focused on the spontaneous expression of participants' feelings about climate change and energy use. Working with collages is an interesting option here (see Chapter 4), in addition to a general discussion regarding the environmental problems that the participants are concerned about. Then, after that initial phase, the groups were exposed to and interacted with expert opinion on climate change and energy use in the second phase

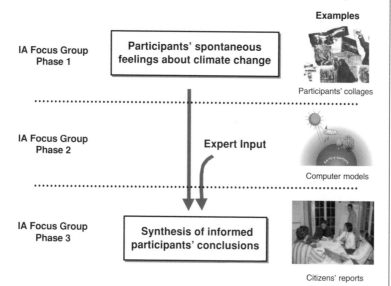

Figure 1.2 The three phases of IA Focus Group processes

of the procedure (see Chapter 5). The scientific input, in particular the computer models, was normally presented and discussed with the support of a second moderator.[4] Finally, in the third phase, the participants made a synthesis of their views after completing the exercise, e.g., in the form of a written citizens report (see Chapter 6).

---

[4] The intervention of a *model moderator* prevented the *group moderator* having to perform an "expert role" during the group discussions. Also within this second phase, participants were given the opportunity to express their initial views and expectations – in this case expectations about the models – before each model was introduced.

the region where participants lived. The groups were given access to expert assessments, usually in the form of computer models[5] and a diverse selection of modeled future scenarios. In some of the focus groups, links to Local Agenda 21 initiatives or other local development initiatives had been established, leading to a broadening of the focus beyond climate and energy.

As the overall goal was to develop and test new tools for public participation in sustainability science, different design versions of participatory procedures within the same general format were developed and tested in the course of the research discussed here. The design described in this chapter was developed and applied by research teams in Barcelona, Frankfurt, Stockholm, and Zurich. Two related methodological designs were developed and applied by teams in Venice and Manchester. These are sketched in the following[6] herein and described in more depth in Chapter 2. The Manchester team designed procedures closer to existing public participation techniques and without using computer models in the group sessions, while the Venice team adopted an approach more closely related to research on citizens' assessments of climate change. These two research teams used different terms to describe the meetings with local residents. For the Italian team, the concept of *In-depth Groups* (Burgess, Limb, and Harrison 1988) was used, reflecting a "research-framing" of their approach, while the British team called them *Citizens' Panels*, reflecting a "policy for real" framing (see also Kitchener and Darier 1998a; 1998b; Guimarães Pereira, Gough, and De Marchi 1999; De Marchi *et al.* 1998). On the other hand, the groups held in Athens were different from the ones conducted by the other teams, since the main aim for that research region was to run 'media groups' that included journalists and citizens.

Before discussing IA Focus Group procedures in more detail, we want to note that a potential problem in any research that uses group discussions is the possibility that certain individuals may dominate such discussions. Inevitably, some focus group participants will have more influence than others. However, an experienced moderator will try to prevent the more talkative or assertive ones from dominating the group process, and encourage the others to speak up (see Merton 1987; Morgan and Krueger 1998a). Indeed, a focus group study on a topic similar to the present project found that dominance by particular individuals can usually be avoided (see Dahinden 1998).

---

[5] The computer models most commonly used within ULYSSES have been: IMAGE (Alcamo 1994), TARGETS (Rotmans and de Vries 1997), PoleStar (Raskin *et al.* 1996), and "Personal CO_2 – Calculator" (Schlumpf *et al.* 1999).
[6] This brief description is based on Querol *et al.* (1999).

Detailed design of IA Focus Groups

Below we describe the design developed and tested by the Barcelona, Frankfurt, Stockholm, and Zurich research teams of ULYSSES in more detail (see also Kasemir *et al.* 1999a).[7]

Recruitment

The aim of the recruitment process was to enlist a broad cross-section of citizens to participate in our groups. This applies both to socio-demographic criteria as well as to environmental attitudes. The latter criterion was considered important in order to ensure that different perspectives on climate and energy were represented in the discussions. Using heterogeneous group compositions means that they can be considered as a kind of micro-cosmos for exploring debates that could take place within the general public (see Jaeger, Schüle, and Kasemir 1999).

To obtain a broad sample of the perspectives of European citizens, we conducted IA Focus Groups in seven metropolitan areas – Athens, Barcelona, Frankfurt, Manchester, Stockholm, Venice, and Zurich. Several focus group discussions were held in each area and, including the pilot sessions, approximately 600 people from across Europe participated in these groups. In addition, special sessions were conducted with regional decision-makers and representatives of the financial industry and the media.

Criteria

In order to get a heterogeneous spectrum of focus group participants, recruitment criteria such as the following were applied:

Place of residence:	All participants should be inhabitants of the same metropolitan area.
Age:	At least one third of the participants should be younger and at least one third should be older than 50 years.
Gender:	At least one third of the participants should be male and at least half should be female.
Occupation and Education:	At least one third of participants should be manual workers (employees or entrepreneurs) and

---

[7] The design is also described in a web-based tutorial. J. P. Van der Sluijs, J. Jäger, C. Querol, À. Gerger, and B. Kasemir (1999). The ULSSES Web Tutorial on Participatory Integrated Assessment. http://www.zit.tu-darmstadt.de/ulysses

	no more than one third university graduates.
Income:	At least one third of the participants should have relatively low income (threshold below the average household income) and at least one third should have relatively high income (some threshold above the average household income).
Attitudes toward the environment:	In order to avoid a "green" bias in our groups, two questions were asked when contacting potential group participants: "Please mention the three most important problems in our society today." At least one third of participants should have mentioned the environment, at least one third of the participants should not have mentioned it. "Would you be in favor of more environmental regulation (taxes and laws)?" At least one third of participants should have agreed, at least one third should have disagreed.

Recruitment was carried out either by the research teams themselves (using random phone contacts and subsequent screening for the criteria) or by professional recruitment agencies. The above recruitment criteria led to highly heterogeneous groups. In some groups this ranged, for example, from an unemployed waiter to a stockbroker with high income, from an industrial worker to a 'cultural consultant', or from an 84-year-old retired teacher to a 23-year-old hotel receptionist. Accordingly, the discussions in the groups were shaped by very different backgrounds and experiences among the participants. These types of discussions needed more careful moderation, but also tended to contain richer interactions between different viewpoints than had been the case with more homogeneous pilot groups conducted within the project.

In general, participant recruitment is one of the most difficult aspects of conducting IA Focus Groups. It is far from trivial to get a mix of participants according to all the above criteria, especially if they should be prepared to attend five sessions.

Process description

In the research discussed here, the IA Focus Group procedures developed for public participation in sustainability science were tested for the specific topic of climate change and energy issues. One version of the general IA Focus Group format is described below.

First phase: Session one

This first phase of IA Focus Groups is usually conducted without providing expert input. At the start, the participants complete a questionnaire that determines socio-demographic data and establishes their attitudes about climate change issues (knowledge, attitudes, and support for goals and mitigation measures). After that, the moderator may introduce the metaphor that describes the participants going on a voyage, during which the IA Focus Group will explore different sites (e.g., climate change information expressed in the form of different computer models).[8] This voyage metaphor can also be used throughout the subsequent sessions. Furthermore, from the very beginning of the sessions, the participants are encouraged to express their own opinions and concerns ("there are no right or wrong answers; there is no need to agree with the others...").

Then, in order to explore spontaneous non-verbal associations to climate and energy issues, the participants are asked to produce collages on their expectations for the future. For this task, the groups are split into subgroups. One subgroup produces a collage on how they think their region could look by 2030 if present trends continue. The other subgroup does the same under the assumption that energy use is reduced by 50 per cent from present levels up to 2030. Each group is provided with a set of magazines containing a wide range of images to choose from. After approximately 30 minutes to 1 hour, the two subgroups present these collages to each other, and discuss them. Experiences with these collage processes are discussed in Chapter 4.

The first session also includes a more general discussion on which environmental problems participants are concerned about. The session is closed with a short feedback round on how the participants had experienced this session, and a short presentation of the program for the following sessions. One tool that can be used in the last part of all sessions are "graffiti cards": pieces of cardboard on which each participant can make a drawing of what he or she thought or felt important about this session. These drawings are then presented to the group and are intended

---

[8] This use of a voyage metaphor and its link to the diary or logbook procedure (see below) was inspired by the approach of the Venice research team within the ULYSSES project (see De Marchi *et al.* 1998).

to enable the participants to express themselves in a more informal manner. A further tool that can be used is the "voyage diary" in which each participant, or alternatively all participants together, can note down their impressions of this leg of their "journey."

Second phase: Sessions two, three, and four

In these sessions, the participants discuss climate change and related regional policy options and mitigation measures. They are provided with computer models and possibly other expert input (e.g., "fact sheets" or expert presentations) as a background to their discussions. A model moderator both introduces the computer models and facilitates the group's interaction with them. In the following, we give an introductory overview of the content of these sessions. The use of models in IA Focus Groups is described and analyzed in more depth in Chapter 5.

One possible way to start the second part of the IA Focus Group process is first to introduce the global dimension of climate change and energy use. Alternatively, the regional aspects of climate change can be introduced in the initial phase of the discussions before moving on to the global scale. In either case, it seems useful to use both a model on global change and one on alternative regional developments. In our groups, the participants were presented with either the IMAGE (see Alcamo 1994) or the TARGETS (see Rotmans and de Vries 1997) model on global change. The group could choose to look at specific scenarios from a pre-computed set (in the case of IMAGE), or request scenarios to be computed directly during the session (in the case of TARGETS). Before the model is used, the participants are asked what information they would expect or like the models to provide, and they are asked to complete a short questionnaire on their expectations of, and previous experience with, computers. The model is then presented and used to support the discussions on different global change scenarios.

During the discussions on regional options related to climate and energy, either a computer tool on regional carbon dioxide emissions or a tool to calculate personal carbon dioxide emissions is used. In the focus groups discussing regional emissions, PoleStar (see Raskin *et al.* 1996) was used, which allows, for example, the calculation of regional carbon dioxide emissions, if technology mix and usage level are specified. Some regional scenarios are computed in advance, and the group may also suggest preferable future changes in different sectors, for example, transport and household, which are then translated into model scenarios between two sessions. As an alternative, a computer tool to calculate personal carbon dioxide emissions (see Schlumpf *et al.* 1999) was employed in some groups. Whichever tool is used, and in whatever specific way, it is important to provide enough time for the group to discuss in-depth desirable (and undesirable) possible future developments in their region.

The participants' interaction with computer models was especially useful in that it helped to address both global and regional issues, and their interdependencies, in the focus group discussions. After the participants interact with the models, they then comment on their experiences with these models in a discussion and by completing another short questionnaire. At the end of each of these three sessions, the same procedure that was used at the end of session one is employed: a feedback round, possibly using graffiti cards and/or voyage diaries.

Third phase: Session five

In the final session of the IA Focus Groups the participants express their concluding assessments. The group does this via the production of a written citizens' report. For this, the research team asks the group to make an assessment of climate issues and related policy options according to a list of questions such as the following:

1. Do you think there is a climate change problem here (e.g., in Stockholm)? World-wide? If so, then what is the problem?
2. If so, what changes need to be made in the way people in this region will be living thirty years from now?
3. What should be done to get there?
4. Given this, how much energy use compared to today is appropriate in total, and in the different sectors (e.g., transport, households).
5. Who should take action? And when?
6. What do you think will be the difficulties in getting there?
7. If you have anything else you want to note down, please do so.

These questions have already been presented to the group in the preceding sessions, so that this task does not come as a surprise to the group in this final session. Often, the participants start with drafting parts of their report in these earlier sessions as well. Usually, the moderation team leaves the room while the group works on their citizens' report for approximately 1.5 hours in the final session.[9] The group is encouraged to note down their agreement on points where consensus develops, but are not required to reach a common position. The reason is that if the participants strive for consensus at any cost, the result might be "trivial" reports that give only the least common denominator and leave all remaining conflict aside.

---

[9] However, some groups preferred the moderators to stay and to help with compiling statements they had made in earlier sessions into the report.

At the end of this final session, the group presents its citizens' report to the moderation team and comments on it in a final discussion round. Experiences with these citizens' report procedures are discussed in Chapter 6. Subsequently, the participants complete a short final questionnaire on issues of climate, energy, and policy options. The process is then closed with the usual feedback round, and a general evaluation by the participants of the whole focus group process.

Analysis

The data obtained from IA Focus Groups requires a more structured analysis than is usual with conventional focus groups. One procedure that was found to be especially useful for this type of exercise is to videotape the group discussions, to selectively transcribe them, and then to scan the transcripts for discussion sequences relating to the topics of primary interest with the help of software that supports qualitative content analysis.

Exploring the patterns of such discussion sequences helps to identify the relevant "ideal types" of lay views on scientific and policy questions. These are evaluated not only on the basis of the number of times a view is expressed but also in terms of the meaningfulness of the vision reflected in it. Ideal types were introduced into social science methodologies by sociologist Max Weber at the beginning of the twentieth century. For an early US reaction to Weber's ideas, see Parson (1937). The application of ideal types to focus group analysis is described in Schüle (2000).

Ideal-type analysis simplifies qualitative data by focusing on possible alternative states of a given social system, and by relating such alternatives to the moral choices this system faces at a given time. This type of analysis is thus especially well suited for studies targeting the views of social actors and their potential impact on future developments. Some results of the analysis of IA Focus Groups conducted with citizens across Europe are discussed in the next section.

Major results on citizens' perspectives

Stakeholder groups involved in the ULYSSES project ranged from ordinary citizens to decision-makers in the domains of public policy, technology development, and financial investment. The main aim, however, was to explore the participation of citizens in IAs of climate change and energy issues. To obtain a broad sample of European citizens' views, IA Focus Groups were conducted in seven metropolitan areas – Athens, Barcelona, Frankfurt, Manchester, Stockholm, Venice, and Zurich. As the views of a single group may be biased, several focus group discussions were held in

Table 1.1 *Number of citizens involved in ULYSSES and CLEAR[a] Groups*

Region	Main Groups	Pilot Groups	Sum
Frankfurt	72	36	108
Venice (approx. numbers)	54	40	94
Manchester[b]	24	16	40
Barcelona	38	16	54
Stockholm	36	23	59
Athens		20	20
Zurich (incl. groups in CLEAR project)	132	92	224
Total	356	243	599

[a] In the Swiss part of the ULYSSES project, the IA Focus Groups were conducted in collaboration with the CLEAR project. CLEAR stands for Climate and Environment in Alpine Regions. Similar to ULYSSES in approach, this project was supported by the Swiss National Science Foundation.
[b] Manchester region, including St Helens.

each area. Including pilot groups, approximately 600 people from across Europe participated in these groups (see Table 1.1). Participants were selected according to pre-established quota so as to yield stratified samples of the population. However, it is crucial to understand that the sample space of IA Focus Groups does not consist of isolated statements of individual participants. The whole point of running group discussions lies in triggering conversations so as to be able to learn from interacting sequences of statements and from the resulting dynamics of opinion formation. This also implies that what matters in the analysis of IA Focus Groups is not just the frequency with which certain terms or words are used, but the context in which they are used. We can call this context "webs of meaning." Such webs of meaning, related to perspectives on climate change and energy use and observed in IA Focus Groups with citizens, are discussed in detail in Chapters 4, 5, and 6 of Part II of this book. Each of these chapters discusses the IA Focus Group approach from a different angle, allowing the reader to experience this adventure in participatory IA through "different glasses," and to be able to select the aspects which are most relevant for her or his own work. Finally, Parts III and IV of the book explore links between this research and ongoing state-of-the-art research on stakeholder participation in sustainability science.

As a more detailed discussion of the views of citizens who participated in the IA Focus Groups is given in later chapters, we give only a rough summary of some of the main results here. The European citizens who participated in the focus groups often saw the prospect of climate change as very frightening. They adopted an ethical rather than an economic approach to framing their discussions of climate impacts. Expectations of the deterioration of basic livelihoods around the world, ecological destruction, and danger to future generations made a wait-and-see policy unacceptable to them. In general, the participants were also in favor of mitigation measures even in the face of scientific uncertainty – that is, they usually based their views of the climate issue on the precautionary principle. In these respects, their opinions can be said to be close to a "deep-ecology perspective." Their views parted company with that perspective, however, when it came to discussing climate change mitigation. The participants readily considered the economic implications of any mitigation measures, and were interested to discuss the costs of such measures. In this respect, their views were closer to an "economic-management perspective." While most participants were supportive of small increases in energy prices, they usually rejected large ones. Although they often saw large reductions in energy use as more desirable than business as usual, they thought that this reduction should and could be achieved without greatly raising energy prices. Developing the products necessary to make this possible was often seen as the task of the research community and of industry. From these results one may infer that climate policy will only be acceptable to the European public if it focuses on developing low-cost options for substantially reducing energy use.

It is interesting to compare these results to those of other major studies of citizens' views. The international "Health of the Planet" survey on environmental attitudes was aimed "to give voice to individual citizens around the world concerning the environment and economic development issues affecting their lives" (Dunlap, Gallup, and Gallup 1993b; Dunlap and Mertig 1997). This survey was carried out in twenty-four nations both in developed and in developing regions around the world, and citizens in six nations (Canada, the US, Mexico, Brazil, Portugal, and Russia) were asked specifically about global warming (Dunlap 1998). Another series of studies has targeted US residents' views on global climate change, and has combined questionnaire survey methods with semi-structured interviews of a small but diverse sample of citizens (Kempton 1991; 1997). In contrast to both studies, the European participants of our IA Focus Groups had the opportunity to debate expert opinions on climate change and energy use in in-depth group debates, and had access to relevant computer models in this process. What are the major similarities and differences between the findings of these other studies and of the research discussed in this book?

First, while both of the other studies found that citizens had a high level of concern about climate change, the findings on which impacts of climate change generated the highest concern differ considerably between them. In the six-country study conducted in the context of the "Health of the Planet" survey, respondents saw global warming effects on natural systems (either by creating various ecological problems or by changing weather patterns) as more worrying than effects on social systems. "Choices that people have on where to live and economic well-being are the least likely realms to be seen as being harmed – suggesting that economists' emphasis on economic impacts (see, for example, Nordhaus 1994) ignores the public's crucial concerns..." (Dunlap 1998). However, Kempton's findings suggest that species preservation is not highly valued in the abstract by the majority of the US public. Instead, rising food costs, for example, were perceived as more worrying than species extinction, and most of his informants justified species preservation in anthropocentric terms. Concerning climate change impacts, our findings are more in line with Dunlap's results. Most European citizens participating in the IA Focus Groups expressed concern with geophysical, ecological, and human health impacts, but not with economic impacts of climate change.

Second, concerning mitigation of environmental degradation in general, the "Health of the Planet" survey overall found some willingness to pay higher prices if these increases supported environmental protection. The role of technology was perceived ambiguously, seen both as a cause of environmental problems, but also as a part of the solution. Concerning these points, our research on the views of European citizens can give more depth to Dunlap's results. While the IA Focus Group participants supported some increases in energy prices, substantial price increases were rejected. The expectations of the roles of technology were mainly to achieve decreased energy use without high costs or loss of comfort. Under these conditions, a strong reduction of energy use was often seen as more positive than business as usual. This is in contrast to Kempton's findings that US respondents saw reductions in energy use much less positively: "When analysts talk about reducing energy use, lay people [in the United States] tend to interpret it as decreasing energy services" (Kempton 1991). Given the much more positive views of ordinary Europeans on this issue found in the research discussed in this book, European policy-makers may have more opportunity to address climate change by focusing on significant reductions in energy use than do their US counterparts. However, on the following issue there is a match between Kempton's results of US citizens' views and the views of ordinary European citizens participating in our IA Focus Groups: he found that average Americans "are aware that measurable environmental disturbance is now global in scale... and they want decisions to be based not only on cost and benefits but also on our responsibility to leave a healthy planet for our descendants."

The feasibility of IA Focus Group participants' expectations concerning decreased energy use will in part depend on investments made in technological innovations. Rather than discussing results of a participatory process with financial investors on this issue (for which we refer the reader to Chapter 7), we want to conclude this section by emphasizing that stakeholder participation is not about reducing, but rather *clarifying* uncertainty and disagreement.[10] Providing narrative scripts of different points of view of different stakeholders, and including multiple scenarios based on these, can support negotiation processes on environmental policy better than developing any single "optimal" description or scenario could. It is in this spirit that we are making various perspectives of ordinary European citizens, who have been exposed to expert opinions on issues of climate change and energy use, available to policy-makers and researchers. While science has long been based on the paradigm of "settling" debates rather than supporting them, with procedures like IA Focus Groups, IA can both provide negotiation support and advance the process of scientific inquiry.

Outlook

Today's global society knows two major institutional settings for the "giving and taking of reasons": parliamentary democracy and scientific research. Of course, reasons are exchanged in all kinds of interactions – and such exchange may even be seen as lying at the core of what it means to be human (Brandom 1998). This makes the role of parliaments and of scientific communities all the more interesting. And it makes the tensions between the two a major issue for the future.

In a parliamentary democracy, issues are debated in public and decisions are then made by electing and/or voting. In scientific communities, issues are debated among specialists and arguments are selected on the basis of peer review processes. Increasingly, these two modes of collective reasoning have begun to interact with each other. Debates about genetically modified food, about nuclear power, about climate change, about internet security, about social security, health care, and military technology are impressive examples from a much longer list. These issues share the property that knowledge claims from scientific communities

---

[10] This paragraph owes much to the very fruitful discussions we had with participants of the workshop on "Uncertainty and Participation in Integrated Assessments," organized by the European Forum on Integrated Assessment (EFIEA), Baden, 10–17 July 1999. Responsibility for errors stays with the authors.

become the subjects of public controversies, and that at important junctures the relevant issues are settled by parliamentary decisions. There is a serious difficulty in balancing scientific expertise and democratic decision-making in such situations. As a result, they require institutional innovations, exercises in "creative democracy" (Burns and Ueberhorst 1988) at the interface between parliamentary and scientific debates.

IA Focus Groups offer an important opportunity in this respect. Already today, conventional focus groups are used as an important means to gauge opportunities for, and the results of, policy interventions. However, this often happens without providing scientific information to the citizens involved and without making the results of these groups accessible to public and scientific dialogue. IA Focus Groups can help to overcome these deficits. If IA Focus Groups are geared to parliamentary debates, they can strengthen the role of parliament as the arena where the whole polity can focus, as through a lens, for a while on the long-term choices with which the polity is faced. One could imagine, for example, that the European Parliament would engage in a debate about European food policies, while across Europe IA Focus Groups were run concerning the same topic. Other examples are easy to find. Instruments like the Enquête-Kommission of the German parliament could be used to give additional depth to such debates.

One might consider the possibility of running IA Focus Groups linked to specific parliamentary debates on a regular, possibly yearly, basis. This would have the advantage of establishing a lasting communication process. Topics could change from year to year so as to establish a comprehensive view of long-term choices relevant for the polity. Evidence about global environmental assessments indicates that in order to be effective such assessments should not consist simply in written reports delivered to some authority, but in an ongoing communication which supports open processes of social learning (Clark and Dickson 1998). IA Focus Groups provide one platform for such communication.

Parliamentary debates linked to IA Focus Groups could take great advantage of Internet technologies. As our experience in the ULYSSES and CLEAR projects has shown, the Internet can be used to make scientific information accessible for IA Focus Groups and for stakeholders in general. This of course refers to the possibility of overcoming geographical distance in information transfer, but it also goes much further. Web browsers provide tremendous opportunities to present scientific information to laypersons. Current systems of parliamentary knowledge management could be considerably enhanced by using IA Focus Groups in combination with web-based knowledge systems. In order to make this possible, such systems should be built directly with the needs of lay users in mind. The use of IA Focus Groups already in the design phase for web-based systems of knowledge management is relevant for many stakeholders in environmental and other issues.

Not only for parliaments and other public policy institutions, but also for many businesses and industries there is a real need for new forms of dialogue that involve scientific communities and the public. A platform that enables different parties to share their perspectives and to develop a synthesized and integrated view of the state of scientific knowledge, including the unavoidable uncertainties arising with any complex problems, could be of great use for solving such problems. Along these lines, the procedures for public participation discussed in this book can be used as a starting point for supporting a plurality of stakeholders to solve complex problems in a cooperative manner.

CHAPTER TWO

Contexts of citizen participation

Clair Gough, Éric Darier, Bruna De Marchi, Silvio Funtowicz, Robin Grove-White, Ângela Guimarães Pereira, Simon Shackley, and Brian Wynne

Climate change: between democracy and expertise?

Climate change represents one of society's most challenging environmental concerns and has been a major factor in changes in the way that environmental policies are debated and informed. Climate change policy faces at least three major challenges: (1) what is known – or not known – about climate change, in particular regarding the relative importance of anthropogenic factors; (2) what can and should be done; and (3) who should do something about it?

Since the 1992 Rio Earth Summit, these challenges have been addressed in several ways: (a) by increasing research and international sharing and integration of expertise on climate change (e.g., the Intergovernmental Panel on Climate Change); (b) by developing international agreements on issues such as the reduction of carbon dioxide emissions; and (c) by promoting national/local strategies to fulfil international agreements (e.g., Local Agenda 21 – community defined strategies for sustainable development arising from the first "Earth Summit" held in Rio in 1992). These challenges all include policy and scientific aspects but also raise questions over the interpretation of Local Agenda 21 (Tuxworth 1996; Selman and Parker 1997; Voisey *et al.* 1996; Young 1996; Young 1997). How local is "local"? What kind of "agenda" is "Agenda 21"? Whose "agenda" is it? Answers to these questions vary according to the perspectives and purposes of those asking the questions in the first place. The spectrum of answers reflects the diversity of views about what could or should constitute the "local" in relation to climate change policy. Nevertheless, there is a general common purpose behind Local Agenda 21 which is to involve "people" – whoever this might include: citizens, public(s), electors, individuals, households, consumers, family, community, stakeholders, local/regional governments, etc. What exactly such an involvement of "people" could mean raises difficult methodological questions and was one of the foci of the research discussed in this volume.

Obviously, an easy answer is to claim that the involvement of all is relevant. However, as the literature of the sociology of science and policy informs us, the actual defining of objects of inquiry and/or legitimate actors is shaped and constrained by the specific contexts from which they emerge. One of our first objectives here is to identify the broader contexts which made it possible for the articulation of a concern about the involvement of "people" in environmental, particularly climate change, issues. In Western Europe, there are two main contextual features that are relevant to environmental policy: (1) a general commitment to "democracy" and the extension of public participation, and (2) a perceived legitimate need to "integrate" and "assess" complex and uncertain expert knowledges. "Climate change" discourses have emerged in the dynamic and context-specific spaces between these two features of the Western experience (relationships between these have been discussed already in Chapter 1 for the specific case of parliamentary debates). Citizens' participation in sustainability science in general, and in Integrated Assessment (IA) of climate change in particular, highlights the uneasy relationship between democracy and expert knowledges as they have been generally understood in the West. The central goal of the research discussed in this book was to develop procedures for facilitating the integration of lay and expert knowledges. This chapter – based on experiences from two case studies, in-depth groups conducted in Venice (Italy), and citizens' panels conducted in St. Helens (UK) – focuses specifically on contexts and conditions for participation in such procedures.

Commitment to "democracy"

The commitment to "democracy" – or at least its rhetoric – has been widespread in the West since the seventeenth century (Held 1987). However this is only one aspect of a broader Western historical trend that also required that an increasingly (self-)disciplined and homogenized population become responsible (i.e., predictable) "citizens" as a condition for successful and lasting "democratic" regimes (Foucault 1981; 1991). Global environmental issues – like climate change – also require the active mobilization and normalization of the population, in this case, as global eco-citizens (Luke 1999; Rutherford 1999). Active "participation" of "people" is now assumed to be a necessary working feature of democracy, as illustrated by the recent renewed theoretical interest in "deliberative democracy" (Bohman and Rehg 1997) and various "participatory" practices such as "citizens' juries" or "planning cells" (Coote and Lenaghan

1997; Renn, Webler, and Wiedemann 1995). In addition, there are reconceptualizations of the notion of "sovereignty" – including sometimes democratic practices of "sovereignty" – away from exclusively "nation-states" at the macro and micro levels. Emerging powerful global organizations (e.g., international institutions, global corporations, international NGOs) and increasingly relevant "local" practices (e.g., regional/local governments, new individual and collective territorialized/ de-territorialized identities), are all contributing to heterogeneous and poly-centered practices around "sovereignty" (Bauman 1998; Castells 1996; 1997; Foucault 1991; Held 1995). The concept of "subsidiarity" in the EU is an example of the reconceptualization of "sovereignty" where the specific implementation of an appropriate policy takes place at the level where it is the most effective overall.

The rise of expertise

In parallel to an increased commitment to "democratic" practices over the past few centuries, knowledge has become increasingly the domain of "scientific" expertise and oriented mainly toward producing end results. Combined with a general increase in expertise (including greater awareness of uncertainty and complexity), global environmental issues created new research concerns for what is now commonly referred to as Integrated Assessment or IA. Integration is necessitated by the perceived need to offer a synthesized *assessment* drawing on various fields of expertise, which takes into account the complexity and degree of scientific uncertainty about the causes and the possible future impacts of climate change (e.g., Parson 1995; Risbey, Kandlikar, and Patwardhan 1996; Weyant *et al.* 1996). Due to the necessarily broad nature of such an ambitious approach, IA is open to different interpretations, including its uneasy relationship with the policy process (e.g., Haigh 1998), although all agree that IA cannot be captured within the scope of a single expert discipline (e.g., van Asselt, Beusen and Hilderink 1996; Bailey 1997; Rotmans and van Asselt 1996; Morgan and Dowlatabadi 1996; Shackley, Risbey, and Kandlikar 1998; Darier, Shackley; and Wynne 1999). This plurality of definitions need not be problematic but it calls for additional clarification on our part.

Combining democracy and expertise: 'Participatory Integrated Assessment'?

One of the results of combining a commitment to "democracy" with technical and/or scientific expertise, is a series of general calls for the "public" – or rather the publics – to have some say in global environmental issues (Lafferty and Meadowcroft 1996) and in IA in particular (e.g., Funtowicz and Ravetz 1991). This is part of a broader and older call for the democratization of science and of policy-making. There are strong *scientific* reasons that such democratization should lead to better quality in the assessment process (Funtowicz and Ravetz 1997). The term "Post Normal Science" has been adopted by some to represent such an extended approach to the use of scientific and other forms of expertise, which is particularly relevant in situations of high stakes, urgency and uncertainty (Funtowicz and Ravetz 1993). The ambiguities identified in IA and in "participation" separately are multiplied manyfold when it is suggested that the public should participate in IA. In fact it is not at all clear "where does the public[s] fit in" to scientifically framed issues (Perhac Jr. 1998; Irwin and Wynne 1996). However, the broader issue here is about the (possible) relationship between expertise (of scientists and policy actors) and the overwhelming majority of the population who do not have "expert" knowledge but have nevertheless a broader set of "lay knowledges" which might be relevant to environmental decision-making. Therefore, the nature of the relationship between "expert" knowledges and "lay" publics is at least as much about the general (mis)understanding of the "publics" – and their "lay knowledges" – by those who have specialized scientific knowledges[1] as it is about the "public(s) understanding of scientific knowledges." Thus, implementing participatory IA can present equal challenges to both expert and lay participants, as the process may call on new types of interactions from each. This is precisely what our research and other recent experiments are striving to do under the broader banner of "public participation" in IA (e.g., De Marchi *et al.* 1998; Bailey 1997; Bailey, Yealey, and Forrester 1999; Jaeger *et al.* 1995; Jaeger 1998; Darier and Schüle 1999).

However, tensions remain in calls for "public participation" as it can be justified as a political "good" in itself (ethical prior commitment) and/or as a technique for the further enhancement of expert knowledges and policy-making (instrumental means) (Fiorino 1990; Gundersen 1995; Kitchener and Darier 1998a; Webler and Renn 1995). We consider that the interface between experts and lay publics must be a contextual and

---

[1] The "lay/expert" distinction is made here simply as an analytical means of distinguishing between those who are professionals in environmental science and policy (and hence ascribed with a certain authority) and those who are perceived as not having "professional" expertise on the topic and therefore generally marginalised and/or ignored within the debate (or more commonly unaware of the debate in the first place!). Also, this distinction should not obliterate the sharp differences which frequently exist among "experts" from the same and/or from different disciplines.

interactive process if both are to be able to make meaningful sense of their respective domains of expertise and to contribute to an integrated assessment. As Laird (1993) puts it: "The education that needs to take place is helping people make the linkages between issues in their lives and scientific or technological policy choices." We include in Laird's definition of "people" not only the lay publics but also the experts; one of our commitments is to try to avoid the notion of *correct* (expert) perceptions and *incorrect* (non-expert) perceptions within the climate change debate (see the discussion by Thompson and Rayner (1998)).

The remainder of this chapter outlines what "citizen participation" in IA could look like in the light of our empirical experiences in Venice and in St. Helens, illustrating some of the richness, diversity, challenges, and opportunities. First, we present the approaches and objectives selected to encourage participation. Then, we describe the different types of expertise used. Finally we conclude with some insights that we consider can be relevant for future participation in IA.

Approaches, contexts, and objectives

The overall goal of the research discussed in this book was to develop and test new tools for public participation in IA. Because of the exploratory character of this research, different design versions of participatory procedures within the same general format were developed and tested. In this chapter, we discuss findings from two case studies conducted within the ULYSSES project, in Italy and the UK, in relation to their use of different metaphors in the framing of the participatory process with group designs based on "research" and "policy for real" framings, respectively. The two approaches featured many similarities – but also differences – reflecting the similarities and differences between the two locations. Further descriptions of the two case studies and their findings are presented in Guimarães Pereira *et al.* (1999), Darier and Schüle (1999), and Darier *et al.* (1999).

Approaches: In-depth groups and citizens' panels

Generally, our approaches were inspired by well-established qualitative methods in the social sciences known as "focus groups," as introduced by Merton and Kendall (1946) and recently refined further (Morgan and Krueger 1998b; 1998c; 1998d) which were adapted to the objectives of the present study (Dürrenberger *et al.* 1997; Kasemir *et al.* 1997). More precisely, our approaches built on two clusters of methods. The first cluster includes the growing qualitative studies using "focus groups" or "in-depth groups" to specifically examine public perceptions of environmental issues mainly for research purposes (e.g., Macnaghten *et al.* 1995; Burgess, Limb, and Harrison 1988; Grove-White *et al.* 1997). Within this cluster there is a small but expanding number of international comparative studies (Harrison, Burgess, and Filius 1996; McGranahan and Gerger 1999; Darier and Schüle 1999). The second cluster acknowledges the limitations of the above "public perceptions gathering" methods when it comes to examining the actual conditions for public "participation." There is already a sizeable body of processes that focus on public participation in policy-making and include, for example, "citizens' juries" and "planning cells" (Kuper 1997; Renn, Webler, and Wiedemann 1995; Coote and Lenaghan 1997). However, the topics reviewed in the course of these participative processes tend to be narrow in focus (e.g., "municipal waste" in a specific locality), and mainly within the jurisdiction of a single institution (e.g., a local government or a local Health Trust in contrast to the multilayers of jurisdictions involved in climate change).

Our own approaches fall somewhere between the two clusters (i.e., between research and decision-making for policy). In designing our approaches, we built on the general format of the ULYSSES project (described in Chapter 1 and at greater length in Dürrenberger *et al.* 1997) by adapting it to our specific contexts. For example, each team used different terms to describe the meetings of local residents. For the Italian team, there were *in-depth groups* (Burgess, Limb and Harrison 1988) reflecting a "research framing" while the British team called them *citizens' panels* reflecting a "policy for real" framing. The other important difference was the presentation of "expert" knowledge within the groups. In Venice, this was achieved mainly through Information and Communication Technology (ICT) using as a metaphor the "Voyage of Ulysses" (De Marchi *et al.* 1998; Guimarães Pereira, Gough, and De Marchi 1999), through which the topic of climate change was explicitly introduced into the discussion as one of the destinations of the metaphorical journey. In St. Helens, expert knowledge was introduced through the direct participation of the chief planner from the local municipal government and the executive director of the local Groundwork Trust, a well-established and active ENGO, through a "policy for real" framing (Kitchener and Darier 1998a; 1998b) in which environmental issues in general were brought into the discussion.

We should stress, however, that neither process represented the exact archetypal (in-depth discussion groups or policy for real) framing because of constraints and limitations beyond our control (namely, resources and lack of a policy organization prepared to entrust the process with real decision-making powers). However, these limitations in no way reduce the value of the material obtained for interpretative purposes. In the case of St. Helens, the project has contributed to the further use and development of participatory methods in informing policy on the part of a local authority.

Local contexts

St. Helens and Venice may appear, at first glance, a strange comparison to those who have visited both places. Yet, there are some striking similarities between parts of the Venice region and St. Helens. Both encompass peripheral (post-)industrial cultures which are undergoing massive economic, social, environmental, and urban restructuring. One of our questions was to examine how people living in such (post-)industrial cultures perceived global environmental issues and what were some of the necessary conditions for public participation. The Municipality of Venice covers the historic center of Venice (the part that tourists see), the mainland (facing the lagoon and containing the industrial centers), and the estuary (the islands between mainland and open sea). The Venice groups were made up of residents from all three areas and were held in Porto Marghera on the mainland. St. Helens is located within Merseyside (the administrative region of Liverpool and its surroundings), though it has many connections with Lancashire and Greater Manchester.

There are indeed many elements of similarity between St. Helens and the district of Porto Marghera in Venice (Jaeger *et al.* 1997b). Both regions:

- have a fairly long heavy industrial history (St. Helens since the eighteenth century; Porto Marghera since the First World War) especially in the energy, chemical, and metallurgical sectors;
- have experienced massive economic and social "adjustment" since the 1980s, such as the closing of all the coal mines in St. Helens which employed up to 20,000 people at its peak, and the loss of 11,000 jobs in Porto Marghera since the early 1960s (a decline of total employment by one-third);
- are located on the periphery of important urban cultures;
- experience multiple "split personalities" – former villages of Newton-le-Willows or Billinge in St. Helens, whose identities are divided between Liverpool (Merseyside), Manchester, and the County of Lancashire; or the diverse identities of the different Venetian areas;
- have local governments controlled by parties leaning toward the Left of the political spectrum while, until recently, national or regional governments were controlled by the parties on the Right.

The political culture and experience of "democracy" and "expertise" is structured differently in the two regions. Since the nineteenth century, trade unions and municipal governments have provided virtually the sole opportunities for participation in political activities for many in and around St. Helens. Because of the long-lasting and unchallenged constitutional, institutional, and political arrangement in the UK, there have been very few meaningful attempts at bridging "democracy" and "expertise." Therefore, there is virtually no culture of meaningful public participation in the UK. The only significant acts of public participation in the UK took the form of blue-collar trade union activism and a few radical municipal governments. However, even these two forms of participation disappeared under the government of Margaret Thatcher, notably through the adoption of anti-union legislation, the defeat of the coal miners' strike in 1984 and the reduction in the powers of – and funding to – local government. The first-past-the-post electoral system tends to produce large parliamentary majorities disproportionate to the actual voters' preferences. The UK electoral system produced a strong bipartisan party system and a political culture where achieving social consensus is not necessary. As a result there is very little public trust in government in the UK, particularly in view of the perceived fiasco on issues such as the nuclear industry and BSE (Bovine Spongiform Encephalopathy). However, there have been interesting changes recently. In the UK, the New Labour government elected in 1997 is committed to "democratization" and "decentralization." The establishment of Scottish, Welsh, Northern Irish and London assemblies – all elected on a proportional electoral system – points to possible future reforms in England and in the UK as a whole. In addition, there have been a series of innovative attempts allowing lay members of the public to interact directly with "expertise" in the policy-making process. For example, "citizens' juries" "citizens' panels," "consensus conferences" and so on have been used on a variety of issues. However, it is too early to say if these experiments will significantly change the UK political culture.

Roughly until the collapse of the Berlin wall, Italian political life was characterized by a strong ideological polarization which defined people not only by the political parties to which they belonged, but also by representative forms of collective action, from unions to (highly politicized) school councils. This situation has changed considerably in recent years, partly as a consequence of the "clean hands" experience (extensive investigation into political corruption). With the fading of old, consolidated distinctions and preferences in the political processes, new forms of political and civic aggregation are surfacing, although as yet these are far from being consolidated. New parties and political coalitions have appeared, in an attempt to remedy the progressive detachment of the citizens. Yet, on the whole, the new factions seem unable to fill the gap between the political sphere and civil society, while the public expresses strong discontent at the "lack of representation" they experience. New forms of aggregation are beginning to provide a channel for public intervention but they tend to address specific issues rather than broadly conceived political projects. Thus public participation rises and falls according to specific circumstances, and is yet to find stable channels for its full expression. In this context the environmental movement is highly dispersed and the Green Party has never been able to consolidate its different components nor has it been able to achieve a significant electoral success. A significant institutional change has been introduced recently that allows the citizens to directly elect a mayor. This has been presented as, and felt to be, an improvement in the mechanisms of participation.

Objectives and practical implementation

Two framings ("research" and "policy for real") were envisaged as providing a means of establishing a dialogue between lay and expert participants. What differed was the ways in which the two teams chose to structure the sessions and the *medium* of interaction between lay and expert participants. However, both framings were designed to find:

(1) if – and how – a participatory dialogue between lay and expert participants can take place; what form such "participation" takes, and what might influence that form;
(2) what is the role and the importance – if any – of "information" (about climate change and about the policy process) for a meaningful dialogue;
(3) what form of "information" (through ICT or face-to-face with "experts"/policy-makers) is helpful in establishing and sustaining meaningful public participation.

The concern of both teams was around the *interpretation* of different types of information that is gathered from different sources by the participants, rather than generating new information *per se*. It was also hoped that the involved individuals (researchers and lay participants) would also "learn" while "participating." This relates to what Laird (1993) terms "participatory analysis" as a "specific kind of learning process while people . . . are engaged in participation."

Both teams convened a series of five-session meetings of between seven and nine local residents selected on a broad range of criteria (age, gender, occupation, residence, etc.) (De Marchi *et al.* 1998; Kitchener and Darier 1998a).[2] Each team provided a facilitator who concentrated on the process, and avoided the expression of views on the substance of the discussion. The research teams worked to create and maintain a distance between themselves and the expertise provided in order to foster a more egalitarian group dynamic. In Venice, this was achieved through the use of a computer, running both global models, supplied by outside research teams, and a simple purpose-built carbon dioxide calculator. Obviously, this is a framing through which the researchers also shared a learning experience with the participants, while assisting them in their interpretation and personal interaction with the computer "expert."

In St. Helens, it was possible for the lay participants to influence the selection of "experts" they wanted to interact with. Two experts participated in the groups. The first expert was the executive director of the Groundwork Trust, an ENGO that is particularly active in St. Helens and whose mission is the implementation of sustainable development and various physical environmental improvements through local partnership and community participation. The second expert was the chief planning officer of St. Helens Metropolitan Borough Council that has mandatory environmental responsibilities, including the implementation of Local Agenda 21.

All of the meetings were recorded and transcribed. In addition, the Italian team produced a web site that contains some of the actual interactions and additional details (http://alba.jrc.it/ulysses.html). For further details about the process in both regions see Darier and Schüle (1999); Darier, Shackley, and Wynne (1999); De Marchi *et al.* (1998); and Guimarães Pereira, Gough, and De Marchi (1999).

The main finding of our analysis shows that participants in St. Helens and Venice always adopted a broad contextualist approach not only about the topic(s) discussed but also to the process itself, the motivations of the research team, the information provided and the perceived objectives. Our joint analysis of the transcripts reveals three main kinds of contextual questions raised directly or indirectly by the participants:

(1) *Contexts:* Why are we meeting? What are the practical objectives and rules of the meetings? Who is behind the meetings?
(2) *Knowledges:* What kind of "information" is being provided to us? How do we discuss the topic(s)? What kind of "information" do we provide?

---

[2] In Venice, a total of six groups each met five times for up to two and a half hours (full details can be found at: http://alba.jrc.it/ulysses/voyage-home/VOYAGE.htm). There was one group in St. Helens, which initially met five times, with two additional voluntary meetings organised by the group themselves and two follow-up meetings (one with policymakers); each meeting also lasted about two and half hours.

(3) *Assessments:* How do we, and others, interpret and assess knowledge? What will be done with the assessments?

If formal IA is about a synthesized assessment informed by various fields of expert knowledges, the involvement of lay members of the public brings a much broader range of knowledges that go well beyond those which might be scientifically accepted, or usually considered directly relevant. Our findings suggest that lay participants involved in IA do not limit themselves to "expert information" but also incorporate personal and collective experiences and values, historical trends, trust, distrust, and expectations about the political, social, information, and economic systems (e.g., Misztal 1996).

Contexts of participation

As previously explained, there are various reasons why the two research teams framed the meetings in different ways (research and "policy for real"). This was also related to the fact that the financial sponsor of the project was the research branch of the European Commission (DG Research, previously DGXII) which has neither a direct policy/implementation mandate within the Commission, nor jurisdiction over climate change policy, especially at the local level. Consequently, each team's framing attempted to construct more plausible and more tangible contexts which participants could relate to more readily. Obviously, the two adopted framings (and the revealing of the identity of the sponsor) directly influenced the initial discussions, for example, the sorts of questions asked at the beginning (such as the "why?" questions).

The presentation of the two framings also carry certain challenges, such as communicating to the participants the reasons for bringing them together and defining the objectives and boundaries as part of the participatory exercise. Adopting a (local) "policy for real" framing (St. Helens) avoided some of the problems by providing a potentially clearer (local) policy focus for the discussions but generated a need to demonstrate institutional commitment and a likelihood of resulting action or policy influence. Enabling the participants to choose and interact directly with policy representatives gave the meetings some degree of policy realism and positive incentives for the group to participate. On the other hand, the research framing (Venice) used the metaphor of the "Voyage of Ulysses," a journey shared by each member of the group. This metaphor allowed each participant to adopt a role (traveler, guide etc.) as they visited and explored the destinations "Information and Communication Technology (ICT)," "lifestyles and sustainability," and "extreme events and climate change." This created potentially clearer rules of engagement for the participants but possibly suffered from a lack of obvious potential for practical and policy actions.

Whatever the advantages and shortcomings of the two adopted framings, in both cities the participants tended to unpack not only the framing but also the broader contexts of the framing itself: Why is the EU paying for this kind of project? What is "research"? What is "policy"? What is the actual purpose of the exercise? The ambiguities that remained outside the two framings generated a sense of vagueness and skepticism among the participants during the initial meetings. Nevertheless, these remaining ambiguities created an opportunity for the participants to define for themselves the purposes and rationale for their participation. Once the participants started to engage in that task, there was a general willingness – albeit conditional – to participate. This development from initial skepticism to conditional willingness to participate is summarized in Box 2.1, and discussed in more detail below.

Box 2.1: Contexts for participation

The two regions drew on different framings for introducing the series of meetings, each of which was associated with particular challenges in engaging the participants. However, despite these differences both regions revealed similar processes through which participation within the groups was established.

Initial skepticism was voiced as participants sought to understand the broader political and practical origins of the meetings. This arose because the precise boundaries of the research were left open by the research teams in order to enable the participants to define their own boundaries as far as possible and so allow the researchers to explore the conditions that allow citizen participation in such issues. The open-ended nature of the groups was eventually recognized as an opportunity by the participants, albeit one requiring some justification as to why participation might be worthwhile.

Two such *justifications* emerged: (i) instrumental – their participation may contribute to better policy decisions; (ii) normative – participation as a good in itself and, in Venice, a third intrinsic justification was identified as participation for communicative reasons.

Once such goals were established the participants showed a *conditional willingness to participate*. Overall, the groups revealed a great potential for fruitful interactions between "expertise" and "democratic processes," providing that mutual trust and an understanding of the reasons for participation are established.

Initial skepticism

At first, participants tried to understand the broader political and practical contexts surrounding the meetings and the specific framing that was offered. Consequently, there was strong skepticism on their part that can be explained by at least three factors. *First* of all, the research teams themselves left the exact boundaries of the research "object" fuzzy. *Second*, as one of the central objectives was about the conditions for "citizen participation" in IA, it was decided to let the participants themselves help to define the boundaries within the contexts of the two framings. It was an exercise that also extended to the participants' ability to have a say in the terms of engagement! In a sense – and up to a point – the process itself became a *sui generis* approach to research. These two factors alone generated incredulity followed by skepticism among the participants. For example, one of the immediate reactions from one participant in St. Helens was skepticism about the practical outcome of the process: "Will anything be done at the end of it all?" In Venice, the participants tended not to comprehend or appreciate the culture of "research". In referring to the experience, participants would use phrases such as "the course", "the lessons", "the teachers", despite repeated reframing in terms of "research" by the facilitators. *Third*, which generated skepticism in St. Helens, was the participants' experience of previous public participation exercises. For example, a participant expressed concern about the final outcome and drew from her own past experience in another participatory process:

SANDRA: And I don't know, maybe I'm just a bit cynical, because what's the point in a way. I'm saying it from experience because I got, for some reason, got involved with [the] 'Pathways' project. And because I'm fairly local I got involved and went to quite a lot of meetings that they gave on topics on Merseyside with John Brown, the regional Director . . . I've seen it all happening, we've seen these policy-makers making these decisions and inherently, well . . . I mean I'll flow with it but . . . you know.   (St. Helens, Session 1)[3]

Although the participants were skeptical at first, they soon realized that the open-ended nature of the framings was also an opportunity for them to explore what they could achieve through the meetings. However, the participants had to rationalize why their participation might be worthwhile.

Why participate?

The participants offered two main justifications for their possible participation: (1) it will lead to better policy decisions and implementation

---

[3] See Darier and Kitchener 1997.

(instrumentalist justification) and (2) it is a good in itself (normative justification). The participants' justifications were similar to the ones outlined in other recent studies on public participation and IA (Forrester 1999) and the broader theoretical debate on "deliberative democracy" (e.g., Gutman and Thompson 1996; Bohman and Rehg 1997).

Generally, the participants understood very well that their participation could assist wider research and policy objectives but from the relatively "passive" position of an observed subject. This implied that they perceived that the ability to act lies firmly outside their realm, as illustrated by the following quotes:

Our own behavior helps the research – we can give our contribution to those who have executive power.   (Venice, Group I, Session 5, Log Book[4])

SUE: So has the EU picked St. Helens to improve St. Helens? Or have they picked St. Helens to be a town to represent other towns in the area, you know, if the people of St. Helens want this, people of this town will want this?
                                                                    (St. Helens, Session 1)

Some of the participants also perceived "public" – or rather "community" – participation as a tool to make the implementation of policy more effective.

JOHN: When you get people from a community doing things for their own community everything is going to last a lot longer because if you see somebody doing anything, I don't say you've got the right, but you feel you've got to stop them making a mess of what you've done...   (St. Helens, Session 2)

The participants also gave a rationale for participation from an intrinsic value perspective (a "good in itself") that obviously varied according to the framing offered. In the context of the St. Helens "policy for real" framing, the participants questioned the broader political issue of who should have a say and who should make decisions:

DAN: Just so you've got like your councillors in St. Helens, you have a vote on we'll do this or we'll do that. I'm not a communist like but I think they should do it [i.e. increase public participation]. They should...let the people have their views.
JOHN: I think there should be more devolution or decentralization [to] communities...   (St. Helens, Session 2)

In the context of the "research" framing in Venice, people also tended to justify their participation for intrinsic ("communicative") reasons rather than exclusively for instrumentalist purposes:

[4] The quotations from the Venice groups are drawn from two sources: (1) material written up on the wall log books and hence selected by the participants as being important; (2) extracted from transcriptions of the sessions and hence selected by the researchers.

The discussion of environmental problems presented to this group has, in our opinion, been only a pretext to encourage a diverse group of people to exchange ideas and opinions.   (Venice, Group III, Session 5, Log book)

One overcomes shyness in expressing one's opinions.

. . .

The pleasure of mutual disagreement and respect.
                                        (Venice Group IV, Session 5, transcripts)

These two rationales ("good-in-itself" and instrumentalism) closely relate to the two intertwined Western features outlined in the introduction, namely commitment to "democracy" and the rise of "expertise."

Conditional willingness to participate

After this initial questioning, the participants suspended their skepticism and incredulity and became quite willing to participate with, however, certain reservations, as expressed by Sandra in St. Helens: "I mean I'll flow with it but . . . you know." This general conditional willingness to participate is illustrated by the fact that none of the participants abandoned the process.[5] In fact, the ambiguity of the framings and the potential practical results of the process enabled the participants to guess or define for themselves the objectives of their meetings, what the relevant topics would be, who the relevant policy-makers should be and what the research was about. For example, in St. Helens, the first two sessions turned out to be another scoping exercise during which the objectives emerged *sui generis*. It became clear that the objectives of the project were mutually constructed/negotiated during the interaction between the participants, the invited "experts"/policy-makers and the research team. The two research teams were quite willing to encourage this process by not taking a strong pro-active guiding role, apart from simply providing the opportunity for the interaction. The willingness to participate was clearly demonstrated in St. Helens when the participants took the initiative to organize two extra (and unpaid) meetings (to which they invited the research team as observers). They also made a 26-minute video directed at local policy-makers that they themselves selected and whom they met in a subsequent joint citizens/policy-makers' meeting. In another example of the willingness to participate, one of the participants in St. Helens, a pub manager, asked his customers to list their "environmental" concerns,

---

[5] Although the participants received a small sum of money for their attendance (St. Helens £20, Venice 80,000 Lire per session) they generally said (in the debriefing period and/or in post-meeting confidential phone interviews) that the money was not the main incentive and that they had stayed throughout the process because they enjoyed it and/or they became committed to it.

thus becoming himself a "researcher." In Venice, participants celebrated the experience by organizing cakes and sweets for their final meeting. The Venice participants also reported how they were discussing their experiences in the groups with family and friends and that they were alerted to climate change in the news. They frequently brought along newspaper cuttings, mentioned TV and radio broadcasts and one group declared their readiness to be reconvened (without payment) and to help to spread information to others. The ultimate demonstration of this, and an indication of their "ownership" of the process, was the unanimous agreement in each of the groups to give written permission for their comments and designs to be made widely available through the Internet.

However, the participants' willingness to participate was always related to their perceptions and experiences of the obstacles and limitations of such a process. The participants acknowledged that changes could happen sometimes as a result of individual initiatives ("All it needs is like one person to actually go...") but that it wasn't easy ("if you formed a group and started to do things I'm sure that the Council would have something to say. You get stopped don't you, even if you're doing good, you still get stopped" (St. Helens, Session 3)).

This explains why the participants tended to be ambivalent and suspicious about "participation" although generally willing to give it a chance, as identified in previous research (e.g., Gundersen 1995). However, there was another challenge waiting for the participants: how would they respond to expert knowledges presented to them through the two framings?

The introduction of expert knowledges

Despite differences between the two regions in the way expertise was introduced, the issues identified by the citizens showed broad perceptions of environmental topics, very different from narrowly framed natural scientific perspectives.

In St. Helens, the topics of climate change and sustainability were introduced into the discussions gradually and indirectly through the prism of local policy. Consequently, environmental issues only emerged within the broader context of the daily life of the participants from a local perspective, for example the fact that their house was located close to a park, or on a hill above the smog. The participants did not talk about "purely environmental" issues but approached the discussion from more holistic and empirical perspectives, which might include environmental concerns.

After the initial question asked by the St. Helens facilitator – "what does the environment mean to you?" – the participants talked comfortably with no need for additional prompting. Responses given by the participants were striking in their breadth, detail, diversity and the specificity of what the word "environment" can mean:

- The earth itself, anything concerning the human race...
- Conditions which we live under
- It means like the fields, parks and everything...
- I think environment covers the lot, it's everything
- Environmental health and safety...
- It's the conditions and the surroundings that we live in. The environment can be filthy or it can be clean and healthy, but we all strive, or we attempt to strive to keep it clean and tidy and a good place to live in.   (St. Helens, Session 2)

The participants were also able to talk about the "environment" using some of the more scientifically framed terms: "'chemicals on food', 'pesticides', 'toxins', 'additives', 'the pollution in the sea'..." (St. Helens, Session 2). Similarly, the earlier introduction of climate change issues into the debates in Venice sparked the expression of a very broad range of effects associated by the groups with climate change:

- North Pole (higher temperature / sea level)
- Nature (Siberia is hot now)
- Ecosystem change
- Life habits (the change)
- El Niño (nobody knows what it is)
- Worsening (for those who love hot weather, it is probably an improvement)
- Seasons (only 2)
- The ice covers that melt
- Acqua Alta – (Venice high tides)
- Reversal (seasons – climate)
- North–south ↔ south–north
- In the end there will be extinction of animals
- New illnesses
- Adaptation
- Behaviour (thought, laws...)   (Venice, Group V, Session 1, Log book)

Compared to experts operating within their professional knowledge context, the participants tended not to be constrained by a need to present themselves as objective – they were freer to openly express value judgments, to invoke knowledge outside their "specialist subject" (or nominal area of expertise) and to place importance on non-technical elements of an issue. From this free-ranging perspective they were able to identify the web of possible contributing factors associated with climate change and the web of possible solutions which may lie outside purely "environmental" concerns and framings. For example, one of the participants in Venice strongly hinted that "environmental problems" were associated with factors beyond the traditionally "environmental" classifications and solutions involved novel and broader ways of thinking: "there are no boundaries to *environmental* problems. For the solutions are those of *imagination*" (Venice, Group II, Session 3, Log book, participant's own emphasis). Venice has certain environmental problems of its own that all Venetians know and live with (their examples were: high water, industrial pollution, and a loss of green spaces). In discussing these, one of the groups developed a metaphorical expression (given in Box 2.2) of the link between these local problems in Venice with environmental issues around the world.

Box 2.2: "Venice is a metaphor for the world"

This group drew a picture of Venice (represented by a stylized map of the islands making up the historic city center) as a planet with moons orbiting around it. The metaphor the group wanted to express with that is that each place has its own environmental problems, but that understanding the specific problems, for example in Venice, can also help to understand environmental challenges experienced by other communities around the world:

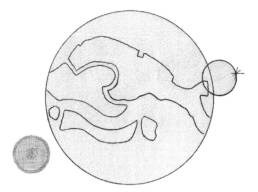

Figure 2.1 "Venice is a metaphor for the world"

"Venice is a planet . . . Venice is a metaphor for the world"

(Venice, Group VI, Session 2, Log book)

This example shows how the lay participants used metaphorical forms to express some of their ideas relating to the social dimensions of environmental change. This metaphorical depiction complements the metaphorical function of model outputs described by Jerry Ravetz in Chapter 3 of this volume.

Lay understandings of complexities and uncertainties

In both regions, disagreement and controversies among experts were made explicit in order to render obvious complexity and uncertainty issues associated with expert knowledge. Obviously, some of the participants were initially disappointed and surprised that the experts didn't know as much as they might have expected them to, which was possibly due to the aura of intellectual superiority that is exhibited by many experts. However, the participants had no problem in understanding and acknowledging the complexities, uncertainties and broader contexts surrounding environmental problems.

Truth as hypothesis: after the news, information and discussion, we hypothesized ways of changing thanks to political, social, economic contributions and those of the whole community.   (Venice, Group II, Session 3, Log book)

The participants in St. Helens offered the following assessment (after their interaction with Richard Sharland of the Groundwork Trust):

... I think environmentally that St. Helens has got a hell of a job with the backlash of industrial legacy that's been left to us ... ;
I think they've got a very difficult task. It takes 2 steps forward and one back. OK, he's making progress but I would think it's a very slow job;
They've [the Groundwork Trust] got all the ideas and they know what they want to do, it's just finding the money to do it;
There's so much to do and making priorities, making one thing a priority and others into the background. Terribly difficult job!   (St. Helens, Session 3)

It seems that participants in both cities had no problem recognizing complexities and uncertainties as such. This might be due in part to the fact that daily life itself is full of uncertainties and complexities – what Bauman calls "ambivalence" (Bauman 1991) – and that participants were quite willing to acknowledge them. This interpretation is supported by the discussion given in Chapter 4 of collages produced in IA Focus Groups, which show the high ability of ordinary citizens to express and accept situations of ambivalence or ambiguity with regard to complex environmental problems. On the other hand, much modern expert knowledge tends to suppress uncertainties and complexities in order to offer convincing, legitimate and neat story lines. This relates to the "first conception of the task of using models" described by Ravetz in Chapter 3, that post-normal science and sociology of contingency in expertise have tried to challenge, in order to render uncertainties and complexities explicit in expert knowledges. In our groups, clearly the (lay) participants were using the models in a manner more consistent with Ravetz's "second conception of the task of using models," in which models can provide knowledge through implicit suggestion.

Lay and expert knowledges meet

If the participants were generally not surprised by the existence of uncertainties and complexities *per se*, they were more surprised following their encounter with experts. For example, the St. Helens participants offered comments on the encounter with Richard Sharland. The first realization was that the policy-maker (one of "them") they had just met was not able to provide answers to everything. However, instead of considering this situation in a negative light, it seemed to reassure the participants that Richard (the "Director") was more like "us" and that he didn't conform to the stereotypical idea of what a policy-maker was (blurring of the "them" and "us" distinction).

> It's amazing to think that he is the Director, in some cases he was not aware of some things that were going on. . . .
> . . . and that is a good news really, because it means that . . . he is a reasonable guy and I would think that he's not over-bound by his own ideas. He's got some rules and regulations against to go by.   (St. Helens, Session 3)

Similar reactions were experienced in Venice when mistakes in calculations were made or when model moderators were unable to provide answers to certain questions. In fact, these "mistakes" contributed to reducing the "lay/expert" divide. However, mistakes or problems exhibited by the computer itself were viewed much less charitably. What seems more important than the actual knowledge an "expert" can offer is the way in which that knowledge is shared. "Mr. Computer has a brain but not a soul, you turn it on and you see immediately that it needs you as you need it . . ." (Venice, Group V, Session 4, Log book). A computer can process data but *interpreting* data requires human judgment to make them meaningful. The computer can replace logical pathways in processing information (the "brain") but human experts apply their own values – applying the "soul" that the computer does not have. In situations of uncertainty and complexity, it is the interpretation of information that is generally contested, rather than the knowledge/information itself.

In this context, credibility and trust are largely dependent on inter-personal skills and the ability to communicate in a way that maintains interest, clarity and a human dimension. Also, an explicit acknowledge-ment of the validity of many different kinds of expertise and a consistent internal coherence (congruence) of the expertise presented are two other essential conditions for a productive lay/expert dialogue (De Marchi *et al.* 1998; De Marchi and Funtowicz 1997). Even if these conditions are met, uncertainties and complexities will remain. However, from a lay public perspective this might not necessarily lead to pessimism or anxiety. On the contrary, it could be a source of optimism. As shown in other studies (e.g., Wynne 1992a), the fact that the experts can be wrong meant that the future remained undetermined and hence forecasts and predictions should be treated with caution, as illustrated by a participant who was "afraid that long term forecasts could make us follow the wrong route" (Venice, Group VI, Session 2). However, the fact that experts could get it wrong also provided opportunities for action and for influencing how the future could evolve.

> Reconsidering data that was thought to be certain, makes us realize how we can be more directly involved personally (*we can do something!!*), because they are not certainties but only *hypotheses*.
> (Venice, Group I, Session 2, Log book, participants' own emphasis)

In conclusion, the participants tended to be reassured by the fact that experts could get it wrong because this fact created the conditions for the empowerment of lay publics in the debate about the future. This didn't mean that expert knowledge had no role at all but that it was only one of many types of knowledge that might be taken into consideration. However, even this approach didn't guarantee success, as illustrated in the following exchange in St. Helens:

KEN: Well I think with this ozone we've got to rely very much on the so-called experts and believe what they tell us.
DAN: Until you can actually look up and say . . . you know what I mean, you can say that. Because you don't know do you? You can't really say "oh yes, it's getting bigger, you can see," you don't know, you know.
KEN: Well I think that's why the message is not getting across really . . .
> (St. Helens, Session 5)

Action = precaution

As we have already seen, there were many facets to the citizens' inter-pretations of uncertainties and complexities and how this should, or should not, affect the participants' perception of their own empowerment, forcing them to make their own assessment. However, the participants were quite confident that the dilemma of uncertainties and complexities shouldn't be used as an excuse for inaction or for maintaining the status quo. On the contrary, the appropriate action was to adopt a precautionary approach to potential problems because, as Josy said in the case of the depletion of the ozone layer, "by the time it gets so far it's too late then if you start using the ozone friendly stuff" (St. Helens, Session 2). This is an example of the degree of implicit sophistication of lay IA which relied here on a comparison with similar cases. In addition, the participants' understanding of the importance of precautionary actions simultaneously created space for possible action while not diminishing the level of anxieties created by uncertainties:

There are possibilities in the face of everything...If only one of the variables [from the set shown to the participants] is not certain, I know that the future will be like that [anyway]; but if it's all the variables that we mentioned before, it might not be so. In this sense I have more hope, I see things positively.

MOD: This feeling is shared?

The debate also at the level of scientists makes me afraid because...they don't know what to do either; then we have reached a point that – I don't know – perhaps we can do something but we must move ourselves, for sure.

(Venice, Group I, Session 1, Transcripts)

Building on their own broad contextualist assessment, the participants concluded that action on climate change in the context of scientific uncertainties should be precautionary.

Conclusions: conditions for participation

We can offer two kinds of assessments as conclusions: (a) the participants' own assessment which can be summarized as a conditional willingness to participate based on a general hope for the future and as a heuristic process for empowerment and precautionary action, and (b) our own assessment of the process and more precisely some of the practical conditions for participation in IA.

Hope for the future

We have already presented some of the recommendations made by the participants themselves, such as, for example, the importance of acting in a precautionary way in the face of scientific uncertainties and complexities. There is, however, at least one other general conclusion that emerged out of the process: citizens' hope for the future. Despite a lack of trust and confidence in governments and in institutions generally, despite growing personal and collective insecurities in the age of globalization, and despite some culturally well-entrenched skepticism (mainly in the UK), there was a general hope for the future. That hope was not necessarily an illustration of an unflagging human spirit but was grounded in historical experience. For example, in St. Helens, participants really thought that the local environment had improved. And therefore this was the best guarantee for the future, and the belief that things could improve because action has been taken or could be taken now:

... the Mersey [River has] been all clean[ed up] ... ,
... there are actually fish in [the Mersey River now],
they're not dumping sewage quite so much as they used to,
it was the EU wasn't it? They set the standards ...
(St. Helens, Session 2)

We think about the future to improve the present!
(Venice, Group I, Session 4)

Participatory IA as a heuristic device for empowerment and action

The participants also considered the heuristic value of the process as a positive outcome, but not mainly for "knowledge" for its own sake, nor for a specific policy end-purpose. Rather, the participants seemed to consider their participation as a learning and empowering process during which they realized that "Only *we* can change our future" (Venice). In addition, participation was also seen as a way to refocus collective decision and action on a problem.

I would like to hope and think that we'd blocked up the hole in the ozone, getting decent weather, that because of what we're trying to do now, or hoping that we're going to do now ... discussions like this will bring up points that are being pointed out whereas when the hole in the ozone was first discovered everybody did something, now it's dropping back off. Perhaps meetings like this will give it another surge, another push in the right direction on all the different things, and just in general clean up everything so that it comes to a high standard and we maintain it; hopefully ... we should be able to do it in 20 years.
(St. Helens, Session 5)

In a sense, we can go beyond the conclusion of Adolph Gundersen's study which showed that his participants' recommendations were "the result of a highly complex cognitive operation, involving judgments of environmental fact and a constant balancing of multiple environmental values against competing political goals" (Gundersen 1995, 130). We would argue that through the muddling participatory process, our participants defined (a) the broader and multilayered boundaries of the environmental object itself, ranging from culture, values, fear, hope, perceived track records of collective institutions, personal experiences, scientific uncertainties, etc., and (b) the conditions and the scope of their personal and group involvement and empowerment in the participatory process itself.

Practical conditions for citizens' participation in IA

We saw above that in the absence of established and habitual interaction between lay publics and scientific and technical expertise, the interpersonal dimension became crucial. It seems that in order to overcome some of the distrust and suspicion expressed by lay publics *vis-à-vis* expertise, it is essential to institute regular occasions for such interaction, thus making expertise more open, transparent and accountable to a wider audience. Notwithstanding this broad conclusion, we can identify three practical conditions for citizens' participation in IA in the meanwhile.

First, the *medium* through which communication takes place is critical and can hold a strong influence over the way expertise is interpreted and used. The choices are many, for example, video films, personal presentations (lectures, informal groups, theatre, etc. . . .), and computer-based interactions (slide shows, models, etc. . . .) may all be deployed to different effect.

Second, *interpersonal skills* are equally important. Useful exchanges depend on the ability of the communicator to relate information to those with whom it is to be shared. This can be an individual's skill in speaking plainly and concisely while bringing a topic to life, the user-friendliness of a computer interface, or the choice of graphical representation of results (see also the discussion of model use in IA Focus Groups given in Chapter 5 and in Guimarães Pereira *et al.* (1999)). The presenter has to be an effective and credible "witness" for a body of people, knowledge and experience. In all cases demonstrating respect for other's knowledge (discursive feedback, user inputs, etc.) is essential. It can be a difficult balance, however; a presentation that is too polished or an interface that is too sophisticated can engender distrust and alienation.

Third, even with appropriate media and good interpersonal skills, *contextual aspects* retain a strong influence on the assessment. Within groups such as ours this was seen through the benefits of distancing the facilitation or moderation process from the provision of expert knowledges, avoiding defensive justification of authority and thus transferring certain control to the citizens in their exchange with experts. The framing sets the initial conditions through which this relationship is established and hence is critical to the participatory process.

Outlook

Public participation is without doubt the least established aspect of IA and is often treated with skepticism by certain users and practitioners. There are many different approaches to implementing a participatory IA but this paper has illustrated that there are certain necessary features to make this involvement mutually productive. There is great potential for successful interactions between "expertise" and "democratic processes" but a mutual trust and understanding of the reasons for participating must be established. If these conditions are met, decreasing public confidence in political processes that are based on apparently isolated scientific evidence, and increasing experience with participatory approaches, will together contribute to improved understanding and implementation of public participation in IA, and in sustainability science in general.

CHAPTER THREE

Models as metaphors

Jerry Ravetz

Introduction

This chapter discusses philosophical reflections on the intellectual adventure of conducting Integrated Assessment (IA) Focus Groups with citizens, as presented in this volume. The task of this exercise was ambitious: to bridge the gap between sustainability science and democratic debate in the climate domain. The science component was mainly represented by models, most (although not all) having the appearance of describing future states of the global climate and their consequences for human society. At first it could seem a daunting, indeed, overwhelming task: it was hard to see how lay participants could meaningfully relate to models whose construction required very special expertise in mathematics and software engineering; and whose comprehension required knowledge of climate science. But having witnessed the debates among the modelers themselves, the research team already knew that IA models are quite problematic products of science. It is freely accepted, even emphasized, among the experts that the models do not provide simple predictions; and so their epistemic status and policy relevance were already open to question. In addition, there was the knowledge that experts are usually "laypersons" outside their specialties, and that policy-makers are generally no more knowledgeable than ordinary citizens. And, in any event, the democratic process involves debate over issues where both expert and lay voices are heard. Hence the IA models were an appropriate vehicle for developing a many-sided dialogue on basic issues.

In the event, the involvement of this "extended peer community" proved far less difficult than anticipated. For, although the content of the IA models might be arcane, their conclusions were not. Indeed, as predictions of the future state of the planet, the outputs of the models lent themselves to discussion and criticism. This latter arose in two headings: the first, how much the general models could tell us that is relevant to our decisions; and the second, what sort of messages they are. In particular, once it was freely admitted that these are not ordinary predictions, categorical statements of what will and what will not be happening, then the lay participants found themselves engaged in an engrossing methodological debate. Given all the scientific talent and technological resources that had gone into the construction of the models, just what use are they if their outputs, whose form is that of categorical statements about the future, are just estimates or even guesses, shrouded in uncertainties?

The IA Focus Group procedures developed within our study could actually be an ideal forum in which such issues could be aired. It could well be that in the open setting of these focus groups, free of any of the commitments and prejudices that afflict any policy debate among vested institutional interests, such questions could be framed and expressed all the more clearly, and with greater force. We are not speaking of an "emperor's clothes" situation, since there has been a continuous and vigorous public debate within the specialist community about the meaning of IA models. But in the context of our research it was possible for plain people to speak plain words about their confusions and reservations about these scientific instruments. And so the learning experience became universal; they learned about the climate change problems in relation to urban lifestyles, and the experts learned about the different aspects of the usefulness of their tools in the general policy process. In these focus groups conducted with citizens, the IA models – which do not claim to make factual statements or reliable predictions – were seen as useful for enlarging the scope of people's imagination about climate change and the role of individuals in that problem. In that context models were discovered to be "poetic." Stimulated by this experience, this chapter explores the question of whether they could fruitfully be seen as "metaphors," expressing in an indirect form our presuppositions about the problem and its possible solutions.[1] Although this approach is very different from the traditional understanding of scientific knowledge, it may well be useful in helping science adapt to its new functions in an age of sustainability challenges and scientific uncertainty.

Models as scientific?

For nearly 400 years, our ideal of science has excluded metaphor; for science is supposed to be about exact reasoning, leading to certainty. In scientific discourse and inquiry the poetic faculty must be tightly constrained lest it lead us astray. The Royal Society of London expressed it

---

[1] This chapter is to some extent a sequel to earlier reflections on the problems of the proper use of IA models (Ravetz 1997a; 1999). I hope that it will contribute to the sense of a largely successful adventure, or voyage, that our study has been for all its participants.

simply (if somewhat obscurely) in its original motto of 1661: "nullius in verba." The facts and the power resulting from natural science now serve as the paradigm for all forms of practical knowledge. The "subjective" studies, or "gossip" in the words of one distinguished physicist (Ravetz 1971), are deemed inferior, existing only because of the present limits of scientific knowledge and the weaknesses of human intelligence.

It is possible that the triumphs of European science over the past four centuries have been due largely to this attitude, of excluding or downgrading the qualitative aspects of experience. Certainly, some confluence of external and internal factors made possible the unique rise of our science, to achieve a degree of knowledge and power that could scarcely have been dreamed of in previous civilizations. But now, at the start of the twenty-first century, we realize that the problems of "the environment" are becoming challenges to the "sustainability", or survival, of our civilization; and that our "urban lifestyles," made possible by our enveloping science-based technology, are largely responsible for this perilous situation. Our simplistic, myopic technology threatens to destroy our own habitat, and our reductionist science, by definition incapable of grasping systems thinking, is inadequate for managing the tasks of cleanup and survival. The quantitative social sciences that are designed around the imitation of Victorian physics become ever more clearly seen as caricatures. Instead of being genuinely scientific in the way that their practitioners so ardently desire, such disciplines are merely "scientistic," misconceived parodies of real knowledge. The modern program of scientists "teaching truth to power," deducing correct policies from incontrovertible facts, is, in the environmental field, in tatters. We now have an inversion of the classic distinction between the hard objective facts produced by science and the soft subjective values that influence policy. Now we have decisions to make that are hard in every sense, for which the scientific inputs are irremediably soft. The goal of the whole enterprise, "sustainability," is now recognized as something other than a simple, scientifically specifiable state. Rather, as pointed out by Kasemir *et al.* in Chapter 1, sustainability (especially when the social and moral elements are included) is something of an "essentially contested" concept in the sense of Gallie. In these circumstances the denial of rhetoric, as part of the traditional reduction of reality to quantitative attributes, can now be seen as a profound metaphysical prejudice, one of the patently counterproductive elements of our intellectual heritage.

All these problems are exposed most sharply in the use and interpretation of environmental models, particularly IA models that are cast in the form of describing future states of the global climate and their consequences for society. These "models" are themselves of an unusual sort.

They are not miniature globes with water and clouds swishing around; and in fact they cannot even be seen. Rather, they are sets of mathematical relationships, embodied in computer programs, which (it is intended and hoped) simulate some of the interactions in the bio-geosphere. To understand how any model works is indeed a task for experts; but to ask what it tells us, indeed why it has been constructed, is open to any interested citizen.

The outputs of the IA models are represented as assertions concerning quantitative indicators, expressed at some future time. But they are not simply "predictions" in the sense of the classical philosophy of science. In our traditional understanding, the statements of natural science are intended to be tested against experience, to determine the truth or falsity of the theory from which they are deduced. However, a computer model is not a "theory" in the sense of the achievements of Newton and Einstein. The models are not expected to be "true" or "false" in the classic scientific sense. Further, in the case of most IA models the outputs relate to times in the future which are too far away for any practicable "testing." And in any event, practitioners now agree that even if one were to wait for the requisite number of years or decades, the actual states of those indicators would most probably be quite different from those "predicted" back in our present. In the sense of the classical philosophy of science, all our models are trivially "false."

Those who develop and use these models must then become creative methodologists. The models are said to have a variety of heuristic functions. Prominent among these is clarifying our understanding of our assumptions. But it is not clear whether this relates to the assumptions made by society in general or by policy-makers about the environment, or merely to the assumptions made by the modelers about structure and inputs of their models. Models also might provide some indications of the way things will turn out in the real world; but then again they might not. All this endeavor with models is very important, as our assessment of the future is genuinely quite crucial in the setting of public policy. But IA models are clearly seen to be lacking in a methodological foundation in the successful practice of natural science. Therefore the justifications of this sort of modeling will not be able to succeed within the framework of the traditional conceptions of scientific knowledge and practice. They are based less on a successful practice of advancing knowledge, and increasingly on an embattled faith.

If these models are not fully "scientific," but to some significant extent merely "scientistic," how are they to be understood as objects of knowledge? Under the challenging conditions of our focus groups, fresh insights could be generated which would not be likely to emerge within the groves of academe. Thus, in one regional case study the discussions gave rise to the notion that climate change models are a form of "seduction" (Shackley and Darier 1998). The term is used in a nonsexual sense following the French philosopher Baudrillard, as "a game with its own rules," and refers rather more to the modelers than to the models themselves. Reviewing the variety and confusion among the explanations of the uncertainties, dependence on special assumptions, and value-loading of the models, they eventually arrive at the explanatory formula "truths/untruths." For the "IAMs [Integrated Assessment Models] are hybrids . . . : a mixture of conditionally valid uncertain and indeterminate knowledge – data, theory and insights – combined together in a fashion which generates further indeterminacy." Further, "several types of ignorance [are] involved, related to processes, phenomena and data."

The authors argue that the advocates of the models alternately use strong and weak claims for them, in order first to recruit possible supporters, and then to keep them on board when the inadequacy of the models becomes apparent. This is what is understood as "seduction"; but it should be observed that the process may well be directed even more to the modelers themselves, to maintain their own sense of worth in the face of disillusioning experience. Such an explanation was offered by Brian Wynne in his classic study of the IIASA (International Institute for Applied Systems Analysis) energy model, whose designers, aware at one level of its quite crippling flaws, had to practice a sort of Orwellian doublethink on themselves as well as their patrons (Wynne 1984).

In historical perspective, the dilemma of the modelers is really quite ancient. The policy-related sciences have been in such a bind for a very long time. The earliest mathematical social science, astrology, struggled constantly with suspicious clients and with methodological conundrums (as the "simultaneous births, diverging fates" paradox). The first applied natural science, medicine, faced harsh criticism and even derision until quite recently. It is a sobering thought that academic medicine, one of the mainstays of the university curriculum for well over half a millennium was, in retrospect, absolute nonsense. Those patients whose condition could be treated by an "empiric" had a chance of effective treatment; those who went to the learned doctors of physic needed to trust their luck, right through to Victorian times. It was only the triumphs of the applications of science in the present century that made success the natural and expected condition for science. Only recently has research science been accepted as the paradigmatic form of genuine and effective knowledge.

Now the sense of the power and limits of science is changing quite rapidly. We know that science can fail to produce a desired good in the form of safety and wellbeing; and we also know that science can produce evil, accidentally or intentionally. The authors of the seduction analysis suggest that we now go beyond "enlightenment rationality and instrumentalism, and to open up discussion to the messy processes of thinking, creating and imagining that we all engage in through everyday practice."

Metaphors and science

In that spirit, we feel justified in searching further afield, seeking other conceptions of knowing, with which we can explain and guide our actions in this still significant practice. Let us consider "metaphor," in spite of the long tradition within science of denying and deriding metaphor as an inferior form of expressing knowledge (for a note on the terms "model" and "metaphor," see Box 3.1). Surprisingly, we find metaphor embedded in the most apparently scientific sorts of discourse. Darwin's theory of

Box 3.1: Models and metaphors

"Model" is a word with many meanings. In this context it refers to computer programs designed to mimic the behavior of particular complex systems. Models are used in the cases where neither theoretical understanding, experimental verification, or statistical analysis are available in sufficient strength. The variables in the model represent observable properties of the system, and the structure of the model represents the relations among them that are known and also capable of simulation. Models normally require "adjustment" elements introduced *ad hoc* to make their outputs plausible; and validation of the models is always indirect.

"Metaphor" is a rhetorical device, meaning "carrying beyond." It refers to the denotation of an idea by a term which literally refers to something else. Its explicit rhetorical use, as in poetry, is to add dimensions of meaning beyond those available in prose. Although the practice of science is believed to be antithetical to poetry, any process of naming, particularly of new theoretical entities, relates them back to other ideas and in that sense is metaphorical. In computer models, the metaphors conveying extra dimensions of meaning tend to be hidden, both in the general assumptions about the world that make models relevant, and also in the particular assumptions about reality and value that shape the model and its outcomes.

evolution relied explicitly on metaphors, such as the "Tree of Life"; and what is "Natural Selection" but the greatest metaphor of them all? Even the concept of "species" so central to Darwinian theory, has functioned as a metaphor for discreteness, fixity, and indeed purity, so that biologists are only now discovering how much they have been biased against recognizing the importance of hybrids (Brooks 1999).

Even in physics, the very structure of basic theories, as thermodynamics, is conditioned by the metaphors embedded in it, as "ideal heat engine" and "efficiency"; and these reflect the perspectives and values of the society in which the theories were forged (Funtowicz and Ravetz 1997). In contemporary policy-relevant sciences, the importation of social values is clear in such titles as "the selfish gene." Overarching metaphors like "growth" are translated into particular sorts of social-scientific language, and are then given very particular sorts of policy implications. One may then legitimately inquire about the extent to which the practices in such fields, in their criteria of value and of adequacy, are themselves influenced by the same social values that provide their metaphors (Lakoff and Johnson 1980; Luks 1999).

Thus we find that in spite of our pretensions to manage so many aspects of our affairs scientifically, that practice is both described and informed by metaphors, themselves embodying societal and cultural values which doubtless shape the practice itself. Reflecting on this state of affairs, we can welcome the prevalence of metaphors, but we can also regret the absence, hitherto, of awareness of their prevalence. For without awareness of our driving metaphors, our supposedly scientific practice is afflicted by a sort of false consciousness of itself. Earlier theorists ascribed this particular defect to other sorts of knowing, assuming that science, by definition, is immune to it. But now we see that such confidence was misplaced. And a practice governed by self-delusion is vulnerable to every sort of distortion and perversion. Recall that we are not talking about the rock-solid experimental sciences of yesteryear, but about the sciences which are both intimately related to policy and also necessarily uncertain because of the complexity of their assigned tasks.

If we then propose to embrace metaphor as an explanation of a practice, in this case the mathematical methods used in environmental analysis, then our conceptions of its objects, methods, and social functions (three related aspects) must come up for review, along with the re-framing of the appropriate criteria of adequacy and value. This is a large task, to be conducted by a dialogue among all those concerned with the problem. The present remarks are intended only to show why such a dialogue is legitimate and indeed necessary, and to indicate the sorts of theoretical lines along which it should proceed.

We may start with Michael Thompson's insight (Thompson 1998) that, while the future is unknowable, this area of ignorance is to be viewed positively, as an opportunity for the growth of awareness through a dialectical process. The core of this awareness is that of our ignorance. In that way, studies of the future can induct us into Socrates' philosophical program, of becoming aware of our ignorance. Since the whole thrust of Western philosophy since Descartes has been to control, deny, and ultimately to conceal our ignorance, this is a radical program indeed (Ravetz 1997b).

We are thus confronted with two conceptions of the task of using models. One is based on the faith that scientific methods can be extended to knowing the future, and hence to bringing it under control. This conception is expressed in what I have called the "elite folk sciences" of reductionist quantification of the natural and human realms alike (Ravetz 1994/5). These include the so-called "decision sciences," along with mainstream economics and the predictive computer modeling fields. Their language is rich with metaphors, but they are all taken from the "possessive individualist" conception of humanity and nature. Their methodology is an imitation of the "hard" natural sciences, and they attempt to operate hegemonically in all the relevant fields. Needless to say, ignorance is a severe embarrassment to such sciences, as it presents itself as a simple refutation of their claims of total knowledge and complete control.

The other conception embraces uncertainty and ignorance, and welcomes the clash of distinct perspectives. Its style is dialectical, recognizing that the achievement of final truth is a false and misleading goal. This conception is permitted only at the very margins of the practice of "matured" science, as in discussions within small colleague communities at open research frontiers. Otherwise, in the pedagogy and popularization of research science, certainty rules. Up to now, that particular conception of science, inherited from a triumphant and triumphalist past, has been successful in that it has provided many more "goods" than "bads" for humanity (or at least its "fortunate fifth"). Hence it cannot be refuted in its own terms. But now that our science-based technology reveals its negative impacts on the natural environment and on ourselves as well, and in ways that cannot be controlled, predicted or even anticipated, the assurance of triumph is weakened. Uncertainty at the policy interface is now recognized, however reluctantly, as inescapable. Hence science as a whole, and especially the "predictive" fields, must now embrace real uncertainty, or sink into undeniable confusion and vacuity.

The dilemma can be seen creatively, if we understand these predictive sciences as telling us less about the natural world of the future, and more about our social and intellectual world of the present. In that sense, we see them as metaphors, providing knowledge not by mere straightforward assertion, but rather by suggestion, implicit as well as explicit. In that way the loss of the pretence of scientific certainty can be seen as a liberation, whereby our discourse about ourselves in nature is opened to the enhanced understandings of metaphor and poetry. This vision is amply borne out by the experience of our focus groups, where the confusion caused by the scientistic understanding of the models gave way to the creativity of discourse about their metaphorical meanings. Disagreement was thereby freed from its negative interpretation, and could then be appreciated as the expression of complementary visions of a complex reality.

Metaphors in environmental modeling

But how are we to find metaphors in the forbidding, frequently impenetrable, thicket of formulae and computer codes that constitute mathematical "models" of environmental processes? We can be sure that they will not be patent, announcing themselves as transferring meaning from some other term to the one under scrutiny. So we look for implicit features of the construct, concerning which perhaps even the modelers themselves may not have been aware. One place is in the assumptions, cast in mathematical form but expressing values as cogently as any *cri de coeur*. For example, whenever we put a numerical value on things at some future time, we are assuming a particular "social discount rate." This expresses the price that we, as individuals or a society, are willing to pay for deferring our use (or consumption) of resources. A high "social discount rate" means that future rewards have little value; it expresses the philosophy "What's posterity done for me?"; conversely a low social discount rate stands for "We are here as stewards of our inheritance." In between, the choice is driven by values and politics, as filtered by fashions in the relevant expert communities. Yet policy conclusions, apparently the outcome of rigorous theoretical logic realized in precise mathematical calculation, can depend quite critically on the size of this concealed quantified value commitment. In the design of permanent structures, either in the public and private sectors, the assumed working life (and hence the quality of construction) will depend quite critically on this assumed discount rate. And in the evaluation of environmental goods, the "present value" of an ongoing resource depends critically on the rate at which it is discounted into the future.

It can be quite instructive to witness an IA modeler displaying the predictions and recommendations of his model to three-digit precision, and then to learn that he has never tested it for sensitivity to the assumed social discount rate. There is a simple relation between decrease of value and discount rate; for example, we may define the "throwaway time" of an object as the length of time required for it to be reduced to a tenth of its present value. This is equal (in years) to 230 divided by the discount rate. So for a 10 per cent discount rate, we throw away before a "generation" of twenty-five years has elapsed; with 7 per cent, the throwaway time is thirty-three years. If we really value the wellbeing of our grandchildren, and have "throwaway time" of, say, sixty years, then our social discount rate is only 4 per cent. The future that we construct through the choice of discount rate, is (in this respect) a metaphor for our conception of the good life in the here and now, as revealed through our evaluation of the future.

Another implicit metaphor lies in the choice of the attribute of the future which is to be salient for our scenarios. There are too many complexities and uncertainties for anything like "the whole picture" to be conveyed at once. So modelers necessarily choose some aspect, which will involve a design compromise between what is scientifically reasonable, and what is humanly and politically meaningful. The early focus on increase of "global mean temperature" related the debate to the capabilities of the leading models, and it also cohered with the comforting assumption that change into the future would be smooth and somehow manageable. It was left to commentators to elaborate on the implications of temperature rise, with melting ice-caps, changing crop patterns, new diseases, etc. More recently, we have become more aware of instabilities and extreme phenomena, occurring on a regional or local scale; the vision is now becoming more "catastrophist." These irregular phenomena are much less amenable to scientific treatment, but they offer convenient "confirmations" of climate change whenever the weather comes up for discussion. Neither focus is "right" or "wrong" in any absolute sense; each has its function, dependent on the context of the debate at any time. Each is a metaphor for a predicament which defies control and perhaps even defies full understanding.

In analyzing these metaphors, I am suggesting a sort of "deconstruction," but not in a negatively postmodern spirit of demystification or debunking. Nor am I asserting that environmental models are simply, or nothing but, metaphors. Rather, as in the analysis of works of creative art, we can use the idea of style to illuminate what the work is about. This is expressed in the less declaratory aspects of the work, but provides a key to its context, framework of ideas, or paradigm, or perspective, or *Weltanschauung* – call it what you will. In the visual arts, the "style" relates less to the explicit theme or subject of the production, and more to silent choices made by the creator, on technical aspects of the work or on particular implicit thematic materials. In written work, style can relate to vocabulary, diction, place of the narrator with respect of story and reader, and so on. "Style" is used by scholars to place works (sometimes quite precisely) within ongoing traditions; and alternatively to tease out deeper layers of meaning.

Among computer models, stylistic differences relevant to users are most easily discerned in their outputs. Even the choice between digital and graphical displays reflects cosmological metaphors. This is expressed in Oriental philosophy between the Yang and the Yin, or in classic computer terms between the IBM of the New York corporation and the Apple of the California garage. Digits provide information that is precise (perhaps hyper-precise) on details, but they fail to convey any sense of overall shape. Graphs are more expressive, but are vague; and a collection of curves all climbing upwards at roughly the same rate does not stimulate either the eye or the mind. The representation of uncertainty is even more fraught. To accompany each principal curve with others that display "confidence limits" can give a seriously misleading impression of the precision and information content of those supplementary curves. It might be best (or rather least worst) to show curves as "caterpillars," consisting of shaded areas with gradations from center to edges; but I have seen hardly any examples of this.

If we adopt maps for our display, we may be involved in another level of inference and interpolation (from the global to the regional for the case of IA models on climate change and its relations to social activities). We also incur a significant risk of conveying a false verisimilitude to users. The partly metaphorical character of maps has not been generally concealed (unlike in the case of numbers). For example, the use of standard colors and conventional symbols is obvious (Funtowicz and Ravetz 1990). When a map makes a patent distortion of what is on the ground, like the graph maps of the London Underground tradition, the metaphor is clear. Even there, it has been discovered that people (and not only tourists!) sometimes orient themselves solely by the Underground map, ignoring coincidences on the ground that could not be conveyed on the plan. (The most famous of these is the pair of stations, Bayswater and Queensway, within a stone's throw of each other in reality and yet unrelated on the map.)

Indeed, we may say that the more realistic and powerful becomes the map display, the more urgent becomes the question of its epistemic character. It is all too easy for maps to become instruments of seduction, where the display is taken for the reality. This can happen even when the given output is only one among several alternatives. Somehow each alternative "vision" gets a quasi-real status: if this and that about the general picture are as we assume, then the detailed future will be just as shown on the screen. The task for users may then seem to become one of making "correct" or "the best" assumptions, to predict the "real" future state. In spite of all the variety and uncertainty that may be built into the model and clearly expressed in the instructions for its use, the combination of deductive structure and compelling display can tend to make its interpretation fatally scientistic after all. Those who use them extensively are at risk of becoming seduced by the assumptions concerning reality and value that are embedded in their structures (Dyson 1999).

There are various ways to guard against such a development. One is for the models to be able to convey the "bad" along with the "good" news. Particularly when regional models are employed, anything that shows the effects of general constraints (as in land or water supply) or contradictions between various goals, is to be welcomed. When they cause discomfort by showing unexpected or unwanted consequences of a position assumed to be good and natural, they can have real educational benefits. Better still, if they are employed within a dialogue, so that the experience of disappointment and disillusion are shared, their Socratic function is enhanced. For then it becomes a public knowledge, that just as men formerly made gods in their own images, so now they construct apparently scientific futures out of their hopes and dreams based on the past.

When embedded in a dialogue full of surprise and shock, the model can then function truly as a metaphor. It is recognized as carrying not a literal truth, but an illumination. And what the bare output (numerical, graphic or cartographical) lacks in enhancing an aesthetic imagination, it can compensate for in its development of our self-awareness. Knowledge of our ignorance is, it was said long ago, the beginning, or rather the prerequisite, of wisdom. This sort of knowledge has been systematically excluded from our intellectual culture for the past 400 years; and it could be that this ignorance of ignorance, and the scientific hubris to which it gives rise, is responsible, in no small measure, for the present perilous character of our total scientific system. While in some ways this is still plausibly in the image of the conqueror of Nature, even more does it remind us of the Sorcerer's Apprentice.

Moreover, the recognition of models as metaphors will have a profoundly subversive and liberating effect on our very conception of science itself. For a metaphor has a reflexive, even ironic character (O'Connor 1999). When I say, "My love is like a red, red rose," I know as well as the reader that this is literally false. There is a deeper truth, which may be explicated later in my story; but starting with the metaphor I draw the reader into a little conspiracy, perhaps in its way a seduction. We share the knowledge that I have said something apparently false and ridiculous, and we will now play a game where I show how this apparent non-knowledge actually becomes a better knowledge than a photographic description. Of course, she/he may not want to play; some people find metaphors peculiar, useless and distasteful.

Healing the amputation of awareness in science

There is a long history in Europe, partly cultural and partly political, of a reaction against metaphor. One can find it with the early Protestant reformers, who wanted the Bible to be understood as a plain history for plain men. This, they thought, would eliminate the corrupted spiritual expertise of the priesthood. Later the same impulse was realized in the forging of a new conception of science. The prophets of the Scientific Revolution all put literature in a separate, and usually unequal, category from the knowledge derived in the experimental-mathematical way. Subsequent spokesmen of science stressed the need for clear thinking, for a hobbling of the imagination, lest the mind be led astray.

But now we find ourselves in a peculiar situation. Beneath the hard surface of scientific discourse, metaphors abound; we have "chaos" and "catastrophe" in mathematics, and "charm" in physics. It is just possible that those who create and popularize these metaphors are unaware of their complex character. They might think of them as cute and suggestive names, rather than as conveying realms of knowledge and presuppositions, which can be all the more powerful for being unselfconscious. In this way the creative scientists are, all unawares, poets *manqués*; in their nomenclatural practice they violate the principles on which their knowledge is claimed to rest.

Were this a matter concerning only theoretical scientists ensconced in academe, it would be of purely "academic" interest. But the pretensions of science, embedded in and unselfconsciously conveyed by the apparently impersonal conceptual instruments of analysis can, in cases of environmental policy, deceive and confuse the scientists as much as their audience. The numbers, graphs, and maps announce themselves as objective, impersonal facts; they are a whole world away from the red, red rose of the poet. Appreciation of them as metaphors requires an even greater sensitivity than grasping that the red, red rose is not a photographic description. But it is all the more difficult, because of the amputation of awareness that is instilled by the standard education in science.

Students of the traditional sciences are still formed by a curriculum which teaches by example that for every problem there is just one and only one correct answer; and the teaching is reinforced by the discipline of the exam. Having been thus force-fed for a decade or more until they emerge as "Doctors of Philosophy," students or researchers generally do not know what they are missing of the total picture of scientific knowledge in its context. Those who know about this amputated awareness do not necessarily think it is a bad thing. Indeed, it was argued, by Kuhn himself, that it is integral to the process of science and essential for its success (Kuhn 1962). The deficiencies and dangers of "puzzle-solving" in "normal science" become manifest only when that process fails in its own terms, when, in Kuhn's words, there is a "crisis." This can occur in research science as a precursor to a Kuhnian "scientific revolution." More commonly, now, it occurs whenever science is in a "postnormal" situation where facts are uncertain, values in dispute, stakes high and decisions urgent. Then puzzle-solving is at best irrelevant and at worst a diversion.

The amputated awareness of science is directly challenged when models are introduced as a means of education about global environmental problems and urban lifestyles. The experience of our focus groups has repeatedly shown that the "plain man's question," namely, "are these real predictions?" will, if accepted at its own level, produce nothing but confusion (see also the discussion in Chapter 5 by Dahinden et al.). If the models are claimed to predict scientifically, refutation follows swiftly; but if they are not predictors, then what on earth are they? The models can be rescued only by being explained as having a metaphorical function, designed to teach us about ourselves and our perspectives under the guise of describing or predicting the future states of the planet. In that process, we all have the opportunity to learn, not merely about ourselves, but about science as well.

In all this, there is another lesson to learned about science. The triumphs of science and the technology based on it are undeniable; no one could, except provocatively or mischievously, say that science is nothing but metaphor. But that science has produced our present predicament, where our urban lifestyles are clearly unsustainable. How is that total system of knowledge and power to be transformed, so that it does not destroy us in the end? Can the understanding which has become the leading problem for civilization, simply turn around and constitute the total solution? My argument, supported by the ULYSSES experience, is that a new understanding of the science that is employed in the policy processes is necessary, and that the awareness of metaphor has its part to play.

Conclusion: ULYSSES and the future

There is a consensus among its participants that this enriched understanding has been an important achievement of the present study. Through the interaction of experts with laypersons, we have found that the question for discussion and mutual learning is not restricted to the properties of this or that particular model, in relation to its user-friendliness. In the many interactions with intelligent and thoughtful laypersons, these methodological issues have come up repeatedly. While related considerations have pervaded the whole work of the present study, the "metaphor" metaphor (so to speak) has even been introduced explicitly in one of the regional case studies. Here, the participatory process has been portrayed as a "voyage of discovery" on which one of the passengers is a somewhat odd "Mr Computer" (De Marchi *et al.* 1998). And, crucially, all participants have learned important lessons, the experts no less than the laypersons. Such an outcome is the essence of post-normal science, that in these conditions the experts also have something important to learn. They can teach the laypersons something from their expertise, but the others can teach them something about that expertise itself. When all sides are aware of their mutual learning, and all sides gain thereby in self-understanding and mutual respect, then (and only then) can there develop that element of trust among participants, which is becoming recognized as the essential element in our making progress toward a sustainable world. In this way, the experience of the study discussed in this book, where (perhaps uniquely) the products of leading-edge integrated assessments of climate issues were exposed to scrutiny and earnest criticism by the supposed beneficiaries of the research, provides lessons of the utmost importance for us all.

A general recognition of models as metaphors will not come easily. As metaphors, computer models are too subtle, both in their form and in their content, for easy detection. And those who created them may well have been prevented, by all the institutional and cultural circumstances of the work, from being aware of their essential character. Furthermore, the investments in the scientistic conception of models, in the personal, institutional and ideological dimensions, are enormous and still very powerful. But the myth of the reductionist-scientific character of our studies of the future, and indeed of all complex systems, cannot hold. Only by being aware of our metaphors, and our ignorance, can we fashion the scientific tools we need for guiding our steps into the future, now appreciated as unknown and unknowable, but where our greatest challenge lies. Real, working dialogues between the community of experts and the "extended peer community" are essential in improving this awareness on both sides. The initiative of the study discussed in this volume has illuminated the problem of the use of science for policy, and it has shown the ways toward its solution, through dialogue, learning and awareness. In this, I hope that the understanding of models as metaphors has played a part.

PART TWO

Experiences with IA Focus Groups

INTRODUCTION

The second part of this book concerns procedures for citizen participation in sustainability science, and results obtained from such participatory procedures. As in Part I on Concepts and Insights, also in the research discussed in Part II, the issue of climate change and its relation to urban lifestyles is used as a case study to examine the possible roles of public participation in sustainability science. In order to allow a meaningful interaction between lay and expert perspectives in participatory procedures on this issue, these IA Focus Groups with citizens consisted of three distinct phases. Experiences with collage processes in the first phase of IA Focus Groups, allowing participants to express their spontaneous feelings on the focal topic of climate change and energy use, are discussed in Chapter 4 by Kasemir *et al.*, and illustrated with examples of collage pictures. Findings include the fact that citizens across Europe saw a future with strongly reduced energy use rather positively, more so than might be found, for example, in a US context. In making collages, the citizens were found to be rather sophisticated in dealing with ambiguity and uncertainty. In Chapter 5, Dahinden *et al.* discuss the use of computer models in the second phase of IA Focus Group procedures. These models were found to be powerful tools for promoting insights about complex sustainability issues like climate change, but future models could be improved, in particular with regard to accessibility to lay audiences. Criteria for this, and for successful facilitation of interactive model use, are discussed. Chapter 6 by Querol *et al.* concerns experiences with procedures allowing participants to summarize their own conclusions in the final phase of IA Focus Groups. Such citizens' report procedures yield the views of lay participants in their own words, and could be very useful in Local Agenda 21 contexts. Findings include the fact that many European citizens see climate change as a real problem, think that mitigation and not just adaptation is warranted, and want action to be taken even in the face of scientific uncertainties. By discussing these procedures for the participation of citizens, we hope to inspire others who want to tackle the challenge of public participation in sustainability science.

CHAPTER FOUR

Collage processes and citizens' visions for the future

Bernd Kasemir, Urs Dahinden, Åsa Gerger Swartling, Daniela Schibli, Ralf Schüle, David Tàbara, and Carlo C. Jaeger

Introduction

In order to respond effectively to the challenge of preparing a sustainability transition, major changes in the socio-economic system of modern society will have to be envisaged. Some earlier and simpler environmental problems could be tackled, for example, by reducing toxic by-products of a few production processes. However, responses to prospects of, for example, climate change will require large shifts right at the heart of our industrialized cultures, especially in the manner in which we use energy and produce greenhouse gases in the process. Referring to reduction scenarios discussed in the context of the Intergovernmental Panel on Climate Change (IPCC), Kempton (1991) has stressed that "if world leaders decide to reduce greenhouse gas emissions by two-thirds, such a large reduction will require consumer and worker co-operation as well as citizen consent that major societal changes are worth the effort." Responses to global environmental change will only be effective if they have clear public support.

Understanding the reactions of citizens to prospects of climate change and related policy options is thus a central element in developing effective climate policies. Studies on this issue can build upon a large body of research on environmental consciousness and behavior in general (see, e.g., the comprehensive overview by Brand 1997). In the last few decades, a variety of studies have focused specifically on perceptions of climate change issues (see, e.g., the overview by Jaeger *et al.* 1993; and by Thompson and Rayner 1998). Bearing in mind the scale of changes needed in the longer run for effective climate protection, the crucial research goal here is to understand the role of the public in supporting changes of a complex socio-economic system. As Dunlap (1998) has stressed, this includes collective action by many players, not just isolated individual reactions in an otherwise static social environment.

Unlike earlier work on citizens' perspectives on climate change issues (see, e.g., Dunlap 1998; and Kempton 1997), the study discussed in this volume has designed research on citizens' perspectives as participatory procedures within the larger framework of Integrated Assessment (IA) processes. This research, mainly conducted within the ULYSSES project (see Acknowledgements), has developed IA Focus Group procedures for this purpose. As discussed in Chapter 1, the reason for this was that integrating participatory methods from the social sciences with natural science research on climate change is necessary to support climate policy-making for the future. As also argued there, such an integration of social science with natural science approaches is especially promising for sustainability science using methods of IA.

Effective methods of participation in sustainability science have to avoid two opposed pitfalls. On the one hand, procedures heavily dominated by expert input run the danger of rendering participation meaningless. On the other hand, procedures that don't take expert information adequately into account are in danger of suffering from information deficits. IA Focus Group procedures were specifically designed so that a balance between lay and expert input into the process is attained. To achieve this, the IA Focus Group procedures consisted of three distinct phases. The first phase allowed the participants to express their spontaneous associations with climate change and energy use, by producing and discussing collages on these issues. Results from this collage work are discussed in the present chapter. Only in the second phase were the groups exposed to expert opinion on climate change topics, before the participants themselves made a synthesis of their views on these issues in the third and final phase of the procedure.

This chapter is organized as follows. In the following section we discuss our research questions and method. We relate this to current debates about the role of social science in improving public participation in global environmental change assessments and politics. And we discuss two expectations concerning the concept of "reflexive modernization." First, that today arguments questioning the idea of progress, which was characteristic for "simple modernization," play an important role in laypersons' conversations about climate change and energy use. And second, that in these conversations the ability to deal with ambiguity and doubt is essential. Later, we discuss results from collage work within IA Focus Group processes in relation to these ideas. These collages were produced for different scenarios of energy use. We then draw three kinds of conclusions from this discussion. First, we conclude how the citizens in our IA Focus Groups assessed a strong energy reduction scenario versus a business-as-usual scenario. Second, there are conclusions about the concept of reflexive modernization in the light of our IA Focus Group findings. And third, the possible implications of the collage work in IA Focus Groups for the IA modeling community are discussed.

Research questions and research method

Climate change is increasingly present in citizens' conversations. International comparative studies (see, e.g., Dunlap and Mertig 1996) show that in many countries climate change is seen as a problem which is *already* occurring. Climate change is usually not perceived as the most important of all environmental problems, and is often confused with other problems such as ozone depletion (see e.g., Bostrom *et al.* 1994; and Read *et al.* 1994). But attention paid to climate change by the media, NGOs, and local politicians (Bell 1994; Mazur 1998) has contributed to the "social creation" of the issue (Hannigan 1995), and to greater public awareness and debate.

This growing body of public opinion about global environmental risks is not sufficiently incorporated in experts' debates. The concept of the *risk society* discussed by Ulrich Beck (1992) and others suggests that in today's society, where global hazards threaten all social classes, scientific results are becoming more relevant for policy decisions, while at the same time providing less and less of a sufficient basis for such decisions. In this situation, social science has a decisive role to play in bridging the gap between public opinion and expert debates on complex environmental issues.

For this purpose, it will be crucial to address a cluster of related problems in social science research:

(1) The constructivist-realist debate about the ontological existence or *real* nature of environmental change. Most theoretical and empirical contributions in the field put much weight on the assumption of whether they take environmental problems as "real" or as "socially constructed" (Buttel and Taylor 1992; Dunlap and Catton 1994). Attempts to integrate the two approaches for the case of climate change have been pursued for a number of years (Rosa and Dietz 1998).

(2) The extent to which global change is understood either as the cause of social change, as its effect, or as being independent from it. This debate is rooted in the contrast between ecological determinism and

socio-cultural autonomy (Alexander and Smith 1996; Crenshaw and Jenkings 1996; Douglas and Wildavsky 1982).

(3) The epistemological discussion on which procedures are most adequate to obtain knowledge for framing and coping with global environmental change. This dispute takes place along a populist–elitist axis, and bestows different weights on what is, or should be, the role of the lay public in GEC assessments and policy formation (see Beck 1992; Funtowicz and Ravetz 1991; Jasanoff and Wynne 1998; Wynne 1995; 1992b).

(4) The contested question of whether social science on environmental issues should develop independently from or in collaboration with natural science research. Is it still useful to proceed with a non-integrated environmental social science, or should both social and natural sciences inform each other (Rosa 1999; Stern 1993; Stern, Young, and Druckman 1992)?

(5) The open issue of whether social science methodologies are useful and legitimate to facilitate participation, and to democratize environmental research and its applications (Renn, Webler, and Wiedemann 1995; Dürrenberger *et al.* 1997; Tàbara 1998).

Exciting developments in the social sciences can be expected in the coming years concerning these issues. We opted for a less theoretical approach in the research discussed here. The focus was to develop and apply methods for empirical qualitative studies of public perceptions related to global environmental change, extending research conducted in earlier comparative studies in the field. Examples of such qualitative studies include the work by W. Kempton (1991), contrasting perceptions of lay people with those of experts in the US. J. Burgess *et al.* (1995) compared public views on global environmental change between Holland and Great Britain. R. E. Löfstedt, (1992; 1993)) studied climate change perceptions in Sweden and Austria. And A. Bostrom *et al.* (1994) and D. Read *et al.* (1994) analyzed the level of knowledge about this problem among different societal groups in the US.

The methodology developed and applied in the present study is the IA Focus Group approach, discussed in more depth in Chapter 1. It extends earlier qualitative research on citizens' views concerning global change with respect to three dimensions. First, while most other qualitative studies have been restricted to analyzing verbal exchanges, we have included *visual* expressions of citizens' associations with energy use and its relation to climate change. Second, we have confronted the study participants with current scientific knowledge on climate change, mostly in the form of IA computer models. And third, we have encouraged the participants to summarize their own views at the end of the process, usually in the form of written citizen reports.

This chapter focuses on the first of these points, visual expressions of citizens' views in the form of collages. We found that collage production can be a very productive tool in IA Focus Group discussions on alternative future developments. As described below, participants in the focus groups were asked to produce collages on such alternative futures using pictures they selected from magazines provided by the research teams. This collage work was used in the focus groups as a projective technique. In the psychological literature, projective techniques are commonly defined as psychological assessment devices using often standardized but purposefully ambiguous stimuli "on the assumption that unstructured material will allow unconscious motivations and fears to be uncovered in the client's interpretation of its content."[1] In order to convey an idea of how such techniques work, two projective techniques often used in clinical and forensic psychology are briefly described below: the Rorschach ink blot test and the Thematic Apperception Test.

In the Rorschach ink blot test, a subject's interpretations of ten standard abstract designs are analyzed as a measure of emotional and intellectual functioning and integration. The test is named after the psychiatrist Hermann Rorschach (1884–1922) who designed the ink blots. Various methods for the analysis of these tests have been developed (Exner 1993). Another projective technique, the Thematic Apperception Test (TAT), was developed by Henry A. Murray and Christiana Morgan from Harvard University. Examiners present individuals with a subset of cards displaying pictures of ambiguous situations, mostly featuring people. Respondents then construct a story about each picture. The stories are then analyzed according to certain scoring systems (Gieser and Stein 1999). Within psychology, there is an ongoing debate on the robustness of findings resulting from such projective techniques (Lilienfeld, Wood, and Garb 2001). But even the critics agree that projective techniques can yield valuable information if they include a careful analysis of the empirical material (Lilienfeld, Wood, and Garb 2000).

The collage work in IA Focus Groups discussed in this chapter is similar to the projective techniques described above in that participants are confronted with unstructured material (images contained in a broad selection of magazines) and react to that in a manner that allows them to express both hopes and fears. The collage work differs from the other

---

[1] Iverson (2001) Psychology Explorer – a glossary of nearly 1,300 terms related to psychology. In: http://www.iversonsoftware.com/reference/psychology/p/projective_test.htm (8 October 2001)

projective techniques discussed in that participants respond to that material as a group rather than individually, and that they actively create new visual forms of expression (the collages) rather than only react to visual stimuli (ink blots or image cards). This kind of projective technique may be especially suited for discovering the evolution of "mental maps" in group settings, a major goal of IA Focus Groups.

The collages produced in the focus groups allow us to better understand how the participants themselves conceive of different alternative futures. Within our focus groups, collages were mainly produced on the issue of different future developments in energy use, which is a key question for climate policy and sustainability. As a concrete task, the citizens in the groups were asked to imagine how their region might look in thirty years' time under two different assumptions: first, if present trends of energy use continue; second, if energy use is reduced to half its current level within the next thirty years.

For this purpose, the group was usually split into two subgroups, each starting from one of these two assumptions. The participants had between 30 minutes and an hour for producing the collages. They were provided with a mix of different magazines (technical and motor magazines, nature magazines, and general magazines concerning society, lifestyle, and hobbies) featuring colored pictures, and also with scissors, glue and pens. After producing the collages, the subgroups presented their collages to each other and discussed them. These collages and the related group discussions were then analyzed for systematic differences in the way these different visions of the future – business-as-usual versus strong reduction of energy use – were conceived by citizens in the IA Focus Groups.

Findings from these IA Focus Group collage processes are discussed below in relation to the concept of *reflexive modernization*, proposed by Beck *et al.* (1994). In an extension of the risk society concept, reflexive modernization is described as a new modernity, where technological and institutional hazards have shattered the trust in eternal progress. Beck *et al.* have argued that in this reflexive modernization, traditional borders between public and private as well as between expert and lay views have become blurred, and multiple and contradictory viewpoints have become the norm rather than the exception. Here, we do not aim at an in-depth discussion about the concept of reflexive modernization, or at taking a definite position as to its validity. Rather, we want to relate our discussion of IA Focus Group collages to the question of what the distinction between simple and reflexive modernization could mean for the concrete case of citizens' views on energy use and climate change.

One may expect that in reflexive modernization laypersons question received ideas of progress in conversations about energy use and climate change. The increasing ability of humans to control large energy transformations is a hallmark of progress as understood by "simple modernization." As a first point, we have investigated whether European citizens still take it for granted that the continuation of current energy use trends will lead to increased welfare for themselves and their children. In addition, reflexive modernization differs from some forms of environmentalist opposition to simple modernization. While these sometimes replace the certainties of modernization by the certainty that a restored tradition of "living in harmony with nature" would solve our problems, reflexive modernization is subtler. Thus, as a second point we have investigated whether European citizens always expect clear-cut arguments in favor of one policy or another, or may see arguments emphasizing ambiguity and doubt as more appropriate.

Citizens' images of the future: findings from IA Focus Groups

In the following, we discuss findings from IA Focus Groups in relation to these research questions. This discussion is based on the analysis of collage processes in twenty-four IA Focus Groups, conducted in four regions from the south to the north of Europe (Barcelona, Frankfurt, Stockholm, and Switzerland). Overall, about 170 citizens participated in these groups. As described above, the participants produced and discussed collages on two alternative types of future developments, business-as-usual concerning energy use on the one hand, and strong reduction of energy use on the other hand. Some of these collages were either unambiguously positive or negative, others explicitly showed different types of ambiguity. In classifying collages as positive, negative, or ambiguous, we looked for images of the types of associations summarized in Table 4.1 in each collage. These types of positive and negative associations had been abstracted from an inventory of images appearing in the collages.

The individual collages were then analyzed for the occurrence of pictures corresponding to these types of associations. The impression gained

Table 4.1 *Association categories used for analyzing the collages*

Positive associations	Negative associations
Emotional and physical wellbeing	Emotional and physical distress
Harmony, natural, and integrated lifestyle	Conflict, alienation, and poverty
Health of natural environment	Degradation of natural environment
Health of human environment	Degradation of human environment

Table 4.2 *Collage types occurring (marked by X) and not occurring (unmarked) in the IA Focus Groups*

	Negative Collages	Ambiguous Collages	Positive Collages
Business-as-usual	X	X	
Energy reduction		X	X

by analyzing the collage pictures in this manner was then checked against transcripts of the collage discussions in the focus groups. This proved essential for gaining a deeper understanding of what the collages meant for the citizens. Sometimes, it also helped to avoid clear misinterpretations. For example, one business-as-usual collage contained a picture of an intact seashore – a positive association of health of natural environment in our classification. However, from the transcript it became clear that the group wanted to express that this was a positive aspect of the past, which would be lost in a scenario of continuing present trends.

In principle, we could have obtained six types of collages in these processes: clearly positive, clearly negative, or ambiguous collages on business-as-usual, and the corresponding three types for energy reduction. From these six possible types, two did not appear: clearly positive collages on business-as-usual, and clearly negative collages on energy reduction (see Table 4.2). The types of collages found in our focus groups are discussed in more detail below. Overall, in the collages obtained in these groups, associations with strong energy reductions were more optimistic than those related to business-as-usual. Business-as-usual was often associated with a degrading natural and human environment. Clearly optimistic visions of continuing present trends of energy use were not found.

But what concrete images do citizens associate with these developments? And what roles do uncertainty and ambivalence play in these images? Answers to these questions are provided below with examples from collages of the different types obtained, and with related quotes from the corresponding focus group transcripts. In this discussion we pay special attention to collages expressing ambiguity. Collages of this type are often more complex and need more effort of interpretation than straightforward positive or negative ones.

Clearly positive and clearly negative collages

Clearly negative collages were only found for business-as-usual scenarios, clearly positive collages only for energy reduction scenarios.

Figure 4.1 Detail of collage on continuing present trends. (Focus Group 4, Zurich)

Business-as-usual and fear

The continuation of present trends was often associated with clearly negative images, expressing fear. One example is a purely negative collage on business-as-usual from the Frankfurt region, including a picture of a young man on a motorcycle together with images of natural degradation, illness and social decline. It was commented on by one of the participants as follows: "BRITTA: 'climate catastrophes, environmental catastrophes, floodings, droughts . . . all the same, still [there will be] people who insist on all their privileges'." (Focus Group 8, Frankfurt region).

Another example is a collage from Zurich on continuing present trends (see Figure 4.1). This collage was presented with the following comments: "RENATE: 'the world is half drowning. There a skeleton, there we have the hands looking out of the water like that, because . . . the level of the water is rising and rising. There we already have graves . . .'" (Focus Group 4, Zurich). As in these two examples, clearly negative collages on continuing present trends of energy use often contained two types of negative images. First, they contained images of climate change and other related disruptions of the natural environment, like desertification and floods. Second, they included images of degrading human living conditions like illness, high inequality, poverty, or violence.

The presentations and discussions of negative business-as-usual collages not only contained depressed statements, but occasionally also cynicism. This was the case, for example, in the following remarks on the role of cars in the society of the future in a collage presentation:

PETER: ... the car industry that continues to grow beautifully and will characterize our country as ever. There are just some little side effects: Here we have someone who is badly wounded, here we have allergies occurring, but the cars are nice and colorful. We have a bright and colorful world, even if prosperity has decreased a bit; this is a world in which things only get worse as it grows and thrives. Germany in 2030.

(Focus Group 2, Frankfurt region)

Other examples bordering on cynicism or black humour came up in two focus groups in Zurich and the Frankfurt region. In both cases, in response to the moderator's question on whether they could not imagine any positive aspects of continuing present trends (of energy use), participants said that mortality would increase. That in turn would be good for the environment (Focus Group 7, Frankfurt region; Focus Group 4, Zurich).

Interestingly, the only time an image of unemployment appeared explicitly in one of the collages was in a business-as-usual collage, not in a collage on energy reduction:

PER: ...in 2030...if we go on the way we do today. The environment will degrade year by year. ...But we think you will remember good old times. That is the first picture to the left. That you will go back in your thoughts how the Stockholm area looked like in 1997, green with lots of nature, next picture...The picture at the far right shows that unemployment will be significant – it is our 25 year old kids who sit there and can't find a job.

(Focus Group 1, Stockholm)

This example also illustrates that dangers to human wellbeing in business-as-usual scenarios of energy use were not only associated with droughts, floods, or accidents, but sometimes with more general problems of industrial modernity as well. A list of such problems is given in this example: "ORIOL: 'We wanted to explore a little the question of violence, problematic things, marginalisation, emigration, psychological problems, drugs...'" (Focus Group 2, Barcelona). This quote, however, is from a group that produced a business-as-usual collage that was not purely and unambiguously negative. First, an image of a pristine coastline was included within the otherwise very negative collage. Second, the participant presenting this collage also said that after they had finished, the group had reconsidered and would have wanted the collage to look more positive than it did. This again stresses the importance of analyzing the discussions of the collages together with the pictures themselves.

Figure 4.2 Detail of collage on reducing energy use (Focus Group 1, Stockholm)

Energy reduction and hope

In contrast to business-as-usual, strong reduction of energy use was often associated with clearly positive images. For example, in one group the collage took the form of a tree with its branches and leaves made out of images of happy children, sporty women, art, fruit, and flowers (Focus Group 1, Zurich). This collage and its discussion was typical in the sense that reducing energy use was often associated not only with mitigation of climate change, but also of other environmental impacts, for example, water quality or quantity problems.

AGNES: Yes, well I think that it should just be kept in equilibrium, shouldn't it? Let's say leisure, the life of a person, as well as the whole, nature around it and water... That is the most important for me, somehow, that it is in equilibrium.   (Focus Group 1, Zurich)

In general, water – both as a leisure and health resource for people as well as in the form of pristine aquatic ecosystems – appeared quite often in the positive collages on energy reduction. This is also the case in the following example (see Figure 4.2):

MAGNUS: Here, cleaner water. Better environment in this corner. The animals are healthier, as we can see here. The flowers look fresher. Fewer cars down here, people move. Everything is going to be better.
(Focus Group 1, Stockholm)

This reflects a general tendency in the IA Focus group discussions: the participants preferred discussing different environmental issues not in isolation, but in a more integrated manner. The two collages discussed above are also typical for positive energy reduction collages in another respect: the future looks bright both for humans and for nature, which are in harmony with each other. Positive feelings expressed in these collages are related to people enjoying themselves in this future, just as much as they are related to a healthy environment. We did not find positive collages on energy reduction that only showed images of healthy plants and animals, without also showing joyful people.

The role technology plays in these clearly positive collages on energy reduction varies. In some of these collages, only low-tech options are included, especially cycling. In other collages, energy efficient and alternative energy technologies play a prominent role. Technologies mentioned include wind and solar energy, electric cars, improved public transport, and occasionally energy-saving buildings.

Only rarely, technological innovation was mentioned without much association with behavioral change:

BARBRO: We believe in high technology. That it doesn't need to be expensive. We have alternative energy sources, . . . we have low consuming engines, we have return bottles, we have clean water. We have beautiful buildings . . . We cooperate with a strategic environmental plan . . . and in short we would like to live here in the city.

RIKARD: What really matters is a clean city and the high technology is a way of getting there.   (Focus Group 2, Stockholm)

More often, technological innovations seemed to be viewed as a complement, rather than an alternative, to changes in lifestyles and behavior, as is illustrated below:

IRMGARD: We thought, we have to reduce everything, that we want to lead a simple life and consume less. That we begin to use the things we have here, that we take solar energy, collectors, that we possibly put windmills on top of the houses. That we . . . take the bicycle more again . . . that the air gets cleaner, that we reuse used water for toilets and all kinds of washing machines, that every person contributes to make an effort to reduce energy . . .
                                    (Focus Group 7, Frankfurt region)

Statements like this imply restrictions that could also be seen as negative aspects of energy reduction scenarios. In some groups, energy reduction was indeed assessed more ambiguously, as we shall see below.

Ambiguous collages

Ambiguous collages were found both for energy reduction and business-as-usual scenarios. These collages can be understood as expressing different types of ambiguity, as discussed below.

Figure 4.3 Detail of collage on continuing present trends. (Focus Group 4, Frankfurt region)

Ambiguous expectations for business-as-usual

Collages on business-as-usual expressing ambiguity came in different forms. For example, in one collage today's life was depicted as very agreeable, while a possible future development was illustrated with dark images: chaos, air pollution, droughts, accidents, waste, and death. However, question marks were put all over this part of the collage, and the words "Today like this! Tomorrow like that?" were included (Focus Group 10, Zurich). Also from the discussions transcript, it is clear that the participants saw a future with environmental degradation caused by continuing present trends of energy use as frightening, but also as *uncertain*. Another type of ambiguity appears in the following collage, presented by one participant as clearly negative at the beginning (see Figure 4.3): "AXEL: 'Yes, we have tried to choose nothing but threatening things. We have Lenin for societal problems, the nozzle there is really aimed at people like a weapon...'" (Focus Group 4, Frankfurt region). However, this purely negative statement was complemented by a hesitantly positive one by a second participant, referring to pictures of beautiful beaches in the same collage: "THOMAS: 'Well, ambivalent. To the right you see the bright side of life, but the scissors are opening more and more. Between poor and rich. Where you can afford to live in clean and expensive surroundings...'" (Focus Group 4, Frankfurt region). This type of ambiguous association with business-as-usual concerns *polarization*: while there is much degradation and suffering, some islands of nature are still intact and some people are still well off.[2]

---

[2] There is another interesting feature of this collage in relation to reflexive modernization. The picture of Lenin was explained as symbolizing demagogy and deception being applied

Figure 4.4 Collage on continuing present trends. (Focus Group 5, Barcelona)

Polarization appears in an impressive manner in a collage from Barcelona, too (see Figure 4.4). The different sides of this collage show contrasting developments of both the natural and the social environment:

OSCAR: More or less all of us have agreed that there would be differentiated parts inside the city, we have made an urban nucleus, a city center ... From here we have made four parts, one very green and beautiful, which are the

in politics, or "that much is disguised, like one saw in the past with communism." The image of the new Frankfurt office tower of a major German bank, superimposed on the picture of Lenin, was meant to express "Capitalism which somehow develops its stylistic blunder." Here the traditional political distinction between left and right becomes blurred and both systems seem to be simultaneously accused of causing problems in "simple" modernization.

While this is connected to negative associations, a feature of reflexive modernization seen rather positively in one of the groups was the changing gender roles in society. This collage includes the picture of a woman wearing a business suit and demonstrating a karate pose, and pictures of a man with a steam iron and of another man with a small child in his arms choosing a pram (Focus Group 4, Stockholm). Even if this should be an exaggeration, it reminds us that "a society in which men and women were really equal (whatever that might imply in detail) would without doubt be a new modernity" (Beck 1994).

respected natural areas, which is maybe where the European Union has spent most money to do all this. We have also made degraded areas on the other side which are the destroyed and deserted areas which maybe haven't been looked at so much. On this side we have put a violent society, "ghettos"... here a society which we believe will be superior, with Superman and lucid people who will have a good time, and not so stressful...

(Focus Group 5, Barcelona)

Up to now, we have seen two types of ambiguity, uncertainty and polarisation, in business-as-usual collages. Another type of ambiguity, true *ambivalence* where the same object or development evokes positive and negative associations at the same time, is harder to put into images. Within the business-as-usual collages we did not directly find pictures of that kind. But in the following example ambivalence was expressed in the discussions related to a collage presentation. While this collage depicted mostly negative associations with business-as-usual trends leading to a high-tech society in the future, ambivalent feelings in relation to energy use surfaced during the discussions:

INA: ...Not that you could do something positive with energy or from energy, that is really all rather, yes, negative.

INGRID: With one difference: global communication. That can also be positive. With the whole world. That is really no problem. That would be quite nice for some people.

ANDREAS: You also can see it as positive if one uses more energy. Because then totally new technologies and new experiences in life become possible.

HANS: It could also be alternative energy.   (Focus Group 1, Frankfurt region)

This ambivalence, which was not apparent from the collage picture but only from the discussions, was another reminder that analyzing discussion transcripts is an important part of collage interpretation.

Ambiguous views on energy reduction

As in the case of business-as-usual, ambiguity appeared in different forms in collages on strong energy reduction. These can again be understood to express uncertainty, polarization, and ambivalence. The example from Barcelona illustrated in Figure 4.5 is a clear case of *uncertainty*. This collage is divided into two parts by a vertical line. One part was marked with the label 'Either we adapt... (*o ens adaptem*)' and showed improved technology as well as low-tech options like transport by hang-glider or bicycle; the other part was labeled 'or we turn backwards (*o tornem enrere*)' and featured images of primitive societies.

FERRAN: ...we have seen two possibilities, that either we adapted and the city continued the same with minor changes...we have included...an engine which pollutes less, which consumes less...and on the other hand we are

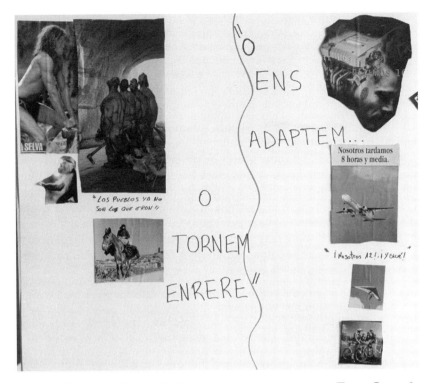

Figure 4.5 Detail of collage on reducing energy use. (Focus Group 3, Barcelona)

not adapting to the reduction of energy, we're not going forward and we're going backwards . . . to prehistoric people, half naked . . . there is the duality that we can see and we don't know what could happen . . .

(Focus Group 3, Barcelona)

In the discussion, the possibility of successful adaptation was seen more optimistically for the case that energy consumption was reduced gradually between now and 2030 as new technological advances appear. For the case that there should be sudden reductions of energy use, expectations were more pessimistic.

A highly interesting example of the second type of ambiguity which was found, *polarization*, appeared in a collage by a group from the Frankfurt region. This group depicted their region with reduced energy use in the future as a boat, on which life is beautiful. However, outside of the boat there are misery and catastrophes. The implication was that a purely regional policy of energy reduction was expected to increase inequalities,

Figure 4.6 Detail of collage on reducing energy use. (Focus Group 1, Frankfurt region)

and that a coordination between regional and global policies was thought to be necessary (see Figure 4.6):

PAUL: The basic idea behind this was, first of all, we have a boat and this boat depicts our region. And as we have fantastically reduced the pollution burden and energy use, in this region, on this boat, there is a paradise, as it were . . . as there is a paradise, so many people want to get in, and that's not what we want. Because, maybe they would destroy our wealth and our paradise. And as you see on the outsides [of the collage], the rest of the world is suffering. What I especially think as well is that such a problem can only be solved globally and can't be approached regionally . . .

(Focus Group 1, Frankfurt region)

Ambiguous associations with strong energy reduction also appeared in the form of *ambivalence*. For example, changing lifestyles under energy reduction were assessed ambivalently in a collage from Barcelona. Here, positive aspects of changing transport behavior were symbolized with a drawing of a smiling man on a bicycle, and a picture of people enjoying horse riding. However, such changes of lifestyle were also seen to have negative aspects: "MARIA: 'We also see society a lot sadder because probably between now and 2030 there won't be petrol and people will have to abandon their cars and even the big cities' " (Focus Group 5,

Barcelona). The whole structure of the collage produced by a group from the Frankfurt region was linked to ambivalence. Very similar to the earlier example on uncertainty from Barcelona, the collage was divided by a vertical line into two parts. Only this time, the parts did not represent different alternative development paths, but positive and negative aspects of energy reduction. One side included flowers, new technologies, and relaxation, and the other side depicted regulation, control, and fights over resources.

KATJA: We now have tried, that was a little difficult, to make two parts out of the whole, on the one hand the positive aspect that a reduction of resource use would entail...and the negative aspect with that, the restriction of the individuals in their actions, in what they can do, as negative aspect of little resource use.... (Focus Group 5, Frankfurt region)

This ambivalence of positive and negative associations did not only hold for the overall scenario, but also for some concrete images. For example, a horse-drawn carriage was placed right onto the middle of the dividing line. This was commented on as follows:

ANDREA: With many things we saw that they are to be seen positively as well as negatively, because this is a personal point of view.... That is why we have put some things in the middle, because it really has to be seen as having two sides. (Focus Group 5, Frankfurt region)

A final example on ambivalence illustrates that expressing ambivalent feelings in concrete images can be difficult. In one otherwise positive collage on energy reduction, an image was included (see Figure 4.7) indicating that preserving the global environment might have to be counterbalanced by "renunciation" (*Verzicht* in German):

HARALD: ...After the rather many positive things, we thought the day – as it says on the left side – may be quite wonderful.[3] But this is confronted with something else; that we couldn't define exactly, because we don't know what the price of this thing is, well, of keeping the globe there in balance. That's why we just wrote: "Renunciation". That doesn't show up really in the picture – apart from the thing with the crowded bus maybe – because we didn't really have concrete ideas there. (Focus Group 8, Frankfurt region)

In fact, two levels of ambivalence appeared here. On the first level, energy reduction was associated with positive aspects on the one hand, and renunciation on the other. On the second level, it was explicitly mentioned in the discussion that different valuations can be associated with renunciation itself – that renunciation is in fact itself ambivalent:

---

[3] "Ein herrlicher Tag," meaning "a wonderful day" in German.

Figure 4.7 Detail of collage on reducing energy use. (Focus Group 8, Frankfurt region)

MARTINA: ... the thing with renunciation ... is then always a question of valua-
tion. So, renunciation can be valued positively or can be valued negatively ...
it depends very much on the assessment of the person in question: What do
I get for giving something up?   (Focus Group 8, Frankfurt region)

In summary, the types of ambiguity found in collages on strong energy
reduction were parallel to those found in collages on business-as-usual:
uncertainty, polarization, and ambivalence.

Regional differences

Up to now we have discussed common aspects of the collages from all four
research regions (Barcelona, Frankfurt, Stockholm, and Switzerland).
For all regions it was the case that clearly negative collages were only

found for business-as-usual scenarios of energy use, that clearly positive collages only appeared for scenarios of strong energy reduction, and that ambiguous collages were found for both types of scenarios. But how did the collages differ between the regions?

Regional differences appeared with respect to the role ambiguity played in the collages. In the German-speaking part of Switzerland (Zurich), collages with little ambiguity – clearly negative for the case of business-as-usual and clearly positive for the case of energy reduction – dominated. In the Frankfurt region, business-as-usual collages were also predominantly negative, but energy reduction collages were more mixed – either positive or ambiguous. In Stockholm, in a sense the situation was the reverse of the Frankfurt case: energy reduction collages showed little ambiguity, i.e., they were predominantly positive, while business-as-usual collages were more mixed – either negative or ambiguous. In Barcelona, both business-as-usual and energy reduction scenarios were dominated by ambiguous collages. But energy reduction collages tended to be more positive than business-as-usual ones here, too. As in Barcelona, in the French-speaking part of Switzerland ambiguity played a crucial role in both business-as-usual and the energy reduction collages. But in the comments on their collages, some of these groups went even further than in the collage images themselves. Occasionally, participants commented on the possibility of a future with energy reduction rather negatively. On the other hand, the business-as-usual scenario was sometimes seen to contain elements of fun and of a life worth living, even if nature had to suffer a bit. Some of these groups conducted in the French-speaking part of Switzerland expressed views that were the closest to a position of "simple modernity," seeing increasing energy use as a part of positive progress, among all views we encountered in the study. It would have been very interesting to conduct additional groups in France to see whether this position would be as strong or even stronger there. However, even for the French-speaking Swiss groups, the collage images remained within the four categories found overall in the study (negative business-as-usual collages, positive energy reduction collages, and ambiguous collages of both types).

The IA Focus Group research discussed here is probably best interpreted as hinting at ideal types consisting, in our case, of typical images associated with business-as-usual scenarios and with strong reduction scenarios for energy use. The sample size does not allow for a statistical analysis by regions. If we restrict statements about frequencies to the basic categories of "none," "some," or "all," and handle them with appropriate care, however, two interesting patterns emerge. First, it seems that across a large part of Europe a perspective of considerable energy reduction is seen as more preferable than a business-as-usual perspective. This is a

highly significant result, which should be compared with similar investigations in other parts of the world. In the light of the results of Kempton
and Craig (1993), suggesting that policy-makers in Europe often view
climate change mitigation much more favorably than their counterparts
in the US, it would be especially interesting to compare our findings
with focus group data from North America. Second, different European
regions seem to differ in cultural ambiguity with regard to complex environmental issues. Whether this ambiguity is better interpreted as a lack of
desirable clarity, or as a sign of reflexive sophistication, will be discussed
briefly in the conclusions.

Conclusions

Assessments of global environmental problems have started with results
from the natural sciences. Yet the complexity, uncertainty, and multi-
plicity of values that characterize this debate have led to an increasing
awareness of the need to integrate expert assessments with the way lay
people frame these problems. Actions directed to mitigate global change
will eventually impinge on stakeholder interests, personal lifestyles, and
public institutions. Tensions about whether policies considered are appropriate and match with public views are likely to spread, as are demands
for higher accountability. In democratic contexts, new and imaginative
channels for including the views of the lay public in sustainability science
and global change politics will have to be devised.

   Therefore, in this section we focus on three types of conclusions. First,
based on a brief summary of the main empirical findings, we highlight
perspectives of European citizens concerning energy and climate developments as expressed in IA Focus Group collages. Second, we raise the
question of how these findings relate to the expectations formulated earlier concerning the concept of reflexive modernization. And third, we
ask whether the expressions of ambiguities in the collage work of our IA
Focus Groups could provide inspiration for IA modelers.

Citizens' perspectives on energy and climate

Here we have discussed collages produced by citizens participating in
IA Focus Groups in four regions across Europe. These collages express
associations by the participants with a continuation of present trends of
energy use, and with a reduction of energy use to half of its current level
within thirty years. Clearly negative collages were only found for the scenario of continuing present trends of energy use. This business-as-usual
was often associated with degradation of the natural environment, such
as desertification and floods, and also with declining social conditions,

such as illness, high inequality, poverty, and violence. Clearly positive collages were only found for the scenario of strong reduction of energy use. This was often associated with a healthy natural environment, illustrated by animals and plants in pristine ecosystems, and to human wellbeing, illustrated by healthy people relaxing in nature and in well-kept urban environments. Technological innovation was often seen to support this goal as a complement, and not as an alternative, to changes in lifestyles and behavior.

Besides these clearly negative or positive collages, more ambiguous collages were found as well. This ambiguity appeared in collages on continuing present trends as well as in those on strong reduction of energy use, and took the forms of uncertainty, polarization, and ambivalence. *Uncertainty* was expressed, for example, in collages concerning the question whether energy reduction would mean going back to primitive lifestyles, or developing a sophisticated low-energy society. *Polarization*, where some people are better off while others are doing worse and some areas are preserved while others are declining, was either depicted separately for the natural and the social dimension, or jointly for both. The latter was the case, for example, with a beautiful beach only affordable for the rich included in the otherwise degraded future of a business-as-usual collage. Finally, *ambivalence*, where the same object or development evokes both positive and negative associations, seemed more difficult to express by means of images than uncertainty or polarization. In one example, the group balanced the image of a conserved globe with the word "renunciation," as they did not find concrete images for the expected negative aspects of energy reduction.

Overall, from our discussion of both clearly negative or positive collages, as well as more ambiguous collages, produced by heterogeneous citizen focus groups in different European regions, we feel confident that one generalization for Western Europe is possible. Business-as-usual with regard to energy use is seen as less attractive than significant reductions in energy use in this part of the world.

IA Focus Group findings and reflexive modernization

Our results are hard to reconcile with a framework of simple modernization. In the focus group discussions with citizens across Europe, belief in progress was far from obvious, and business as usual was not taken as the clear reference case for a desirable future. While this rejection of one of the hallmarks of received ideas of progress is in line with the concept of reflexive modernization, one could try to apply a "flat" environmentalist perspective to our data. This is especially relevant with regard to geographical differences. One could argue that the richer a country, the stronger its "postmaterialist" orientations and therefore its environmental concern. In such a view, the ambivalence found in the Barcelona data would be explained by a lower level of per capita income, and the more clear-cut results from Zurich by the higher income there. However, this interpretation is not really convincing. First, the alleged link between postmaterialism and income per capita does not withstand empirical scrutiny (Dunlap and Mertig 1996). Second, negative elements are contained in all business-as-usual collages from Barcelona, and strong energy reductions do not evoke unambiguous fear in this region either. Moreover, various forms of uncertainty, polarization, and ambivalence have been found in all regions under study.

It seems more appropriate to distinguish between two kinds of decision contexts: those characterized by well-defined preferences and those characterized by feelings of ambivalence (Smelser 1998). Human life always involves both kinds of contexts, but they are not necessarily treated on an equal footing in different circumstances. In particular, simple modernization is focused on the first kind of situations. In policy-making, decision analysis, risk management and related fields, simple modernization emphasizes choices which can be judged by unambiguous preferences. Reflexive modernization does not deny the relevance of these situations, but it combines them with the second kind. Open debates acquire increased importance, and so does the ability to express and accept situations of ambivalence. Our data support the view that ordinary citizens in Europe do not frame the climate change problem in a perspective of simple modernization; rather, a framework of reflexive modernization corresponds better to our observations.

Inspiration for IA modelers?

There is a serious gap between the many layers and kinds of uncertainty present in sustainability science in general, and climate change research in particular, and the graphic images of catastrophic events capturing the public imagination. While our research indicates that the general public is able to deal with ambiguities regarding climate change, research in the same project has shown that current IA computer models are not yet very suitable for communicating scientific uncertainties to laypeople (Chapter 5). A bridge between the way laypeople and experts express uncertainties is required, if the uncertainties discussed in climate change research are to play a role in supporting a more differentiated public debate.

While graphs and maps are well suited for scientific audiences, additional visual aids may be important for stakeholder audiences. This is especially the case if these should not only include policy-makers (see Alcamo, Kreileman, and Leemans 1996) but also wider stakeholder groups, including citizens. The citizens participating in our IA Focus Groups repeatedly said that pictures would make it easier for them to grasp the model outputs. Using pictures to visualize different scenarios would probably be particularly rewarding for issues of uncertainty, polarization, and ambivalence.

Uncertainty in IA modeling has been discussed by Pahl-Wostl *et al.* (1998), van Asselt and Rotmans (1996), and Shackley and Wynne (1995), and different modeling approaches have been explored, for example, by the teams developing the TARGETS (Rotmans and de Vries 1997) and the ICAM (Dowlatabadi and Morgan 1994) models. Visual work in this context might gain inspiration from IA Focus Group collages, where uncertain developments were indicated either by superimposing question marks on a visual representation of one possible development, or by positioning contrasting images of alternative developments side by side. *Polarization* – who loses and who gains, what is conserved and what is destroyed – is not easy to tackle in IA modeling. Agent based approaches may lead to advances here, and experiences from IA Focus Groups suggest that contrasting images could be used to visualize developments for different agents or in different areas. *Ambivalence* is not easily expressed visually, and usually needs additional explanation. In the collages, ambivalence was expressed by contrasting images of positive and negative aspects of the same scenario, or by balancing a concrete image of one aspect by an abstract representation of a contrasting aspect, for which no concrete image was found.

Such ambivalence does not refer primarily to assessment in the sense of describing possible developments, but rather in the sense of judgments about desirable and undesirable aspects of such developments. Judgments about desirable and undesirable aspects of environmental policies are especially relevant in open debates on complex problems, where a consensus of all stakeholders is not easily reached. Such issues probably cannot be addressed or communicated by models alone. Judgment needs human values and discussions. This need to combine discussions on values on the one hand with access to expert assessments on the other was the reason for developing the IA Focus Group method. Public participation in sustainability science along these lines allows participants to express their own perspectives, for example in collage production and discussions, before giving them access to integrated computer models as discussed in Chapter 5.

CHAPTER FIVE

Citizen interaction with computer models

Urs Dahinden, Cristina Querol, Jill Jäger,
and Måns Nilsson

Introduction

This chapter looks at how computer models were used in IA Focus Groups within the study discussed in this volume. In these groups, different computer models – ranging from complex and dynamic global models to simple accounting tools – were used in the second phase of the procedure. Based on a total of 52 IA Focus Groups with citizens, conducted in six European and one US cities, selected empirical results are presented. The analysis of the results focuses on the added value of using computer models during the meetings of such groups, the lessons learned about the models themselves and the ways in which they are used.

The terminology in this field is far from clear. For the purpose of this chapter, we define computer models as all kinds of software tools that include a realistic representation of some social, economic or environmental processes. Integrated Assessment Models (IAM) are included in this definition, but also simpler and non-dynamic tools. On the other hand, by this definition, we are excluding computer games (SimCity and the like) and educational software with text only.[1]

Why use computer models in participatory processes for sustainability science in general, and Integrated Assessment (IA) in particular? We hypothesize that computer models are powerful tools for promoting a numbers of insights about complex sustainability issues like climate change. Computer models provide direct access to expertise and due to their flexibility and interactivity might be better able to support learning processes and decision-making. In particular, computer models might help in understanding the *spatial dimensions* of climate change and the links between the global and the regional level, the *temporal dimension* (long-term perspective), the *uncertainty* involved in the science, the economics, and the modeling, and possible *policy options*. In order to fulfil

---

[1] The reasons for these exclusions are not that we would consider computer games or educational software as useless or inferior to what we define as computer models, but simply because our study has a different focus.

these tasks in participatory IA, we assume that computer models must be *user-friendly*. If the model cannot be used easily by non-experts, it will be of limited use in a participatory process. We hypothesize that a further important characteristic is *transparency*. If the model remains a black box spitting out results without any further explanations, it can hardly inform learning processes. Finally, we believe that if users do not attribute any *credibility* to a model, it is unlikely to be accepted as a support for decision-making.

The next section describes the methodology of this research, which integrated a number of computer models in IA Focus Group procedures. We then present the empirical findings, testing the assumptions and hypotheses outlined in the previous paragraph. Following that, suggestions are made for how IA procedures that plan to integrate computer models should be designed, and how computer tools should be adapted or built in order to be helpful for participatory IA. General conclusions are presented in the final section.

Method: integrated assessment focus groups and computer models

Integrating models in IA Focus Groups

As already discussed in the preceding chapters, the ULYSSES project has developed a particular method in order to allow informed citizens to express their judgments on climate policy. Within the project, there is some diversity in the terminology of this approach, but most teams use the term "IA Focus Groups" for their work.[2] An IA Focus Group consists of a mixed group of citizens, who are provided with basic information, have access to one or several computer models during their deliberations, and reach a collective conclusion, say a policy recommendation for the issue under consideration. The basic methodology has been used in the following seven urban regions throughout Europe: Athens (Greece), Barcelona (Spain), Frankfurt (Germany), Manchester (UK), Stockholm (Sweden), Venice (Italy), and Zurich (Switzerland). Furthermore, one partner project with a similar approach has been carried out in Pittsburgh, Pennsylvania (US).[3] While the same basic methodological template was followed by most research teams, there was some methodological variation between the regions, for example, with regard to the selection of models, or the application of specific elements (e.g., the citizen report).

---

[2] The Venice team uses "In-depth Groups" (IGs), the Manchester team "citizens' panels."
[3] An overview on which models where used in which regions is given below in Table 5.2.

We discuss the implications of this diversity for the findings later in the chapter.

The placement of models within the IA Focus Groups procedure was the following: within the overall IA Focus Group process discussed in Chapter 1, computer models were usually used in the second part of the procedure. The process was normally split into five sessions of 2.5 hours carried out on different days. The second part consisted of sessions two to four, and was focused on discussions of global and regional change supported by access to computer models. Two computer models – one with a global perspective and one with a regional one – were generally used in separate sessions. Most of the research teams presented an IA model of global scope (either IMAGE, TARGETS or ICAM)[4] in the second session, and a computer model of regional scope (either PoleStar or a CO_2 Lifestyle Calculator) in the third or fourth session. The selection of two models for each IA Focus Group had the aim of complementing the global/local spatial dimensions with the impacts/measures dimensions in order to enhance debate on regional solutions for global environmental problems. Generally the presentation and debate on the models was between 1 hour and 1.5 hours for each model. We estimate that the presentation and interaction with the two models did not exceed one third of the total discussion time. The final part of the IA Focus Group procedure was devoted to expressing concluding judgments by the participants themselves, for example, in the form of a citizens' report, and on giving feedback to the research team concerning the whole IA Focus Group procedure.

Which models have been used?

The project teams used a number of computer models, addressing mainly global (IMAGE 2.0, TARGETS, ICAM 3.0) or mainly regional dimensions (PoleStar, IMPACTS, OPTIONS, CO_2 Lifestyle Indicators). Descriptions of these models are given in Alcamo (1994), Rotmans and de Vries (1997), Raskin *et al.* (1996), and Schlumpf *et al.* (1999).[5] It is important to note that most of these models were not specially developed for use by lay people, but rather for assisting technically trained professionals in research and policy-making (for example, public officials, members of parliament, business representatives, NGO staff etc.). This is true for IMAGE 2.0, TARGETS, ICAM 3, and PoleStar. Therefore,

---

[4] A description of all models is given in pp. 107–111.
[5] For a description of the ICAM model, see http://hdgc.epp.cmu.edu/models-icam/models-icam.html#icam

considerable effort was necessary to prepare the models for use in the IA Focus Groups. On the other hand, some of these models (IMPACTS, OPTIONS, CO_2 Lifestyle Indicators) have been designed in the course of the CLEAR project to be used directly by lay citizens.[6] A brief description of the models is given below.

Overview

Table 5.1 gives an overview of the models and their use (process design) in the IA Focus Groups. With regard to the model content described in Table 5.1, two types of models can be distinguished that share some features:[7] One group includes the three global models IMAGE, TARGETS, and ICAM. All of them have a long-term perspective, and two of them (TARGETS, ICAM) address uncertainties explicitly. The other group encompasses the three regional models (PoleStar, IMPACTS, and OPTIONS, CO_2 Lifestyle Indicators) that have no specific time horizon (PoleStar, CO_2 Lifestyle Indicators) or a mid-term perspective only (IMPACTS and OPTIONS: thirty years). Furthermore, only part of the regional models (IMPACTS and OPTIONS) address uncertainties explicitly.

As displayed in Table 5.1, three categories of model use can be distinguished:

(a) *Indirect access:* these models were not accessible during the group session for technical reasons. The IMAGE model, for instance, cannot be run on a personal computer while the group is meeting, because it is a large model with many input and output variables. Similarly, some teams also felt that PoleStar was too cumbersome for a long online presentation to a lay audience and gave only a brief introduction to the model, focusing on input data. Output (scenarios) was produced between two sessions, and presented at the next meeting of the group.

(b) *Facilitated access:* these models (TARGETS, ICAM) could be run on a personal computer and the output was presented on the spot. However, the user interface was not so simple that an untrained individual could learn it within a few minutes. Therefore, a model moderator presented and operated the model, facilitating its understanding in accordance with the questions and demands of the participants.

(c) *Direct access by participants:* IMPACTS and OPTIONS, as well as the CO_2 Lifestyle Indicators, were especially designed for lay users,

---

[6] See http://CLEAR.eawag.ch/models

[7] For a more elaborated discussion of how models can be typologized, see Van der Sluijs and Jaeger (1998).

Table 5.1 *Model description and model use in LA Focus Groups*

	Model description				Model use
Model (literature)	Space	Time horizon (into the future)	Uncertainty	Policy options	Interaction in IA Focus Groups
IMAGE (Rotmans 1990 (Alcamo 1994).[a]	global, with regional information	100 years	not explicit (several given scenarios)	technology, lifestyle changes	indirect access via model moderator
TARGETS (Rotmans 1994; Rotmans and de Vries 1997)	global	100 years	explicit (typology)	implicit in typology	facilitated access
ICAM[a]	global, with regional information	100 years	explicit (stochastics)	economic (CO$_2$ tax)	facilitated access
PoleStar (Raskin et al. 1996; Nilsson 1997)[b]	regional	user defined (here: 30 years)	not explicit (several user-defined scenarios)	technology, lifestyle changes	facilitated or indirect access
IMPACTS and OPTIONS (Pahl-Wostl et al. in press)[c]	regional, with some global information	30 years	explicit	economic technology, lifestyle changes	direct access by participants
CO$_2$ Lifestyle Indicators (Schlumpf et al. 1999)[d]	personal	user defined (here: not explicit)	not explicit	technology, lifestyle changes	direct access by participants

Note: [a] See http://hdgc.epp.cmu.edu/public/icam/icam.html
[b] See www.tellus.org/polestar.html
[c] See for the IMPACTS model: http://CLEAR.eawag.ch/models/impactsE.html and for the OPTIONS model: http://CLEAR.eawag.ch/models/optionenE.html
[d] See http://CLEAR.eawag.ch/models/cozweiE.html and http://alba.jrc.it/ulysses.html

Table 5.2 Model use by region (number in cells: number of LA groups with citizens)

	Global model			Regional model			No model	Total of groups in region
	IMAGE	TARGETS	ICAM	PoleStar	IMPACTS and OPTIONS	Lifestyle indicators		
Athens	2	1		2				2
Barcelona	3	3		5		2		7
Darmstadt	5	5		8				9
Manchester							5	5
Pittsburgh			3			3	2	5
Stockholm	2	2		7				7
Venice	3	3				6		6
Zurich		4		4	6	1		11
Total of groups	15	18	3	26	6	12	7	52

Sources: Own data, Stocks 1998.

and therefore did not need a model moderator as support. In the beginning of the model presentation, the few necessary technical hints were given by the group moderator. After that, participants were navigating through the models on their own, in small groups of two to three persons.

Model use by region

Table 5.2 gives an overview of which models were used in which regions in groups run from 1996 to 1998. Both pilot and main groups are included in this table.[8] The total number of groups in a region (last column) is lower than the line total (groups working with a specific model), because most groups used more than one model. The table provides some important information that has to be kept in mind in the data analysis and interpretation of the findings. First, the model selection is not independent of the region. Some models have been used in one region only (e.g., ICAM in Pittsburgh), others in several regions, but none in all regions. Therefore we do not focus on interregional comparisons (e.g., whether IMAGE was received differently in Barcelona than in Stockholm). Second, the total number of groups run with each model is not constant, but ranges from three (ICAM) to twenty-six (PoleStar). While these small numbers are too low for any kind of statistical analysis, they are nevertheless sufficient to meet the exploratory intention of this study, which is to identify tendencies and patterns in model use. Furthermore, since many of the findings are not model-specific, but touch upon issues that are relevant for many, if not all the models, we can state that we have a quantitatively sound basis. Last but not least, we do not know of any other study that has empirically investigated the use of computer models in such a comprehensive way.

Other means of providing expert information

All research teams combined the use of the computer models with one or several other means of providing expert information, such as a fact sheet, a magazine article, a short expert hearing, etc.

---

[8] Further regional information:
   Athens: Additionally, this team ran one focus group with experts and four groups with media people. Because of time constraints, no data was available as this chapter was prepared from the two citizens groups listed in Table 5.2.
   Darmstadt: In two PoleStar groups, the model was used to present current data; in the remaining six groups, the model was used to present data and to calculate scenarios.
   Manchester: Two Groups in Manchester, two in an other town (St. Helens)
   Stockholm: Three Pilot and four main groups
   Venice: Two Pilots and four main groups
   Zurich: Seven Groups in Zurich, four Groups in Basle.

In two regions, some focus groups were run without access to a computer model. These regional teams provided expert information to the groups either by the oral presentations of an "expert" (Manchester, quotation marks also in the original source) or by written information (Pittsburgh). The Pittsburgh research team used a brochure that was developed in an outreach project for informing laypeople about climate change (Morgan *et al.* 1994).

Diversity and robustness of the findings

Due to the exploratory character of the project, a strict standardization of the design was not considered to be a feasible approach. Taking this into consideration, we have focused on the analysis of results that were documented in several, if not all regions. These findings seem to be robust, in particular because they were visible despite methodological and cultural differences between the regions.

International comparisons between the regions are not the focus of this chapter. For such an endeavor, it would be necessary to discuss very carefully whether differences in the findings have their origin in cultural or methodological variations.

Robustness

To what extent are these findings robust? We have mentioned above that there was considerable variation in the selection of models and other information input and the way these tools were used in the IA Focus Groups. Therefore, a reader might ask to what extent our findings are sensitive to, if not biased by, these methodological differences.

Answering this question in detail would require an extended methodological study which is beyond the scope of this chapter. Nevertheless, we want to express our judgment as authors that we share with many colleagues in the project, that the methodological and cultural variations were of minor importance for the kind of general findings presented here. Most colleagues shared the impression that despite the given methodological and cultural variations, the findings of each region about the models are quite similar to each other. The following points provide some evidence for that judgment.

First, all teams were striving for a fair presentation of the models in the IA Focus Groups. In other words: no team was presenting a model that they considered as absolutely useless for the citizens. If a team reached that conclusion, it decided not to show the model, rather than "proving" its uselessness by presenting it in a bad way. This approach was motivated by both respect for the work of the modelers as well as respect for the citizens who were not brought into this process in order to deliver empirical evidence to support the prejudices of the respective teams.

Second, in order to check and increase the validity of the findings, a draft of the analysis presented in this chapter was circulated to all teams involved, giving them the opportunity to criticize and comment on this synthesis. These comments have influenced the balance of evidence as presented here. Furthermore, most colleagues shared the impression of strong similarities between the regions.

What might be the reasons for these surprising similarities? We see at least two possible explanations. First, climate change is clearly an international issue. Cultural differences come into play to some extent in the perception and management of this issue, but several triggering events are international by definition (e.g., environmental conferences like Rio de Janeiro, 1992 and Kyoto, 1997). In other words, all regions are exposed to a similar stimulus that is transmitted, perceived, and responded to in culturally different ways.

Second, the regions included in this study are from a relatively homogenous background with regard to political and economic parameters. While there is some variation within the sample, all research teams are working in industrialized nations. In fact, most of them are members of the European Union with a shared policy approach on climate change.

In sum, it is plausible, but not trivial that citizens from a rather homogenous region discussing a truly global issue come to similar conclusions on a general level. On the other hand, in the following section we do not want to downplay findings of regional differences that were especially visible with regard to more detailed issues (e.g., policy options).

Findings

In the previous section, we described the methodological approach of this study. In this section, we present some of the empirical findings. As documented in the methodological section, these findings and conclusions are synthesized from a considerable number of realizations, in different European and one US cities, with different moderation techniques and different sets of models used. Therefore, it should be emphasized that the results presented here are tendencies and not unanimous conclusions. Even the results within one region show a wide range of responses to the computer models, for example: "the participants' spontaneous reactions ranged from deep disappointment to active interest and from active rejection up to deep emotional concern about the information provided by the computer models ... Disappointment or rejection occurred particularly in cases in which a video animation, a computer game, uncontested facts or regional policy measures were expected" (Schüle, Haffner, and Jordan 1998: 3).

For all these reasons we focus on the evaluation of features of models that we consider helpful, rather than comparing and evaluating models directly. The section starts with what citizens were expecting from the model use before knowing in detail the options and limitations of these tools. We then present findings concerning the thematical issues to be illustrated by the computer models (global–local dimensions, temporal scale, uncertainty, exploration of policy options).[9] We end with a discussion of the extent to which the key requirements of models (user friendliness, transparency, credibility) have been met or not.

What do citizens expect concerning expert information and computer models?

Before presenting any model or expert information, the citizens were asked what they were expecting of a computer model, and what they would like to know. First of all, they had no specific expectations and most of them were unable to answer the question. This is not very surprising, since they were usually learning about computer models for the first time, and had not yet developed any specific product preferences. Many said that they would like to hear first what the models are and what they can do. On the other hand, they had no difficulty in posing a list of questions they would like to have answered by an expert. The list of topical questions brought up by participants is long and we will not present it here comprehensively. The questions were related to the following broad topics:

- general understanding of climate change (e.g., causes and effects of climate change)
- general understanding of related environmental problems (ozone depletion, deforestation, acid rain, etc.)
- impacts of climate change (global, regional and local, e.g., food production, demographics, health, sea level, migration, etc.)
- determination of policy goals (e.g., risks of no intervention, etc.)
- determination of policy means (e.g., what would happen if petrol use was reduced)

---

[9] Quotes from the discussion are included in order to illustrate the way these topics were addressed. In general, the quotes are complemented with pseudonyms in order to guarantee confidentiality. However, for the Venice groups no pseudonyms were added, because the statements are taken from the logbook, a kind of group diary which was approved by all members of the respective group.

It is also worth mentioning that none of the citizens at this stage asked for information concerning expert disagreement or uncertainty.

This condensed list of topics addressed in the questions illustrates that participants were not concentrating on a few narrowly defined issues, but rather struggling for a broad understanding. Obviously, not all the questions of the participants could be answered by the model or by the model moderator. However, there was at least some overlap between the citizens' questions and the model capabilities.[10]

Space and time

Most participants considered global information as necessary for the discussion, but they were more interested in regional and local aspects. For example, the participants in the Venice groups were looking at the maps from the IMAGE model and searching for a better definition of what was happening in Italy. However, this approach also led to frustration, because the coarse geographical resolution of the output was not sufficiently detailed to provide enough regional information, as desired by the participants.

In addition to the spatial dimensions of climate change and climate policies, participants also discussed the temporal scale. As shown in Table 5.1, the models differed substantially also on this scale, and participants preferred in general the short-term perspective.

The Stockholm research team found that when the global-scale models were presented, it proved difficult to keep the discussion to the global perspective (Nilsson, 1998). The discussions often drifted from energy and carbon dioxide into more local-type problems such as recycling, traffic jams, local air pollution and polluted waters. In Stockholm, PoleStar was used to support discussions of the local situation, and to carbon dioxide emissions that people might be able to control themselves. Once local realities became the focus of the discussion, the groups' interest switched away from the model as they had much more to contribute themselves. The local perspective reduced the groups' "learning mode" and they became more active in sharing their own knowledge. The Stockholm research team thus concluded that most people have much more to contribute when asked about the local issues that they experience in their own lives than global issues.

These findings concerning the interest in spatial and temporal scale support the hypothesis brought up by Meadows that most people focus

---

[10] The Barcelona research team counted that, in their research region, roughly half of the participants' questions could be explored with the models.

their attention on processes that are close in time (the following weeks and years) and space (family, neighborhood, business, nation) (Meadows *et al.* 1972). In other words: climate change as a global and long-term risk lies beyond this horizon of "here and now" and thinking about it is unusual and challenging.

Uncertainty

Only a few of the models deal with the issue of uncertainty in an explicit way. Furthermore, as shown in Table 5.1, there was some variation in how this topic was dealt with. However, the general reactions toward uncertainty in science were similar, independent of the specific presentation: It was a shock for most participants. "VERONIKA: 'I'm scared by the uncertainty in science. I thought that science would know better'" (Zurich). A typical reaction was that if uncertainties are so high, there was no justification for further discussion of this issue. "KAREN: 'The amount of uncertainty in the distribution in ICAM invalidates the model – you can't predict the future'" (Pittsburgh). The main approaches for dealing with uncertainties in the models used were to treat uncertainty typologically (as in TARGETS) or probabilistically (as in ICAM). While the small number of groups confronted with the probabilistic approach does not allow for a robust comparison (only three groups used ICAM as compared to eighteen groups with TARGETS, see Table 5.2), participants seemed to have somewhat less difficulty with the probabilistic approach. One explanation of this might be that probability distributions are more familiar to a lay audience (e.g., from the weather forecast) than the typology of the cultural theory of risk.

Because of the larger number of groups conducted with TARGETS, we illustrate participants' problems with uncertainty display with examples from groups using this model. The reactions toward the TARGETS approach of addressing uncertainties were mixed. Some participants reacted positively, appreciating the attempt to show multiple perspectives.

STEFAN: Well, I found it very interesting and found it quite good that one had on the one side facts as background information, they are built in [the model], as fixed data or data assumed as established. And that from the facts you draw conclusions for future developments based on the different assessments of possible points of view.   (Darmstadt)

However, other participants had difficulties with the TARGETS approach. One difficulty was understanding what was meant by these three perspectives of the cultural theory of risk. Rather than taking them as ideal types of positions in the debate, they thought that each perspective was associated with a specific, "real" scientist. Consequently, they were curious about the names and research sponsors of these individuals. Furthermore, some participants were concerned that reducing social complexity by means of a typology with three categories was too rigid and too simplifying. They were rather sceptical towards attempts to classify human beings, and not willing to identify with one of the three perspectives.

In sum, the approach chosen in TARGETS to convey uncertainty was difficult for many participants. The underlying subjectivism was rarely appreciated as an attempt to promote an honest and pluralistic debate, but rather as an unwillingness of scientists to take sides and stick to (unpopular) positions. One participant felt that this approach was an indication of opportunism of scientists to produce a model that everybody can take as supporting their own views. Others were concerned that the model could be misused to support any political position.

KERSTIN: In my view, there are two types of experts: those contacted by industry, who are certainly bringing in another point of view than those who are contacted by environmental organizations or even politicians. I think that, depending on where an expert comes from, different views and predictions are given. (Darmstadt)

The quote shows that this concern was raised as a rather general problem of science, running the risk of being instrumentalized by specific interest groups.

In summary, many IA Focus Group participants reacted negatively when confronted with uncertainty display in integrated computer models. This contrasts with the finding of the collage procedures (see Chapter 4) that participants were quite sophisticated in dealing with uncertainties there. The reason for this contrast may be the combination of two factors. On the one hand, the public seems to expect science to come up with certain and definite answers to even the most complex problems. The way the scientific community has communicated with the public in the past may have contributed to this expectation, which is beyond what most scientists would claim to be feasible in discussions with their colleagues. On the other hand, it may also be the case that dealing with uncertainty is easier for laypeople in the medium of collage production and related discussions, which is closer to most people's experiences than integrated computer models. Bridging this gap between citizens' and experts' manner of dealing with uncertainty will be a challenging task for the modeling community.

Exploration of policy options

Several of the teams in the ULYSSES project noted that the participants found it difficult to explore the impacts of particular policy options with the available computer models. The Pittsburgh research team suggested on the basis of the analysis that participants felt that models can limit creative thinking about policy options. Further difficulties are indicated in the following quotations:

LUCIA: I think it lacked a bit of... data on intervention from the population.
(Barcelona)

DAISY: It would be helpful if models could tell us the different impacts of different policies to help us decide which policy is best.   (Pittsburgh)

Many policy decisions concerning climate change are taken on a national or even regional level. Thus, it is not surprising that the regional models were better able to explore policy options. Participants had an active role in using the model. And even in the case of PoleStar, where the interaction with the model was indirect and mediated by a model moderator, they could develop their own scenarios, rather than being confronted with predefined expert runs. As the following quote illustrates, participants appreciated this interactive element:

HANS: If people are only reading something, they have a hard time imagining a specific scenario... This model (PoleStar) is good for me as an average citizen, because there are points of reference, visually and with numbers... One has to work with something: If you want to paint, you need a brush.
(Zurich)

Despite the perception that the regional models were better suited for exploring policy options than the global models, participants critized the fact that the former were not addressing this topic in a convincing manner. For example, in Stockholm, groups complained that PoleStar said nothing about feasibility, to what extent the measures suggested and tried are realistic, given economic, social, and political constraints. Since the model is static and does not provide any quantitative barriers for scenario development, it is up to the users to critically evaluate their own selection of variables. This lack of restriction stimulated the discussion, because citizens had to evaluate the feasibility of certain measures themselves. On the other hand, they felt also somewhat abandoned with that task. It was seen as crucial to have some kind of costing feature to find out which different measures are really possible.

Some research teams found that the lay participants mostly wanted a tool that would directly relate to their own consumption and lifestyle, including food consumption, packaging, and waste recycling. The CO_2 Lifestyle Indicators met this demand in many respects. Policy decisions were translated into individual lifestyle choices. This representation of policy choices was understandable and accessible to each participant.

In fact, the policy problem was translated into a moral problem: what are my options for addressing climate change policy? While a model of individual behavior only, it also stimulated discussion on collective choices and changes. For example, in the transportation sector, participants wondered how public transport could be promoted relative to individual driving. The model also stimulated discussions on equity, simply by international comparisons of per capita emissions (e.g., the US and India).

Overall, however, there was a sense that it was not possible to explore policy options sufficiently with the models provided and thus to explore how one could contribute on a regional, or even very local, scale in response to issues of climatic change and sustainable development.

Models in comparison with other input

Many participants believed that if greatly simplified and adjusted to the preferences of lay audiences, the models could become a useful tool in climate change discussions among lay citizens. Despite the obstacles that had to be overcome with the currently available models, some participants had the feeling that the computer models were better able to support a systematic and analytical discussion of climate change issues than other, possibly more attractive sources of information: "FERRAN: 'Yes, [a video] might have been more delightful, but to have the data to be able to compare, or to analyze or to see; I think it is better to have numbers or a graphical representation.'" (Barcelona). However, few of them thought that they themselves would prefer to use the currently available models in order to get acquainted with climate change issues.

Some groups were designed to experiment also with other scientific information input (participant interaction with invited climate experts, video show, fact sheet). In the Stockholm IA Focus Groups, the citizens praised direct interaction with experts as preferable to any other type of scientific information. In Manchester and Pittsburgh some focus groups were run without using any computer models. In Pittsburgh, the participants in those non-model focus groups were asked explicitly whether they would have liked to work with a computer model. They showed some interest. The findings from Manchester look somewhat different. Computer models were not the chosen option, no matter whether they were explicitly offered or not. Rather, participants had no strong opinion either for or against computer models.

A first explanation for these contrasting findings could be that trust in science is the key variable that determines whether participants showed some interest in scientific information, irrespective of the form (paper, computer models, etc.). This trust in science seemed to be higher in the Pittsburgh IA Focus Groups than in those run in Manchester.

However, as a second explanation for these contrasting findings, the Manchester team notes that the issue of trust might not be limited to science, but encompass further public institutions:

An explanation for these contrasting findings could be located in the different levels of public trust in the various cities/countries, not only about level of (dis)trust in "science" *per se* but also (dis)trust in "government", (dis)trust in "public participatory processes" and also (dis)trust of individual agency.

(Éric Darier, personal communication)

A third, more general explanation is that a scientific perspective on the issue of climate change is of limited relevance for most participants. This is consistent with the findings of several teams and cross-regional comparisons that found that participants tended to want to debate the climate change issue from within a much broader range of perspectives (ethical, political, moral, economic, inter-personal) rather than exclusively from a narrow "scientific" perspective (Darier and Schüle, 1999; Darier *et al.* 1999).

Synthesis and suggestions

Feasibility of the approach

As a first and general synthesis, it is fair to say that these findings provide evidence for the feasibility of integrating computer models with citizen deliberation. Keeping in mind that most of these models were not designed for non-experts, this is not a trivial result. This indicates that computer models *per se* are not a barrier in such participation processes. We are aware that feasibility is only a necessary, but not sufficient requirement for suggesting the wider use of models in participatory procedures for sustainability science in general, and IA Focus Groups in particular. Other criteria would include an evaluation of the process by the participants, scientists (here: the modelers) and also policy-makers. For obvious reasons, we are focusing on evaluation by the participants.

How the model moderator should facilitate interaction with models

The model moderator, in addition to presenting the model, should encourage participants to ask for clarification, to make comments, and to discuss among themselves. As for any moderated group discussion, it is important that the model moderator both guarantees a discussion flow between participants, and keeps the limits of the discussion *sufficiently open, but without losing focus.* The experience in the present study was that on some occasions it was necessary for the model moderator to move the debate forward when it got stuck on a single very specific issue, or when participants started a rather rambling discussion. It is very important to redirect discussion if it strays out of scope.

Whatever the range of the computer model options (with regard to input and output variables, action and policy options), the model moderator should not limit discussions to what the model considers nor to the model assumptions. In this regard, the model moderator can ask questions such as: "Which other aspects not included in this model do you think are worth considering?"

We consider the following three points as essential for a successful facilitation of the interaction with the models. First, the model moderator should be fully prepared and have access to proper support material. This includes the ability to provide explanations for counterintuitive results of the models. Second, the model moderator should be able to stimulate discussions. Model moderators should not give lectures about the models, but translate abstract information into a less abstract form and make it more digestible with reference to participants' daily life. Third, participants should perceive the moderator as neutral with regard to the model and its messages. If the model moderator is an overenthusiastic model developer or a too negative model moderator, the exercise outcome will be less valid than if a careful, respectful, and unbiased moderation takes place.

Suggestions for computer model design

On the basis of our findings, we see the following suggestions as important for redesigning given, or developing new, models for participatory IA: *Space:* For a global issue like climate change, a model should provide some global information; however, the focus should be on the region where participants come from. Regarding *time*, participants were more interested in short-term than long-term perspectives. The *complexity* of climate change and its representation was certainly challenging for most participants. In that respect, model presentations should be kept as simple as possible, focusing on a few key processes that are modeled and explained very carefully.

As described in the Findings section, participants reacted rather negatively toward the explicit discussion of uncertainty. "VERONIKA: 'If science is unable to agree, how should we be able to make any statement about climate futures?'" (Zurich). Despite these reactions, we suggest that *uncertainty* should be addressed explicitly in every model. Funtowicz and Ravetz have suggested that the NUSAP notation scheme[11] for dealing with quantitative information could be considered as a good start (Funtowicz and Ravetz, 1990). Besides the communication of uncertainty in quantities, more efforts are necessary to explain the qualities of uncertainty, its various sources, and the approaches to deal with them.

Participants had a strong interest in exploring *policy options*. The findings with regard to that point were mixed. On the one hand, we had the impression that in some groups interaction with the computer models did increase a sense of agency. Manipulating the models and visualizing a diversity of scenarios conveyed the impression that the real world can be modified, too. This is especially true for those scenarios with policy interventions, supporting the view that collective action could make a difference for the future.[12] On the other hand, the models often created a sense of a gap between their own (lay) understanding and the models (scientific knowledge), giving people an impression that little can be done to combat climatic risks.

Furthermore, most models were only of limited help in evaluating the feasibility of the suggested policy interventions, for instance with regard to the political and societal institutions involved. The following quote illustrates this view:

BODIL: The greenhouse effect is certainly a frightful problem, but for our group, the model made us confused more than anything else. To accept that the world will go under or persist in believing that freedom resolves all problems are both naive attitudes. But the big questions are what can we do and how?
(Stockholm)

INGO: Basically, I consider it as sound to approach the issue top-down. Whether this is feasible is an other story. It is certainly easier to address such a topic in the Landtag (regional parliament) than at the European level.
(Darmstadt)

Most of these questions had to be left to the consideration of the participants. Although quantitative modeling of regional policy options is a relatively new research area, IA processes that are provided with more information on this issue would certainly be better able to meet the demands of the users.

---

[11] The notation consists of five qualifiers: Numeral, Unit, Spread, Assessment, and Pedigree (NUSAP). The last three qualifiers address various aspects of uncertainty: Spread conveys an impression of the inexactness. Assessment expresses a judgment on the reliability and indicates the strength of the data. Pedigree conveys an evaluative account of the production process of the information and indicates the scientific status of the knowledge.

[12] It remains open whether this sense of agency is a strong motivation for concrete action or whether it is a virtual experience only with little impact.

With regard to the rather technical requirements of *user friendliness* and *transparency*, we can rely on a number of suggestions given directly by the participants. The responses reflected some high expectations, especially with regard to the use of multimedia techniques (e.g., sound, music, video clips etc.) and the wish for interactive approaches. The following quotations illustrate the desire for color, sound and graphic illustrations:

PER: We are lay people. We need clear, simple and 100 per cent pedagogical information to be able to understand why we are doing this. And these are graphs and tables that we do not understand . . . but if we get it presented in a clear-cut way which stimulates our fantasy . . . because we cannot understand at all what is said there.   (Stockholm)

MONICA: with graphics and colors, because one image is worth more than a thousand words.   (Barcelona)

VICTOR: I would like to see an industry or a factory and see how it emits CO_2 . . . a visual practical example.   (Barcelona)

The wish for more possibilities for interaction with the computer was expressed, for example, by participants from Stockholm, where it was generally felt, amongst those with computer experience, that they would want to sit down and try it out themselves, instead of watching. They wanted to have a more interactive model, where you could go in and change, for instance, the temperature and see what happens to the sea level. By being able to isolate such steps in the complex causal chain in climate change, it would become easier to understand the relationships. Then, it would be easier to grasp what the model is trying to show.

Furthermore, participants in Stockholm suggested that an interactive model for focus group use would likely benefit from features such as selection buttons of a multiple-choice character. This would compromise the transparency but increase user friendliness. Transparency is absolutely necessary in scientific work, but may be less useful in focus groups, where there will be no time to check background data and assumptions anyway.

A number of teams reported that the call for more interactive computer use was also put in terms of the use of computer games. Participants in both Barcelona and Pittsburgh referred to the game SimCity and thought that something similar for climate change and sustainability issues would be useful in an IA Focus Group setting.

Last, but not least we as researchers have also some suggestions based on our experiences with the models:[13] User friendliness can hardly be

---

[13] See also the list of model characteristics that are of specific relevance to the participatory context given in Van der Sluijs and Jaeger (1998).

underestimated as a criterion. Keeping the user of software in mind also means distinguishing between different levels of expertise. We have the impression that many model developers focus on the highest level of expertise only. In contrast to that, we suggest planning for at least three levels of model use.

(1) *Beginners:* Lay people with limited knowledge and time. Provide quick tours and demonstration views that give a first impression.
(2) *Advanced:* Students with some background understanding, more time available, but not experts in any of the fields. Provide comprehensive documentation.
(3) *Experts:* Peers that might invest only little time, but care about details. Provide possibilities for digging deeper.

Another element of user friendliness is the availability of demonstration views. Based on experiences made in the present study, we recommend the use of models – or demoviews – specifically configured for these kind of exercises in IA Focus Groups. Nevertheless, even if the characteristics of the computer model were ideal for use in IA Focus Group discussions, their usage could be suboptimal, if the model presentation and moderation are unsatisfactory. To avoid both the dissatisfaction of participants and failure to achieve the participatory IA aims, we found that it was necessary to have an appropriate preparation of the model moderator before the IA Focus Groups exercise, and an adequate design of the variables of the model to display, as well as proper adaptation of the model screen interface.

Finally, we feel that many of these models focus too much on quantitative aspects and give too little information about qualitative aspects. For the model development, this means that more context has to be added to the models, say documentation of definitions of variables, ranges of variables discussed in the literature, sensitivity of variables, outputs with interpretation, etc.

Conclusions

Our analysis aimed at identifying the key features in the models that were particularly suitable or unsuitable for focus group discussions. We have shown that some of the key issues (e.g., the spatial and temporal dimension, uncertainty, etc.) could be conveyed by means of the models. This communication was not without irritation, which is an interesting result independent of the particular model used.

Only a few of the models were specifically designed for this kind of activity. It is therefore not surprising that the research teams generally concluded that most of the models used were not very suitable for focus group discussions. This suggests that if computer models are to become effective in focus group activities, new ones will have to be developed. The experience of the present study could guide that development.

From our experience with developing a participatory IA procedure which incorporates the use of computer models, we would like to stress that computer models should support the discussion, provide new information and insights, but not dominate the process. Great care and effort has to be taken in the preparation and implementation of this kind of IA Focus Group, but on the basis of the experiences so far, we would encourage continued exploration and development of this technique for public participation in sustainability science.

CHAPTER SIX

Citizens' reports on climate strategies

Cristina Querol, Åsa Gerger Swartling, Bernd Kasemir, and David Tàbara

Introduction

Citizens' perceptions of climate change have been explored in various empirical studies with quantitative and qualitative methodologies. Dunlap (1998) explored lay perceptions and levels of understanding of climate change in six countries with a quantitative poll. In order to understand perceptions of climate change, Kempton (1991) compared lay perceptions with those of scientists in the US with a qualitative technique, while Bell (1994) looked at differences between media and public discourses on climate change. Other studies can be found in Löfstedt (1992) and in Read (1994). In the study discussed here, however, the objective was not to look at the perceptions of the lay public *per se* but to study in which ways citizens can provide reflected and informed opinions, and participate in sustainability science in general and in Integrated Assessments (IA) in particular.

For this purpose, IA Focus Group procedures (see Chapter 1) were developed in the ULYSSES project. While in the first two phases of these procedures collages were produced and models were used (see the discussions in Chapters 4 and 5), the final phase of the IA Focus Groups was mainly devoted to the formulation of citizens' reports – written assessments by the participants themselves. These were usually prepared by first drafting steps and discussions in earlier sessions. What is the problem? What should be done? How should it be achieved? Who should do it? Which barriers are foreseen? These are some of the questions discussed by the participants and addressed in their citizens' reports. While citizens' reports are only one of the outputs from IA Focus Groups,[1] they are conclusions by the participants in their own words.

---

[1] Other data outputs of IA Focus Groups include audio and video recorded group discussions; visual expressions by the participants in the form of collages or "graffiti cards"; completed questionnaires and diary notes of participants; scenarios developed with the help of computer models in an interactive manner; and research notes from post-meeting interviews.

This chapter focuses on experiences with citizens' reports in the final phase of IA Focus Groups. Participants' assessments and recommendations for addressing climate change and urban sustainability are discussed, together with the methodology of citizens' reports and related procedures conducted in 30 IA Focus Groups. The chapter is organized as follows. In the second section, the design of citizens' report processes is described. In the third section, the contents of the participants' written assessments of IA Focus Groups are discussed. Finally, an assessment of the writing exercises is provided, followed by some concluding remarks.

Method: citizens' report procedures in IA Focus Groups

The purpose of asking the citizens participating in IA Focus Groups to write up their conclusions in citizens' reports was two-fold: (i) it was considered essential that the participants in each group had the opportunity to conclude what they agreed to be important; and (ii) the citizens' reports were intended to be useful for researchers and potentially for policy-makers to improve their understanding of citizens' perspectives and recommendations concerning climate change. The citizens' report procedure should help the participants to focus on some target issues and give them a sense of tangible accomplishment at the end of the process. Because they are summaries of the groups' conclusions rather than of individual opinions, and an integral part of the group process helping to focus the discussions, the citizens' report procedures differ from other forms of gathering written comments by citizens on issues of environmental assessments (see, e.g., Webb and Sigal 1996). But the report writing should not be the focus of the whole IA Focus Group procedure. It was not highlighted as the main point of the group processes, which was rather the actual debates among participants.

Within the ULYSSES and CLEAR projects, experiences with different group designs were made. This chapter centers on thirty IA Focus Groups carried out with citizens between 1997 and 1998, and does not concern groups conducted with specific social actors (policy-makers, journalists, or entrepreneurs) in the projects. The groups conducted with citizens during the pilot phase of the projects are also not considered. These pilot groups have been analyzed already elsewhere (Kasemir *et al.* 1997), and were too diverse to be appropriate for inclusion in the synthesis presented in this chapter. The overall IA Focus Group designs developed

Table 6.1 *IA Focus Groups and output materials reviewed for this chapter*

Region	IA FG analyzed in this chapter	Number of participants per group	Output materials reviewed
Athens	2	5; 5 (10)	excerpts from transcripts
Barcelona	5	7; 7; 8; 8; 8 (38)	5 CRs
Frankfurt	6	6; 6; 7; 7; 6; 10 (42)	6 CRs
Manchester	3	7; 8; 7 (22)	1 CR + excerpts from transcripts
Stockholm	4	7; 8; 10; 11 (36)	4 CRs
Venice	6	9; 9; 9; 9; 9; 9 (54)	excerpts from 6 CRs (logbooks)
Zurich	4	6; 5; 5; 7 (23)	4 CRs
TOTAL	30	225 participants	26 CRs + other materials

Note: CRs denotes Citizens' Reports

and applied by the Barcelona, Frankfurt, Stockholm, and Zurich research teams, as well as by the Manchester and Venice teams, are discussed in Chapters 1 and 2 of this book. The groups held in Athens were different from those conducted by the other teams, since the main aim for that research region was to run "media groups" which included journalists and citizens. For this chapter, only the Athens groups which were conducted exclusively with citizens are considered.

Four of the thirty IA Focus Groups reviewed for this chapter did not produce written citizens' reports. For these cases, extracts from discussion transcripts have been used. For the rest of the groups, fully translated citizens' reports were considered for the analysis in this chapter. The six Venice groups reviewed wrote a specific type of group report, the so-called "logbooks." Table 6.1 gives an overview of the materials reviewed for the present chapter.

As the overall goal of the study was to develop and test new tools for Participatory Integrated Assessment, different versions of a shared overall procedure for IA Focus Groups in general, and citizens' conclusions in particular, were designed. Below, we describe citizens' report procedures by first giving the example of a procedure designed in four of the study regions, and second, discussing each region's specific characteristics (Box 6.1).

Specific characteristics of citizens' report procedures used in the different research regions are described below. Before going into these details,

Box 6.1: An example of citizens' report processes

The research teams of Barcelona, Frankfurt, Stockholm and Zurich designed the following basic procedure for the citizens' report task:

Participants were informed in the *first session* that they would be asked to write a report in the course of the IA Focus Group process. A general report structure was suggested to them along the following lines:

- Do you think there is a climate change problem?
    Here (e.g. in the Stockholm region)?
    World-wide?
  If yes, then what is the problem?
- Given this, how should we live in thirty years' time here (e.g., in Stockholm)?
- What should be done to get there?
- Given this, how much energy use compared to today is appropriate in total, and in the different sectors (e.g., transport, households)?
- Who should take action? And when?
- What do you think will be difficulties in getting there?
- If you have anything else you want to note down, please do so.

These suggested questions were distributed as photocopies. During *sessions one to four*, participants in some groups wrote sentences, drew pictures on file cards, or started to draft the collective citizens' report. Some other groups also used individual or collective diary notes written at the end of each session or at home between two sessions. These cards, drafts or diary notes were then used in the final session as a starting point for writing the final citizens' report. In a few groups, the moderator was asked by the participants to act as a rapporteur during the earlier session, writing down what the participants wanted to document for later review. In these rare cases, the moderator typed the notes and made them available for everyone in a later session so that the participants could revise them. When this procedure was followed, the reports tended to be longer and to contain more detailed assessments.

In the *fifth session* the group worked on their own (unless they requested assistance from the moderator) on the citizens' report for approximately 1.5 hours. The group was encouraged to note down those points where consensus developed, but they were not required to address only agreed issues. This was because striving for consensus at any cost might lead to "trivial" reports, giving only the least common denominator and ignoring the extreme positions. Nevertheless, it was found that only a few groups specified differences in views among participants. At the end of this final session the group presented their citizens' report to the research team and commented on it in a final discussion round.

we want to remark that the fact that two different sources of citizen's assessments have been employed (written reports from twenty-six groups on the one hand, and transcripts of discussions from four groups on the other) could indeed influence comparability across groups and regions' results. However, our main intention has been more to discover commonalties among European groups' assessments, and less to compare them. Therefore, this variability of sources was not supposed to be a handicap, but, on the contrary, the inclusion of results from more groups should increase the robustness of our findings. We consider that it was more appropriate to include the excerpts and summaries of transcripts we had from those four groups which did not produce Citizens' Reports (two groups in Athens and two groups in Manchester – see Table 6.1 above) than to leave that material aside.

Barcelona

Groups began to draft the report from the first session by means of a participant acting as note-taker. All participants were encouraged to use cards to express key ideas or to make drawings for later reference. It was explained to the participants that the addressees of the report were mainly the study's researchers and that, to some extent, their debates and reports would reach EU officials. However, the research team also pointed out that since the exercise was part of an exploratory research study, the team could not guarantee that the participants' views would be taken into account by the policy community.

Frankfurt

The purpose of requiring participants to write citizens' reports was to analyze the results rather than to use them directly as an input for policy-making. At the end of the first two sessions participants were asked to write topic statements on file cards. During the third and fourth sessions a list of sectors was suggested to the participants for which they might consider specifying targets and measures. For the final session these materials were typed and printed by the research team and distributed to the participants for them to edit during the final session. These corrections were typed and mailed to the participants, and a further round of editing and mailings took place. As one group was organized with a link to the Local Agenda 21 initiative, the resultant citizen report was mailed and presented to local decision-makers involved in the LA21 process.

Manchester

In this study region the group processes were designed closer to a 'policy for real' framing at the local level, as discussed in Chapter 2. As the approach developed was bottom-up and the discussion was less focused on climate change, the group that wrote a citizens' report decided by itself on the subjects to be included. Their final report was presented – in a special session – at a joint meeting with the citizen group and some local policy-makers. Another group, instead of being prompted to write a citizens' report, was asked to express: (a) to whom they would like to address their concerns; (b) how they would like to communicate their concerns; and (c) what they would like to say (Darier 1997).

Stockholm

A specific characteristic of the Stockholm groups was that the participants were told that their reports should be written as if the addressees were not only the research team, but also policy-makers and that to some extent – indirectly through research reports – their report would reach EU officials. Each participant was also requested to write diary notes at the end of each session. During the final report-writing session the moderators were available in case the participants had questions. For the last two groups, the participant acting as note-taker wrote the draft report on a computer; all diary notes were copied and distributed and were also available in a document on the computer.

Venice

In Venice the groups were designed within a "research" framing, as discussed in Chapter 2, and the groups followed a metaphor of the participatory process as a common voyage. This framing made it appropriate not to ask groups to write a citizens' report, but to make them write, during all sessions, logbooks (or voyage diaries) which contained unstructured impressions of the groups' voyage experience. The Venice In-Depth Groups were encouraged to use flip-charts that would provide them with an informal tool to help them formulate their ideas in writing. The fifth session was dedicated to working on the logbooks. The logbooks were displayed in a special web site on the Internet for participants and anyone else to see.

Zurich

At the end of each session participants were asked to note down ideas by means of drawings on file cards. Participants were also prompted – if they wished – to write in their personal diaries at home between sessions. In the fifth and final meeting the group reports were written by the citizens on overhead projection slides. The process of report writing lasted for about 2 hours and was undertaken without the facilitators present. Then the groups presented their citizens' reports to the research team in a final discussion round at the end of the fifth session.

Different variations of the procedures adopted for the report writing led to different report formats, types of content, and extension. With regard to structure, some reports contained developed sentences, whereas others consisted mainly of listings of concepts. With respect to extent, some reports consisted of one page while a few were up to five pages long. As examples, two citizens' reports with rather different formats are reproduced below.[2] A summary of the citizens' most commonly stated assessments and recommendations for addressing climate change is then provided in the next section, together with a discussion of some specific characteristics of the report results.[3]

Stockholm Citizen Report: group D
11 participants, 31 March 1998

1. Problems related to climate change

Here in Stockholm:

One of the effects of climate change is a warmer climate with milder winters. In the future we will have a rise in the water level and the number of beaches will be reduced; we do not know to what extent.

---

[2] All twenty-six citizens' reports reviewed for this chapter can be found in English on the project web site at: http://www.zit.tu-darmstadt.de/ulysses (Documents section, Annex B to WP-99-4).

[3] A tabulated cross-regional summary of all assessments and recommendations present in the citizens' reports can be found in Querol *et al.* (1999).

In an even longer perspective we can have an ice age due to the Gulf Stream changing its course...It can become so cold that it will be uninhabitable.

Globally:

We foresee that natural disasters have a powerful strength; these natural phenomena have not taken place because of climate change but it has contributed to their being greater. The existing facts on climate change, which we have received, are credible in spite of the uncertainty behind them. We are aware that there are different opinions and thereby no clear-cut answers. We feel that the prognosis regarding the future is very much governed by the source and we realize that it is a power struggle in order to reach the goals of the interested parties.

2. and 3. In the event of problems, this is the way we should live in 30 years time in Stockholm and this is what should be done

We ascertain that climate change is a problem and can become much worse if we do not take measures....we suggest that the existing environmentally friendly resources such as electric buses, electric cars, underground, etc. should be developed. Stockholm can be improved by using water as a transport route and directing through traffic around the cities on ring roads. Choose environmentally friendly sources such as wind power, bio-fuel, solar energy, etc. Households should take greater responsibility considering that we are so densely populated and we have the power to influence the choice of products, services, and energy sources. Sweden can also exert influence through political decisions by subsidizing eco-friendly alternatives.

4. Energy which we believe is suitable to use and save

Energy consumption is at the lowest during the night. Would it be possible to plan for energy consumption during the night so that some of the energy will not go to waste? The existing energy should be used without increasing the quantity. This should be achieved by households and industries using appliances and machines that are low in energy use.

5. Who should do this and when should it be put into practice?

Households and industries should bring about the changes together as soon as possible, but within a reasonable amount of time and before the situation has gone too far.

6. Difficulties in reaching the goal

It is uncomfortable taking environmentally friendly measures today. It is also expensive... We believe in creating laws for people to act in an environmentally friendly way but this should be done through awareness. This should be done through more reliable information, but the dilemma is how? Should it be done solely through interest groups/organizations? How do we influence the people and persuade them to take responsibility? The information should be channeled through the main means of communication such as TV, newspapers, radio, and schools.

Our solution will take time but is fairly sure: by moving the city center to small attractive surrounding communities, the distances will be decreased and so also the emissions. People will become closer to one another and become more harmonious, violence will decrease, people will become more involved in their surroundings and therefore also more conscious of the environment, taking more responsibility for it.

Excerpts of a Venice logbook: group B
9 participants, 2 June 1997

From Session 2:

THE EARTH IS BURNING Truth or alarm?
Is it enough to commit ourselves [to make changes], or do we accept to be controlled? (One always prefers his/her own conscience).

From Session 3:

Truth as hypothesis: after the news, information and discussion, we hypothesized ways of changing thanks to political, social, economic contributions and those of the whole community.

From Session 4:

Is it better to adopt the "theory" of being afraid about the future, or else search the consensus about "common sense" to avoid the worse... If one prefers the second theory, what tools and strategies can one use?

From Session 5:

OPEN LETTER FOR ALL PRESIDENTS
[extracts]
You should:

(1) Disseminate to the populations exact information about the re-search methods and results of studies being conducted about environmental issues; informing people will develop into aware-ness and responsibility toward a problem.
(2) "LISTEN" to us and you should take into account the obser-vations made by all the different NGOs and from individual citizens.
(3) Educate people through all possible channels so that people learn to love and respect Nature and the environment, also using in appropriate ways all technology available.
(4) Be more sensitive about this environmental problem. That will allow people to engage in more dynamic and direct precaution-ary actions to deal with this problem.
(5) Establish common objectives to be attained according to the urgency of the problem, by setting well-defined steps....

Findings from citizens' reports

The analysis of conclusions formulated by the participants in thirty IA Focus Groups cannot be statistically representative for the European general public. However, results from these groups involving 225 citizens in seven European regions give indications of how citizens might frame issues of climate change and sustainability. IA Focus Groups, in which participants debate for approximately twelve hours and have access to various types of expert information can lead to richer insights than could be obtained, for example, in a 45 minute interview, or a 10 minute opinion poll.

An analysis of citizens' reports from these groups can capture this richness only in combination with findings from the full range of outputs of the IA Focus Group processes, including discussion recordings and transcripts, diary notes, and collages. For this reason, the analysis given in this chapter should be considered in combination with the discussions of other phases and other types of output of the IA Focus Group processes, given in earlier chapters of this book. What the written reports do provide, however, is a synthesis formulated by the participants themselves of what they had discussed during the five meetings.

Results summary: most common assessments and recommendations

The groups' statements mainly pertained to the following five issues:

(1) Assessment of causes and impacts of climate change
(2) Actions suggested in specific sectors
(3) General implementation strategies
(4) Who should act, where and when
(5) Perceived barriers to action

The summary of the more frequently stated conclusions on these issues provided below indicates the general patterns arising from a synthesis of all groups' statements.[4] As the reports did not give a ranking of concerns, nor comment on the perceived feasibility of all measures suggested, the issues mentioned most frequently are not necessarily those regarded as the most important ones by the groups. Given the exploratory nature of the ULYSSES project, it should also not be inferred that the recommendations typically proposed by these IA Focus Groups would automatically be accepted by the general citizenry. However, the review below provides a synthesis of what was commonly seen by 225 citizens participating in IA Focus Groups across Europe as causes and impacts of climate change they were particularly concerned about, and as actions they themselves would support. Main points of these citizens' views are briefly summarized in Box 6.2, and then discussed in more detail below.

Assessment of causes and impacts of anthropogenic climate change
Among the ten groups that commented explicitly on the existence or non-existence of climate change, no single report suggested that anthropogenic climate change does not exist. Nevertheless, a report from Barcelona did indicate disagreement within the group regarding the evidence proving the existence of climatic change. In this report it was

---

[4] For the specific participants' statements, see the overview given in Annex A of (Querol *et al.* 1999).

Box 6.2: Overview of common points from the citizens' reports

While the reports are not representative of all European citizens, and were produced in an experimental atmosphere, there are some interesting agreements:

(1) Climate change causes and impacts of concern:
- anthropogenic climate change is seen as a reality
- energy use, deforestation, and transportation are among the major perceived causes of climatic change
- increasing natural hazards, sea-level rise, and ecological effects are among the major impacts expected
- deforestation and stratospheric ozone depletion were discussed as causes and effects of anthropogenic climate change.

(2) The discussions of responses to climatic change frequently cited potential emissions reductions in the transport, energy and household sectors, and waste management and urban planning were also addressed.

(3) Citizens felt that implementation of the mitigation measures would require some economic instruments, increasing public awareness and, to a lesser extent, legislation.

(4) The call was made for action by citizens and governments at the local level and many felt that this action must be taken immediately.

(5) At the same time, barriers to implementation were recognized. These were often seen as related to asymmetric power relationships, and to ingrained lifestyle patterns.

Furthermore, adaptation to climate change was usually not discussed in the citizens' reports. Rather, citizens were concerned about the causes of anthropogenic climate change and their mitigation.

stated that there were three views within the group: (a) climate change exists "because it is evident"; (b) "it exists because scientists say so from evident consequences"; and (c) "we cannot know it." In a report from Venice participants indicated that, although there was uncertainty around the climate change issue, they believed that such climatic change existed. For the three regions in which the groups responded to whether climate change is a problem "now or in the future," most of the reports stated that the groups saw it as a problem on both temporal scales. For the two regions which addressed explicitly whether climatic change was a problem in "their region or world-wide," the groups saw it as a problem at both spatial levels.

The citizens' reports usually don't indicate how important the participants thought climate change to be in comparison to other environmental or societal problems. This was generally addressed in all groups' discussions, but only one group from Stockholm explicitly commented on this in its citizens' report: "It is hard to determine what priority should be given to the climate issue when compared to other societal issues. Other issues like unemployment seem more urgent to resolve." This group also reported that there are other environmental problems to which they could relate more easily, such as acidification and traffic pollution, since these were perceived to be more visible and concrete than climate change.

- The most commonly reported causes of climatic change were: emissions of CO_2; population growth; the hole in the ozone layer (see below); energy use; deforestation; industry emissions; transport emissions; increase of private traffic; unsustainable consumption patterns; politicians' inaction or short-sightedness; and economic interests and lobbies. In contrast to the majority of groups referring exclusively to "human activities," three groups reported that there could also be "natural factors" producing climate change.
- The majority of the reported impacts of climatic change were "geophysical impacts" and, among them, the more commonly specified were: increase of natural hazards; temperature increase/change; changes in seasons; melting of ice caps; sea level rise; storms; floods; droughts; and the hole in the ozone layer (see below). In a second term, three "ecological impacts" were most frequently stated: desertification; effects on flora; and effects on fauna. Interestingly, most groups reported only one direct "human impact": health problems or diseases. The following human impacts were specified only by two groups: plagues or losses in crops; nutrition changes; and starvation or death.

Whilst economic implications were at times commented on in the course of the group discussions, there was no single report which specified impacts on the economy. It could be the case that citizens are influenced by the standard news coverage in newspapers and TV programs on climate change, which focus on the geophysical and most obviously visible impacts. It could also be argued that ecological and human impacts derive from the geophysical ones and, therefore, those primary and direct climate change impacts are more likely to be mentioned.

Interestingly, two items were reported to be both causes and impacts of climate change. One is the "destruction of forests," which was assessed by four groups as contributing to climate change (as less carbon dioxide absorption takes place), and also assessed by another three groups as an impact (in the sense that extreme weather events contribute to the destruction of forests). The other issue mentioned, both as cause and impact, is the "hole in the ozone layer"; this was assessed by four groups as a cause of climate change, and another four groups mentioned it as an impact. While this may illustrate the confusion between greenhouse effect and ozone layer depletion, it was not the intention of the research teams to correct or teach participants when they misinterpreted the information provided. There could be at least two interpretations of mentioning ozone depletion in connection with climate change. From a climate science point of view, climate change and ozone depletion are only weakly connected. Thus, their intertwining by the citizens could be seen as a lack of understanding that would need more education. In contrast to this, Thompson and Rayner (1998) have argued that many citizens may perceive ozone depletion and climate change as two parts of the same wider problem of humankind's disturbed relationship with nature in industrial society. According to them, the connection many people make between these two issues may thus be sensible from a citizens' point of view.

Actions suggested in specific sectors

The measures suggested for addressing climate change apply to a wide range of sectors and sub-sectors, as well as different implementation modes. On some occasions, the groups defined sector actions without specifying the implementation mode, while other statements contemplated a general implementation strategy without specifying any sector. For example, there were groups suggesting that more information and communication are needed, but only on some occasions was it specified to whom the information should be addressed and for what purpose. Due to this diverse degree of specificity among group statements, suggested sector actions are summarized in this section, and, in the following section, the reported implementation strategies are outlined.

The measures most commonly reported to be critical for addressing climate change pertained to transport and energy. These were followed by the household, waste and urban planning sectors.

- The more commonly stated measures within the transport sector were those related to the "organization of mobility": limiting of cars in the city center; more cycling facilities; and spatially distributing the placement of facilities. Also reported were those measures related to "public transport": improvement of public transport quality. To a somewhat lesser extent the reports also mentioned: improved technology for cleaner transport modes (usually suggesting electric vehicles but also solar or ethyl-alcohol ones); and less individual use of cars.

- Concerning the energy sector, the groups suggested measures related to "energy sources": clean or renewable energy sources; and to "energy efficiency." Five out of nine groups, which were explicitly asked to specify in their reports a recommended reduction level of energy consumption, suggested a 20–30 per cent reduction for the time horizon of about thirty years considered in the citizens' reports (this was framed as to be addressed by households and/or transport consumption).
- Typical measures regarding the household sector referred to "technological improvements": renewable energy sources; efficient appliances; and insulated housing. Measures pertaining to "citizen behavior" were also frequently identified: reduction in the consumption of electricity, goods and water; reduction of room temperature; and purchasing seasonal or regional food. Some of the measures referred to the "housing services": improvement of heating and water supply systems.
- It was typically recommended for waste management that recycling should be promoted and that production of waste and packaging ought to be minimized.
- A frequent measure regarding urban planning was increasing green zones.

Actions pertaining to sectors such as industry, land and resource management, as well as the service sector, were also suggested but to a much lesser extent. The industry sector was not specifically addressed when suggesting measures, despite the fact that industry emissions had been the most frequently reported cause of climate change. This can be understood in terms of the influence of the research design of the discussions. Participants were encouraged to focus on the sectors of energy, transport and households, as these are critical sectors for the greenhouse effect, as well as areas that are more directly related to the citizens' own experiences and lifestyles. The types of measures tackling the industry sector, which were mentioned, were mainly centered on technology improvements.

Two major conclusions concerning the type of actions proposed are that no measures of an "adaptive" type were proposed (which might have been, for example, suggestions on urban engineering solutions to mitigate the effects of sea level rise on the coastline, or agricultural adaptation to guarantee food supply). All proposed measures were oriented toward addressing the causes of the human-induced climate change and not the effects. Second, regardless of the sector goals, the groups' recommendations were not limited to material measures, like infrastructure changes (for example, concerning energy and goods supply systems) or technological improvements (for example, renewable energy sources; efficient devices). Procedural measures were suggested by the groups as well, both collective action (for example, shared housing) and individual action (for example, changes in personal consumption habits).

Implementation strategies

The groups' suggestions concerning the actual implementation procedures to pursue the mentioned measures have been clustered into four categories of strategies. From these, the more frequently mentioned strategies pertain to "horizontal support measures"[5] and to "economic or market instruments," followed by "legislation or regulation" and "citizen behavior." Below, the more typically stated instruments are listed for each type of strategy, but, as mentioned above, it cannot always be stipulated which sector actions these instruments were meant to be pursuing.[6]

- The most frequent measures that can be regarded as horizontal support measures were: increasing and improving information contents (clear, accessible, consistent, less academic, pedagogical information and eco-labeling); improved communication (targeted advertising, campaigns in the mass media); and awareness raising and education of different social actors. To a lesser extent, suggestions were made regarding institutional partnerships and research.
- Economic or market instruments that were typically recommended were: promotion of subsidies or lower prices (i.e., for public transport, for clean energy sources and technologies, and for eco-friendly household appliances). In addition, but to a lesser extent, the following measures were suggested: promotion of funding/investments; incentives; increase of prices of fossil fuels; and eco-taxes. Accounting for the number of groups that referred to what can be considered as "positive incentives" (subsidies, lower prices, and other incentives) and "disincentives" (higher prices, taxes), most groups suggested incentives (eighteen groups) compared to the number of groups that suggested disincentives (eight groups). The addressees of incentives and disincentives were both producers and consumers.

[5] "Horizontal support measures" is a termed employed by the policy community.
[6] See Annex A of Querol *et al.* (1999) for greater detail.

- Legislation or regulation: Under this category, there were fewer specific instruments suggested. Most typically, the groups suggested laws and standards for emissions' reduction; regulation for industry; and penalties when the law is not fully implemented.
- Citizens' behavior: The participants also referred to the individual's own capacity to implement measures. Typical suggestions to be considered under this type of strategy were: lifestyle changes toward environmentally conscious consumption; and citizen organization and participation in order to channel concerns and group power.

No written report suggested implementation mechanisms which could be related to "flexible mechanisms" like carbon dioxide trade permits or joint implementation. While this does not mean that such flexible mechanisms would not be acceptable to citizens, it seems that these mechanisms are not the most natural way to deal with climate change from most citizens' points of view. Only two citizens' reports suggested technological or economic assistance to developing or neighboring countries. The citizen groups typically recommended measures that do not imply that other communities or countries should undertake the burden of action against climate change, nor that developing countries should limit their population growth or their expectations of raising living standards.

Who should act, where and when
Nearly all groups made recommendations about which actors should take measures to respond to climate change. There were fewer groups specifying the spatial and temporal context in which the actions were to take place.

- *Who*: Typically it was suggested that the actors who should take action are: citizens or everybody; and a range of governmental actors. These were followed by scientists and researchers; producers and business; household administrators and landlords; and environmental and social movements.
- *Where*: For the only two groups which specified the location of actions, the following was suggested: at the local level and in each town; supraregionally; Western countries should aid the developing ones; and everywhere.
- *When*: In the twelve groups which addressed this issue, it was suggested that action should be taken now or immediately (eight groups), and as soon as possible (four groups). This indicates that the citizen groups recommended more immediate action than what is stipulated in the Kyoto Protocol.

It should be noted that among the groups of actors that were seen as responsible for taking action, not all were regarded as specifically contributing to climate change, but as having specific roles in a joint effort to address it.

Perceived barriers to action

Only a third of the groups were asked to take this issue into account, while half of the groups addressed it directly or indirectly. The barriers that were brought up by most groups were, first, those related to what could be termed managerial and implementation barriers and, second, those related to lifestyle barriers.

- *Managerial and implementation barriers*: The obstacles typically reported were power relations (economic interests; lobbies), and the lack of action from governments or politicians (i.e., measures or agreements not being implemented; politicians not willing to introduce measures).
- *Lifestyle barriers*: The groups often reported the following issues as impediments to implementing or achieving goals: laziness; and induced consumption needs or individuals not being prepared to lower their living standards.

Other obstacles mentioned, but to a lesser extent, pertained to the following categories: economic costs or market barriers; cognitive barriers (i.e., to get people or certain groups to understand that everybody must help); social and cultural barriers; and moral barriers (i.e., egoism, indifference).

It appears, therefore, that the groups typically assessed politico-economic relations as major barriers to implement suggested actions and strategies. On the other hand, difficulties related to social consumption patterns and lack of awareness were less commonly mentioned. Furthermore, the stated economy-related barriers were connected to the power held by economic pressure groups, and not so much to the potential economic costs of undertaking measures, or the potential market (in)competitiveness of environmentally friendly or energy saving goods and services.

Other issues that could have been raised as barriers were not mentioned in any of the reviewed reports, like lack of appropriate technology, lack of means, or lack of knowledge. What some groups did report were negative side-effects that might result from implementing some measures. For example, one group from Zurich reported "job reduction" and "keep(ing) the social peace" as barriers. This outcome indicates that the citizen groups generally held a rather holistic view, which considered the inter-linkages between the global climate change problem and other social problems.

General comments on the citizens' reports

Although the IA Focus Groups were focused on climate change issues, and on the areas of energy use, transport, and households, both participants' discussions and their assessment reports contain many other issues. The participants did not *dis*integrate or isolate interrelated issues of their concern; participants often addressed issues that were not targeted explicitly in the expert information provided. The groups received and discussed information on some predefined policy options (as presented in the form of computer model scenarios, by invited experts, or other means) but, to a larger extent, they also formulated and debated their own recommendations. In some group discussions, the participants pointed out that they, as citizens, would like to receive information or guidance on actions that they could personally take. Therefore, the "areas of action" stated by participants in their reports were broader in scope than "policy areas" as normally defined by policy-makers, who often limit themselves to considering strategies over which they have jurisdiction, and put less emphasis on measures that are mainly undertaken on a voluntarily basis and that imply a change in lifestyle.

The groups were told explicitly that they could express disagreement in their reports but the reports expressed a high degree of consensus. Only in very few reports did participants point out on which issues the group disagreed. This was the case, for example, in a report from Stockholm which expressed disagreement about whether or not to phase out nuclear energy. Another example is found in a report from Barcelona where participants wrote: "It is proposed to ban the circulation of private vehicles in the commercial city center, but the majority do not agree with this prohibition."

The summary of the most typical statements across reports has been rather unproblematic. Besides the diversity of report structures and contents, the reports reviewed did not contain incompatible recommendations. Only two apparently contradictory measures have been found between two reports. Barcelona Report C suggested increasing car parking fees, while Barcelona Report E suggested a price reduction or free use of car parks. However, from the context in which those measures were formulated it is clear that in the first case parking lots in the city center were intended, while in the second case the discussion concerned parking lots on the outskirts of the city to be used for park-and-ride. Thus, in both cases the basic idea was to limit private car use in the city centers by promoting public transport. This is one example which shows that it can be essential to consider the context in which statements are formulated. Reviewing data from citizens' reports should thus be combined with a more comprehensive review of the different outputs of IA Focus Groups.

In contrast to the actual group discussions, the citizens' reports rarely reflect unanswered questions that the groups posed to themselves. An exception, however, is illustrated in the report from the Stockholm region reproduced above, that asks: "Would it be possible to plan for energy consumption during the night so that some of the energy will not go to waste?" Another report, from Venice, suggested: "Maybe the whole thing [climate change] is due to natural evolution."

The limited number of groups and citizens' reports per region does not allow the determination of robust cross-regional patterns. Nevertheless, some regional characteristics have been encountered which can be explained by local conditions. For example, the fact that the Barcelona citizens' reports were more likely to suggest "more recycling facilities" than the Frankfurt reports may be related to the higher availability of recycling facilities in Frankfurt as compared to Barcelona. Also, with regard to implementation strategies, the Frankfurt reports suggested eco-taxes more often than in any other research region. This could be related to the fact that in Germany there already exists a public debate on the issue and – to some extent – public acceptance of this strategic measure. However, the inverse case is also possible, that policy measures are already well established in a region and therefore not considered to be a high priority among its citizens. This means that regional differences regarding measures proposed in citizens' reports have to be interpreted in their specific environmental, political, and socio-cultural contexts.

Assessment of the report writing exercises

Below, we first discuss how the citizens' conclusion procedures were experienced by both participants and researchers in each of the regions, and then give an overview of the general strengths and weaknesses of these procedures.

Assessment of the writing exercises by research region

At the end of the final meetings, participants were generally asked for feedback on the overall IA Focus Group experience. Although they were not systematically asked to comment explicitly on the writing tasks and subsequent outcomes, participants usually made comments regarding these tasks as well. Below, some of the participants' comments[7] are discussed together with observations by the regional researchers.

Assessment from Barcelona

The researchers observed that groups became more confident with the writing tasks as sessions proceeded. It was an effort for the participants to do preparatory drafting and to write the citizen reports, but they undertook the task as part of the discussion exercise, accepted their limitations and carried on. Regarding the resulted reports and the level of group agreement, participants were generally rather satisfied as illustrated by the quotes below:

JOAN: It is a lot what we agree on! Isn't it?   (Barcelona Group A, Session 4)
VICTOR: I think that we have said rather reasonable things given our knowledge.
(Barcelona Group D, Session 5)

Participants generally saw the reports as useful, but sometimes expressed doubts as to whether the policy community would pay much attention to what they as citizens said:

MOD: Do you see any difficulty with the report? How do you see that it is yourselves who have to write the report?
MARCOS: If it is really to be taken into account, I think that is fabulous.
SIMON: Everything done to approach citizens' opinions is good, but that they are taken into account this is another thing.
(Barcelona Group E, Session 3)

Assessment from Frankfurt

Researchers reported that for analytical purposes the entire process and style in which the citizen reports were written worked well, but that the reports on their own would be insufficient and difficult to use for policymaking. For the participants, the process of report writing was generally evaluated positively, although some participants remarked that they had problems writing their ideas on the file cards. In some cases, questions concerning the basic topic of the session had to be clarified by the moderators. When participants were asked to provide suggestions for policy targets and recommendations, some participants found it difficult to distinguish clearly between "targets" and "measures." For this reason, in some groups these two topics were discussed and reported together. Moreover, in some of the groups, participants had difficulty in making

---

[7] The names of participants have been changed in the quotes provided.

recommendations for each of the sectors suggested by the research team. In such cases, the participants themselves combined different sectors and recommended measures valid for all of them.

Assessment from Manchester

As indicated above, in the Manchester study region, a local "policy for real" framing was intended. Researchers reported that one group did not express enthusiasm about writing a report for policy-makers when a speaker presented to them the LA 21 process taking place in Manchester, and participants realized that this initiative – which intended a high degree of citizen participation – had not reached any of them. For this reason participants felt reluctant to write a report for local policy-makers who had not shown a clear initial commitment to the issue. For the group that wrote a citizens' report, researchers observed that participants showed a general sense of uneasiness and confusion around the task of writing a report due to the lack of a clear and specific focus for the exercise, and due to an obvious lack of a mandate from governmental institutions. The situation was different in the third citizen panel, in which a well-known and trusted environmental NGO participated, and in which the council made clear to the participants that it was interested and committed to the process (Darier 1997).

Assessment from Stockholm

The moderators have reported that although the participants often took the report task very seriously, many felt uncomfortable making formal claims about what should be done to address climate change issues locally or globally. While some participants were not convinced that policy-makers would have any reason to take their views into account in the actual policy-making, some of the others felt uneasy about making an analysis of climate change that might later be judged by experts and policy-makers. An interesting comment raised by a participant was related to the issue of whether reports themselves would reflect the richness of the group discussions:

GUDRUN: This stuff that we have said in this paper is only one aspect, but I am thinking about the fact that we have said so much more than this. Will that also appear, I mean, will be it conveyed to the EU?

(Stockholm Group D, Session 5)

The two Stockholm groups that had drafted their citizens' report on a computer with the help of participants who were skilled typists and computer users had no problem in finishing their reports within the available time, and seemed more content with their final report than the previous two groups.

Assessment from Venice

As indicated above, in the Venice region a "research" framing was developed. Researchers reported to be concerned with the legitimacy of asking laypersons – who are not used to writing reports and who do not know each other – to write a formal report with policy recommendations. For this reason, the Venice groups were asked to report their views in a less formal way; the groups first used flip charts and, in the fifth session, completed the log books. Moderators reported that there was no opposition to these tasks; nevertheless, in some groups, there was an initial – though not lasting – inertia. It proved very rewarding for the groups to have the project homepage with their log books presented to them. The opinion of the researchers was that if the participants knew beforehand that what they were saying would "go out of the room," they would be more willing to carry out the writing exercise.

Assessment from Zurich

The moderators observed that participants seemed to take the writing tasks very seriously and almost all participants felt satisfied with their work. There was initial uneasiness concerning the task of making drawings on file cards as participants did not feel confident; nevertheless, most became familiar with it and started to enjoy it after the first try. In relation to the use of personal diaries, some participants took their diaries home to write down their thoughts between the sessions, while others did not write anything.

Some of them were astonished that although at the beginning of the writing exercise there were different opinions, a consensus was found. In some groups, the two-hour period provided for writing the group report proved to be too short; when the moderators returned to the meeting room, the participants were still engaged in serious discussion and it appeared that they could have continued for some considerable time.

General strengths and weaknesses of the writing exercises

Among the major limitations, it was found that participants had some difficulties in formulating their concerns, opinions, and suggestions into synoptic and formal written recommendations. The writing exercises are a more demanding task than debates. This might be due to lack of experience in working in a group context, lack of experience in writing formal documents, the complexity of the issue at stake, or lack of time. The fact that the participatory processes were part of a research project and not directly of a policy process seems to have led to a certain degree of confusion or skepticism concerning the citizens' report task – in some study regions more than in others.

Among the major strengths, the citizens' report provided the participants with a new opportunity and channel to express themselves by means of an additional format.[8] The participants took the report task seriously, felt generally satisfied with the report outcomes, and pleased by the degree of agreement they had achieved in their reports. The preparatory drafting exercises for the reports also helped participants in focusing their debates. This was observed when, on many occasions, it was the participants themselves who asked their group partners to return to the topic being reported, when their discussions started to lose focus. Furthermore, the successive drafting steps of the group reports enabled the groups to keep track of which insights and positions from the discussions they considered relevant and worth a mention.

We want to emphasize that citizens' reports should be considered in combination with other outputs like transcripts of the actual group debates or researchers' summaries of these discussions. However, citizens' reports following a comparable structure are more than a tool to help researchers keep track of what views were expressed in a series of IA Focus Groups (as a full transcript of a single IA Focus Group of twelve hours can exceed one hundred pages, this in itself is no trivial feat). Rather, we believe that Participatory Integrated Assessment outputs, to serve as input for policy, ought not to be limited to researchers' summaries of the group discussions. Since citizens' reports are written by the participants themselves, they have a higher validity than researchers' interpretations of the recorded discussions on their own. A combination of facilitators' summaries of the discussions and citizens' reports seems to be the most advisable option.

Concluding remarks

Effective decision-making on today's complex sustainability issues increasingly makes it necessary to involve a full spectrum of stakeholders. Without integrating, for example, the points of view of citizens, local policy-makers, and industry representatives, environmental policy runs the risk of getting stalled in the early implementation phase.

---

[8] This was the case for people with difficulty in expressing themselves in public, such as a very old housewife who worked on the citizens' report draft over the weekend and read her notes aloud at the beginning of the next session.

The study discussed in this volume has developed IA Focus Group procedures to address this need. This chapter has focused on the procedures and results of writing exercises carried out in the last phase of these procedures. Findings from 30 IA Focus Groups conducted in seven European regions with 225 citizens have been reviewed. Our concluding remarks pertain first to recommendations by the participants and second to methodological conclusions.

Citizens' views on climate change and mitigation measures

Interestingly, while the groups were not required to formulate a consensus report, the group reports showed a high level of consensus within and also between groups. Results first concern citizens' assessments of climatic change. None of the group assessments reviewed here concluded that climate change does not exist; most of the impacts mentioned were of a geophysical nature, and sometimes also pertained to ecological effects. The only human impacts frequently noted were health problems or diseases, whilst only two groups mentioned plagues or losses in crops; nutrition changes; and starvation. Interestingly, there was no single group that specified impacts on the economy explicitly in their citizens' report.

A second group of results centers on recommendations of measures for addressing climate change and their implementation. Following the research design's focus on energy, transport, and household issues, measures most commonly mentioned pertained to these three areas. Among these, the transport and energy sectors were mentioned most often, followed by measures concerning households. In addition to the topics suggested by the research teams, waste and urban planning issues were addressed by the participants. For implementation, the most commonly advocated strategies were related to governmental actions like information and communication improvements, economic instruments, and regulation, and to citizens' behavior like lifestyle changes and citizen participation. Five groups that explicitly recommended a reduction level of energy consumption suggested a 20–30 per cent reduction within the time frame of thirty years considered in the citizens' reports. Interestingly, no measures of an "adaptive" type were proposed; all proposed measures were oriented toward addressing the causes of the human-induced climate change and not the effects. Furthermore, none of the groups' reports reviewed here suggested implementation mechanisms related to "flexible mechanisms" like carbon dioxide trade permits and joint implementation. It seems that these mechanisms are not the most natural way to deal with climate change from most citizens' points of view. The citizen groups typically recommended measures that do not imply that action against climate change is delegated to other communities or countries.

A last group of results concerns the actors seen as responsible for taking measures, and the perceived barriers to action. Actors typically mentioned were citizens or everybody; and a diversity of governmental actors. These were followed by scientists and researchers; producers and business; household administrators and landlords; and environmental and social movements. The groups that addressed the issue of timing explicitly suggested that the actions should be taken now or as soon as possible. This indicates that the citizen groups recommended action long before the Kyoto Protocol deadline of 2012. The typically reported barriers to action were related to power relations (economic interests, lobbies), the lack of action from governments or politicians, and to lifestyle-related barriers like laziness, induced consumption needs, or individuals not prepared to lower their living standards.

The overall findings from the citizens' written assessments reveal a fair degree of understanding about the globality and interconnection between climate change and other issues. The citizens' assessments were based on a holistic perspective as their reports contemplate a broad spectrum of policy areas and implementation strategies. Participants often addressed issues that were not targeted explicitly in the expert information provided. Furthermore, their reported measures and strategies for action appear to be realistic, sound, and based on a precautionary standpoint. The latter point may be a particular European perspective. It would be interesting to compare this with a similar study in the US context.

Remarks on methodology

From our experiences, we conclude first that neither researchers' summaries of the discussions, nor participants' reports on their conclusions, are adequate on their own to convey the full richness of IA Focus Groups debates. Rather, a combination of both seems to be more useful for this purpose. Second, regarding the citizens' report structure, a balance has to be found between a pre-structured and homogeneous format of citizens' reports, which helps to seek patterns and compare results across groups, and a more open and spontaneous report structure, which may capture the views of the groups in more depth. Specifically, in order to apply Participatory Integrated Assessment (PIA) across very different social contexts, diverse tools, designs, and output formats should be kept as simple and as flexible as possible. Participatory processes in such cross-cultural settings need to take cultural differences into account very carefully.[9] If PIA methods were to be applied jointly in several world regions, considerations on the contextual differences, especially between the North and the South, would be necessary for adapting the methods to the different local conditions.

The findings from the exploratory IA Focus Groups conducted within the present study pertain to the area between research on citizens' views on climate change, development of participatory techniques, and "planning-for-real" exercises. The latter is relevant for the relation between citizens' conclusions in IA Focus Groups and citizen participation in Local Agenda 21 (LA 21) processes. It has been argued that local climate action strategies should evolve into a broader and more democratic framework of LA 21 (O'Riordan and Jäger 1996). LA 21 aims at encouraging the participation of all sectors of the community to formulate "local action plans" toward sustainability for the twenty-first century. In general, the IA Focus Group method looks very promising for supporting LA 21 processes. However, citizens participating in IA Focus Groups were not asked to define priority settings for actions, detailed implementation mechanisms, or indicators for monitoring the implementation and effectiveness of measures in their conclusions. Thus, further developments in IA Focus Group design, especially concerning citizens' report procedures, are necessary to realize the full potential of IA Focus Groups for use in LA 21 procedures, as in other participatory processes in the context of sustainability science.

---

[9] We are indebted to Bill Clark and Ortwin Renn for helpful discussions on this topic, on the occasion of the EFIEA workshop on uncertainty in Integrated Assessment, Baden, Austria, July 1999.

PART THREE

Further forms of participation

INTRODUCTION

While the first two parts of this volume have focused on the IA Focus Group approach to public participation in sustainability science, the third part relates this research to further forms of participation explored in recent projects and programs. It starts from one of the central findings of the focus group work discussed earlier, namely that citizens throughout Europe tend to be in favor of climate change mitigation by reducing overall energy use in the future. In Chapter 7, Kasemir *et al.* discuss a participatory exercise with representatives from venture capital and young technology companies and from the European Commission, that explored options of how to initiate significant reductions of fossil fuel use by early-stage investments into ecologically sound energy innovation. The participants considered changes in tax exemptions, subsidies and government guarantee schemes to be at least as important as carbon taxes. Taking a long-term perspective, Tuinstra *et al.* then describe in Chapter 8 how the Dutch COOL project studied options for drastic (50–80 per cent) reduction of carbon dioxide emissions in the long run. Central to this project were participatory processes at three different scales: the Dutch national context, the European, and the global scale. Common lessons from the research discussed in the earlier parts of this volume and from the COOL project are discussed. In Chapter 9 Downing *et al.* then change the focus of the discussion from climate change mitigation to regional adaptation. They discuss experiences from a participatory approach to developing drought management options for southern England's Thames region as an example of adaptation to possible climate change impacts. This project involved key stakeholders from water service companies, public authorities and consumers, and developed a portfolio of scenarios in a participatory manner. The issue of methodologies for scenario development, relevant for all research processes discussed in this volume, is then explicitly tackled by Anastasi in Chapter 10. His remarks are inspired by his rich experience with scenario development, including work for the OECD and the UN, and in Shell's Group Planning. Among the challenges and opportunities he discusses are the need to develop integrated rather than single issue scenarios, and to combine quantitative analysis with narrative elements. The latter could profit greatly from a more intense use of participatory processes, like the ones developed in the projects discussed throughout this volume.

CHAPTER SEVEN

Venture capital and climate policy

Bernd Kasemir, Ferenc Toth, and Vanessa Masing

Introduction: why venture capital?

In the long run, a sustainability transition will require major shifts in our socio-economic activities. As an example, consider the challenge that climate change issues pose for Europe. An effective European climate policy ultimately needs to achieve drastic reductions in greenhouse gas emissions. In order to keep the risk of major disruptions of human and natural systems moderate, global emissions would need to be below current levels in the long term (see Wigley, Richels, and Edmonds 1996). But population and per capita emissions in developing countries will continue to rise significantly for some time to come. The EU and other developed regions have a special responsibility to lead the way in reducing global emissions, not only because of their economic ability to initiate change, but also because their per capita emissions and cumulative historical emissions far exceed those of developing countries.

The IA Focus Group research discussed in the preceding chapters has shown that many citizens across Europe see scenarios of significantly lower energy use and greenhouse gas emissions as desirable (see also Kasemir *et al.* 2000). But how could such a future be realized? The feasibility of such scenarios depends on interacting patterns of lifestyle changes and technological changes. One option to induce technological change toward low-carbon products and processes is to make them more competitive by putting a tax burden on carbon emissions. This would not necessarily lead to welfare losses. Under the term "double dividend," positive economy-wide effects of properly recycled environmental taxes have been discussed (see Welsch 1996, for a Europe scale analysis). Schneider and Goulder (1997) have argued that a carbon tax is an economically efficient instrument to induce technological change that could make emission reductions cost effective and possibly inexpensive over the long term. But there are other options for supporting technological change toward a low-carbon society. A major factor is investment in such new technologies. The financial industry could play a key role in supporting sustainable development (see Schmidheiny and Zorraquín 1996). In particular, large insurance companies could profit in the long run from supporting climate mitigation (Tucker 1997; Karl, Nicholls, and Ghazi 1999), and are indeed already active in this field (Knoepfel *et al.* 1999). Less attention has been given so far to the role of early-stage investment in young companies that are developing energy efficiency and renewable energy technologies. Supporting venture capital investment in such companies could be an effective policy measure with economic as well as environmental benefits, especially in a context of high unemployment as is the case in much of the EU today (see Jaeger *et al.* 1997a).

Venture capital is equity investment provided by individuals or professional firms for starting, developing, or transforming privately owned companies (for a short introduction to venture capital investment, see Box 7.1). Venture capital investors typically keep their engagement in a company for three to seven years, and make their profit in the form of capital gains at the "exit," i.e., when the company is listed on a stock market or is sold to another investor. It is of major concern to venture capital firms not only to select the best performers, but to help them actively in growing as fast as possible. Venture-backed companies indeed grow faster and create more jobs than most other businesses (for experiences from the Netherlands, France, and the US, see EVCA 1996). Although the venture capital industry developed later in most of the EU than in the US, in the last decade it has become increasingly established in Europe as well. The European Commission (1998) has stressed the important potential of venture capital for job creation in Europe.

Since the adoption of the Fifth Environmental Action Program in 1992, a major emphasis of the EU's environmental policy has been on the integration of environmental concerns into economic and sectoral policies (see European Commission 1993; and European Communities 1994). However, this integration has been hampered by the fact that trade-offs rather than synergies between environmental and economic goals have often been at the center of debates. Supporting venture capital engagements in ecological energy investment would offer the chance of creating synergies between European economic and environmental policies. However, to be effective in supporting climate policy, venture capital investment should be targeted specifically at new energy efficient and renewable energy technologies, and investments in the early stages of company development should be particularly encouraged. This will not be easy as venture capital in Europe is much less focused on investing in new technology based firms compared to venture capital in the US, and as the interest of European venture capital in supporting start-up and early-stage companies has declined since the mid-1980s (see Murray 1998;

Box 7.1: **Basics of venture capital investment**

- *Definition:* Venture capital is equity (share) capital provided by individuals or professional firms alongside management to *start*, *develop* or *transform* privately owned companies that demonstrate the potential for significant growth.
- *Actors in venture capital investment: Investors* seek the chance to participate in outstanding performances of small innovative companies, to diversify their investment portfolio, and to save taxes. Mediated by *venture capital professionals*, who also assist at the strategic level in developing the business, these investments offer innovative *entrepreneurs* the chance to realize their ideas. Venture capital has enabled the rapid growth of entire new industries such as personal computing and biotechnology.
- *Main stages of venture capital investment:* Venture capital can be invested in different stages of the development of a business. Some of the earliest stages are seed investment, financing research and development of an initial business concept, start-up financing supporting product development and initial marketing before products are sold commercially, and expansion financing provided for the growth of a company that is breaking even or trading profitably. Some of the subsequent stages are replacement capital that helps to purchase existing shares in a company from another venture capital organization or shareholder, and buy-out capital to enable current operating management and investors to acquire the business. The figure below shows the distribution between these stages by percentage of the total venture capital invested in Europe in 1996:

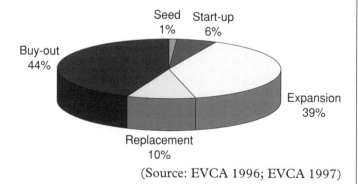

(Source: EVCA 1996; EVCA 1997)

for the distribution of stages of businesses financed by European venture capital, see also EVCA 1997).

This chapter discusses options for improving synergies between venture capital investment and European climate policy that were explored in a policy exercise study conducted within the ULYSSES project. This participatory process included a workshop involving representatives of the European venture capital community and of young technology companies, and a subsequent round of interviews with representatives of the European Commission.[1] In addition to discussing a set of options explored in this participatory setting, this chapter describes findings from this study pertaining to questions of European harmonization. If policy measures for supporting venture capital engagement in ecological energy investment (i.e., investment in energy efficiency and renewable energy technologies) were implemented, should this be done rather at the European or at the member state level? The results of the study indicate that views of representatives from the private sector differ rather markedly from views of European policy-makers on this question.

The chapter is organized as follows. The methodology of the study is described in the next section, followed by the results on options for lowering barriers to venture capital engagement in ecological energy investment in Europe. Conclusions on differences in views between workshop representatives from the private sector and interview partners from the European Commission concerning European harmonization of related policy measures are discussed at the end of the chapter.

The policy exercise methodology

The design of the study discussed here was a further development of the policy exercise concept, aimed at making the process specifically suitable for the participation of private sector representatives. For this, the construction of story-lines of investment patterns by the participants was crucial. In this section, we first discuss the overall design of the study, and then focus on this process of constructing story-lines of investment patterns.

Overall study design

The study discussed here was based on the general concept of policy exercises. A policy exercise (Brewer 1986; Toth 1986; 1988a; 1988b) is

---

[1] This Policy Exercise study was conducted by the ULYSSES project teams from the Potsdam Institute for Climate Impact Research (PIK) and from the Swiss Federal Institute for Environmental Science and Technology (EAWAG) between May and November 1997. For a detailed description of the process and the results, as well as lists of the workshop participants and the interviewees at the European Commission, see Toth *et al.* (1998).

a flexibly structured process designed as an interface between analysts and policy-makers. Its function is to synthesize and assess the knowledge accumulated in several relevant fields of science for policy purposes in the light of complex practical management problems. It brings together scientists, representatives of the major social actors concerned with the issue under discussion, and support staff. A policy exercise usually involves only a small number of participants. As in other participatory methods of qualitative research, such as focus groups (Morgan and Krueger 1998a) that were the basis of the IA Focus Group method described in earlier chapters, intense discussion among participants representing an interesting mix of different perspectives is aimed at. This type of research seems especially suited for exploring new issues where opinions are not yet entrenched, in contrast to more established issues of debate, where opinion formation has to a large extent already taken place. For the latter type of issue, questionnaire studies, for example, involving more participants in a less in-depth manner may be more suitable.

A policy exercise is carried out in one or more periods, each consisting usually of three phases (preparations, workshop, evaluation). At the heart of the process are scenario writing and scenario analyses. In the first phase, a series of plausible future development scenarios are prepared, that integrate issues from various fields affecting the practical problem at hand. In this framework, specific policy options are then tested during interactive sessions at the workshop. A basic feature of the policy exercise concept is that the participants are involved in the preparations from the beginning. The policy exercise does not necessarily yield new scientific knowledge, but rather a new, better structured view of the problem. In recent years the policy exercise approach has increasingly been used to address global change issues (see Klabbers et al. 1995, 1996; Toth 1995; Mermet 1992) and a wide range of public policy problems beyond the environment (Andriessen 1995; Joldersma et al. 1995; Wenzler and van't Noordende 1995).

In the specific policy exercise on Climate Policy as a Business Opportunity for Venture Capital in Europe discussed here, three actor groups were involved in order to study options for synergies between European climate policy and venture capital investment in innovative energy technologies. These were representatives from venture capital companies, from young technology firms, and from the European Commission (see Figure 7.1).

For logistical reasons, the interaction with these participants was carried out in two steps. A workshop with representatives from venture capital and young technology companies was complemented by a subsequent round of interviews with representatives from the European Commission. While this two-stage format worked well in general, a certain drawback

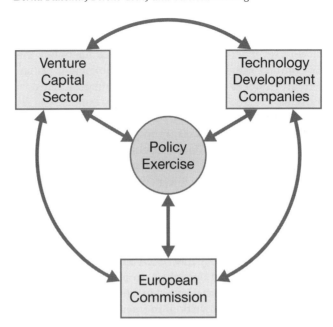

Figure 7.1 Actor groups involved in this policy exercise

was that sometimes both sides seemed to assign responsibility for missing action to the party not present.

Workshop participants included representatives from six venture capital companies in Belgium, France, Germany, and Italy, selected so that companies specializing in ecological energy investment were represented as well as companies who considered this field as not attractive compared with more conventional investment options. Representatives from seven young and innovative technology development companies in Germany, Switzerland, and the UK had been selected in order to include experience in energy conservation as well as renewable energy, and from the building sector as well as well as from the transport sector. Furthermore, a representative of an association in the sustainable energy sector, and of the unit responsible for socio-economic research on climate change within the European Commission, also contributed to the discussions. After the workshop, interviews were held with representatives of the European Commission to obtain their views on the suggestions made by the workshop participants. These included representatives from Commission units responsible for issues of economic and financial affairs, competition, energy, environment, and research, as well as from the Forward Studies Unit.

After an introduction to process and goals of the workshop, and a short briefing on climate change issues using results of the IMAGE model (Alcamo 1994), the workshop participants were invited to discuss opportunities for venture capital investments in energy efficiency and renewable energy technologies. They did this by developing plausible scenario stories of how selected technologies could achieve significant market shares (and thereby contribute to the EU's reduction targets for greenhouse gases) by 2010. The focus was on the use of energy efficiency and renewable energy technologies, especially in private households and the passenger transport sector. More details on how the scenario stories were created are discussed in the following section. The scenario stories and the discussions were then evaluated to identify common elements with the potential to enhance venture capital investments in energy-related technologies. On the basis of these workshop discussions, the research team made a summary of the major points addressed and discussed these in interviews with representatives from the European Commission.

The structured creation of scenario stories describing fictitious but plausible investment paths for selected technologies was essential for this exercise. It took some time for the participants to get used to working in this manner and to refrain from immediately discussing a collection of policies and measures they thought the EU should implement. By creating a situation that mimicked actual decision-making by different actors, this moderation technique helped to utilize fully the expertise of the workshop participants, who routinely take decisions on investment or production rather than on public policy. This may also have been important in the light of research suggesting that although venture capital experts may be good at making systematically consistent decisions, they may not always fully understand the criteria they use in this decision-making (Zacharakis and Meyer 1998).

Developing scenario stories in a "backcasting" mode

Introducing the creation of concrete scenario stories for investment patterns into policy exercises can result in procedures that are much more suitable for private sector participants. For this reason, the workshop participants were asked to develop hypothetical but plausible story-lines of how selected low-carbon technologies could achieve significant market shares by 2010. They were asked to consider two background scenarios for this. The common element in these scenarios was the assumption that the EU had committed itself to a 15 per cent emissions reduction target for 2010 (the EU negotiation position before the Kyoto Climate Conference). The major difference between the two scenarios was in the climate policies of the other OECD countries (especially the US and Japan). These story-lines were created in small parallel working groups. An evaluation of common elements in the different story-lines was the basis of developing more general suggestions in plenary discussions. These suggestions were then discussed in subsequent interviews with representatives of the European Commission.

A central element of the process that was unusual for most participants was the task of constructing the scenario stories backwards from the end point. That is: "If this technology is to have a significant market presence in 2010, this-and-this action must be undertaken by sector X in year Y at the latest." The participants were offered the following metaphor for this process.

Think of this process as building a house: in order to move in on date Z9, one needs to have finished painting by date Z8, in order to finish painting by Z8, one needs to have the walls finished by date Z7, and so on. The important difference is, however, that our stories should contain not only the temporal sequence, but, equally important, the causal chain of actions and reactions by various actors as well.

This approach was intended to help the participants concentrate on necessary stages in the interactions between the three actor groups. Only at the end were they supposed to see whether they would arrive at a plausible scenario needing first actions to take place not earlier than the time of the policy exercise (1997), including policies and measures the EU could implement currently to make the end results possible.

The creation of scenario stories was conducted in three iterations of small group work, with plenary discussions in between. For the first working group session, the workshop participants were spilt into two homogeneous working groups, representatives from venture capital companies on the one hand and those from young technology firms on the other. The rationale behind this was to allow the participants from each of the two sectors to clarify their points of view internally as a preparation for working in mixed groups later. In the first of three iterations of this procedure, it was not easy for the participants to work in the backcasting manner discussed above. Indeed, one of the groups focused directly on discussing general criteria for investments in energy efficiency and non-carbon energy technologies. While the second group used the procedure suggested, it took some time for the participants to get used to consistently work backwards. This group decided to assess hot water production technologies. Working backwards from the year 2010, in which a significant market share was to be obtained for alternative hot water production technologies, a scenario story along the following lines was developed.

By 2005 at the latest, production lines would have to be established by technology companies. This would mean that between 2000 and 2005 subsidies and standards would have to be introduced by the EU. These should already be announced prior to implementation as far back as possible, preferably in 1998, so that venture capital would become interested at that stage in time and would invest by 1999 or 2000. This was considered to be essential as seed and start-up phases were almost concluded for most of these sectors, and capital needs in the growth stage were large. The EU might implement a system of CO_2 emission allowances, e.g., limit CO_2 emission per litre of hot water produced. Overall, all participants agreed that it was of major importance that the EU or/and the national governments set signals so as to create market perspectives as early as possible and review them every 2–4 years.

It was interesting that in this first scenario story created at the workshop, there were only relatively few interactions between the venture capital and the technology sectors, and quite a number of expectations concerning actions by the EU.

This pattern changed in the subsequent two rounds of small group work, where the working groups were mixed so that they included both venture capital and technology company representatives, and where the participants had become more accustomed to working with scenario stories in a backcasting mode. This is illustrated with the example below from a working group in the last session. In this case, the participants decided to discuss in more detail the interactions between venture capital, technology and the EU without envisaging a specific technology example for this. The result is captured in the flip-chart diagram shown in Figure 7.2, which also illustrates the format that had been suggested to the small groups for developing the story lines.

This scenario story (in the discussions as well as in the diagram) showed markedly clearer interaction patterns between the different groups than was the case with scenario stories developed in the first phase of the workshop.

Overall, the policy exercise worked well. The suggestions developed by the participants at the workshop were an interesting input to the interviews with representatives from the European Commission, as discussed below. Most participants said that they had profited significantly from the experience, and would like to participate again in a similar exercise or recommend others to do so.

Results: how to support ecological energy investment?

Climate protection by reducing carbon dioxide emissions relies to a large extent on technological change. While early-stage investments in

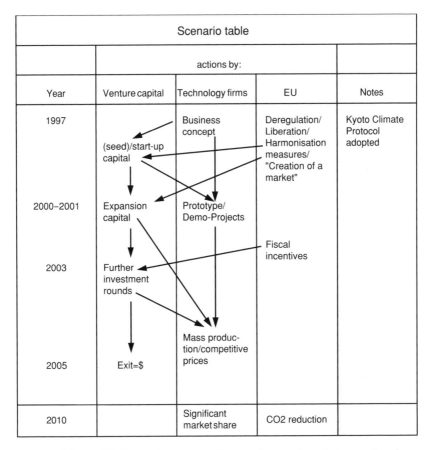

Scenario table				
	actions by:			
Year	Venture capital	Technology firms	EU	Notes
1997	(seed)/start-up capital	Business concept	Deregulation/ Liberation/ Harmonisation measures/ "Creation of a market"	Kyoto Climate Protocol adopted
2000–2001	Expansion capital	Prototype/ Demo-Projects		
2003	Further investment rounds		Fiscal incentives	
2005	Exit=$	Mass produc- tion/competitive prices		
2010		Significant market share	CO2 reduction	

Figure 7.2 Scenario story outline on interactions between the three actor groups

innovative technologies will be crucial, at the moment ecological energy investment is not a focus for most venture capital companies in Europe. On the one hand, high capital intensity, long timescales of innovation, and not always clear advantages from the consumer's point of view in parts of the energy sector make it especially necessary for small new players in this field to target suitable and favorable niches in a focused manner. On the other hand, disadvantages like the dominance of the market by a few large players, or the non-uniformity of the European energy market, would have to be overcome, before venture capital could be expected to support climate policy by investing on a larger scale. Policy measures would be necessary to make this possible, supporting a high growth potential for ecological energy solutions.

Results concerning policy measures suggested by the representatives of venture capital and technology companies at our workshop, and discussed with representatives of the European Commission in subsequent interviews, are briefly summarized in Box 7.2. More details on these measures, and their potential harmonization across Europe, are given in the following sections.

Box 7.2: Results on participants' views concerning policy measures

One of the major findings of the study discussed here was that carbon taxes, while seen as useful for supporting ecological energy investment in general, were not seen by the study participants from the private sector as the primary incentive for supporting private investment in this field.

- First, other suggested policy measures for supporting ecological energy investment in general included abolishing subsidies for fossil fuels, government export credit insurance for fossil fuel technologies, and renewable energy and energy efficiency obligations.
- Second, measures for lowering entry barriers for new companies in this field could include privatizing government monopolies, supporting selected ecological energy technologies, and simplifying and harmonizing technology-specific regulations as well as taxation and administrative requirements for technology companies across Europe.
- Third, the European venture capital sector in general could be supported by harmonizing venture capital regulations across Europe, simplifying cross-border investments, strengthening and harmonizing government guarantee schemes for investments in new technology companies, and providing tax breaks for "business angels." For supporting venture capital engagement in ecological energy investment in particular, lower taxes on gains, higher depreciation allowances, and allowances to defer tax liabilities arising on the exercise of share options until the shares are sold were suggested for ecological energy investments.

Supporting ecological energy investment in general

The general growth potential of a business sector is essential in determining whether or not venture capital will be invested there. Concerning ecological energy investment, this depends to a large extent on the relative growth potential of energy efficiency and renewable energies compared to more traditional energy solutions, especially fossil fuel burning. Policy measures that level the playing field, or even tip the balance toward more ecological energy solutions would be strong incentives for investors to get involved. As policy measures for increasing the share of ecological energy solutions in general have already been discussed extensively in the literature (see e.g., von Weizsäcker, Lovins, and Lovins 1997), here we focus mainly on different expectations concerning European harmonization or not of related policy measures.

The workshop participants from venture capital and technology companies saw liberalization and deregulation of energy markets as essential. Subsidies for coal production were seen as especially distorting. They also suggested that policy-makers eliminate tax exemptions that discriminate against the energy sector in general (e.g., abolish tax exemptions in the transport and building sectors, or bind them to energy efficiency). Furthermore, they thought that government export credit insurance schemes, which reduce the risk of doing business abroad, should be abolished for the export of large conventional power plants. They also suggested renewable energy and energy efficiency obligations, such as requiring automobile manufacturers to ensure that a certain percentage of their new cars sold in Europe are energy-efficient models, in the spirit of the widely noticed Californian approach. The workshop participants discussed all these issues on the European level. This holds also for a possible carbon tax, which was seen as giving incentives to reduce emissions, and thus to support ecological energy investment. Our workshop participants from venture capital and technology companies expected a carbon tax to be easier to introduce at the EU level, since most member states would be against introducing such a tax at the national level for fear of creating competitive disadvantages within Europe.

While our interview partners from the European Commission agreed with the workshop participants on the effectiveness of many of the suggested measures, they were more reserved about the feasibility of introducing them in a harmonized manner across Europe. Coordination between national governments and EU authorities was seen as necessary for changing subsidies or tax exemptions. Concerning government export credit insurance, interviewees from the Commission pointed out that attempts to reach harmonization here on the European level have failed so far, as national governments did not allow the EU to touch this politically sensitive tool. Our interview partners from the Commission agreed that obligations for clean vehicles in the Californian style would be highly effective. However, they were doubtful about the feasibility of such measures. In this case, coordination across Europe was not seen as the major problem but rather the likely resistance of the car lobby. Finally, the Commission representatives, while generally very much in favor of a carbon and energy tax, pointed out that years of negotiations had shown that the process of agreeing on such a tax at the European level is very difficult. In contrast to our workshop participants from the private sector, they expected it to be easier to introduce carbon taxes on a national basis.

Lowering entry barriers for new companies in this field

The attractiveness of a business sector for venture capital investment depends not only on the general growth potential of this sector, but also on the possibility for new players to enter that market. As venture capital works by buying part of a young company and supporting its expansion, a business sector where there is high growth but also high entry barriers for new players is not very attractive for such investment. Here the interests of the venture capital community may serve as a proxy for more general aspects of the health of a business sector. As true innovation often comes from new entrants in a market, the growth of a sector with high entry barriers for new players might not be very sustainable in the long run.

Workshop participants from the venture capital and technology sectors proposed that the EU should enforce decentralization measures such as privatizing government monopolies on the one hand, and limiting the dominance of large energy suppliers, perhaps by supporting small local combined heat and power generation, on the other. They also led a more general and intense discussion about setting standards. They remarked that the information technology sector has become much more attractive for venture capital since the introduction of standards relating to aspects such as the compatibility of interfaces, computer languages, and character sets. Similarly, standards concerning compatibility of building or vehicle components could allow small companies to operate in a more secure business environment. EU-wide standards would also help to harmonize the scattered European market for energy-related products. However, the participants warned that such standards should not be set arbitrarily by politicians alone, but should emerge at the industry level. Further, participants suggested supporting regional marketing campaigns for selected renewable energy technologies. And, finally, the participants remarked that both taxation and administrative requirements of small and innovative companies and also technology-specific regulations should be simplified and harmonized across Europe. This would decrease the need for cost- and time-intensive legal consultations and technical adaptations, which are difficult for small companies.

Most EU interviewees agreed that decentralization of the fossil energy supply sector would be a highly effective policy measure for lowering entry barriers. On the other hand, centralized systems were sometimes seen as advantageous in the sense that public policy could operate more easily in a more unified system than in one that is completely market based. Denmark, for example, with its centralized energy supply system, was more easily able to introduce co-generation and other schemes than would have been possible with a more decentralized system. An important obstacle to achieving a homogeneous level of decentralization throughout Europe was seen in differences in traditions concerning centralization or decentralization in different member states. Concerning standards, feelings were mixed. One counterargument was that advanced technologies were changing so rapidly that regulations would immediately become outdated. A contrasting view was that setting standards could provide a stimulus for innovation, although it might be difficult to impose them at the EU level. It was felt that there would only be voluntary agreements on this issue in the near future, as the EU had no instruments to enforce binding standards. Most of the interviewees from the Commission believed that specific market entry programs could indeed be effective for allowing small-scale operators to develop new technologies. However, there were some qualifications, including the point that "administrators are not very good at selecting winners." Finally, all interviewees from the Commission agreed that simplifying and harmonizing *technology-specific regulations* across Europe would be effective in ameliorating the business environment for small technology companies. However, the actual implementation was seen to be up to national governments, as the EU could only give recommendations here. In contrast to that, most interviewees did not consider the European harmonization of *taxation and administrative requirements* for technology companies as a priority. It was believed to be more important that such procedures should be transparent and non-discriminatory.

Facilitating venture capital backing for these new companies

Even in growth markets with low entry barriers, venture capital investment does not follow automatically. Venture capital investment in general is still weaker in the EU as compared to the US. In addition, the workshop participants saw the market potential for ecological energy solutions as very promising, but also as rather insecure. This was because much of this market potential depends on political processes that are rather hard to predict, and as there is not yet enough experience on what advances in energy technologies consumers will consider relevant and worthy of integration into their spending patterns. In order to improve the chances of venture capital backing of ecological energy investment, measures to support venture capital financing in Europe in general were seen as necessary, as well as measures supporting such investment in ecological energy solutions in particular.

First, from the point of view of venture capital companies, venture capital fund structures across Europe are extremely complex and inconsistent, and often discourage investors. In particular, in the case of cross-border investments the transaction costs can be prohibitive. Therefore, in accordance with EVCA (1996), participants suggested that efficient fund structures should be provided at the local, trans-national, European, and global levels.

Second, supporting "business angel" investment was suggested. This is capital provided to start-up companies by wealthy private investors, usually providing smaller amounts of funding at an earlier stage than most venture capital firms are able to invest. A British workshop participant suggested that tax incentives similar to the capital gains tax roll-over relief and retirement relief in the UK, giving great encouragement to business angels and entrepreneurs alike, should be introduced at the EU level.

Third, the participants mentioned government guarantee schemes to support the financing of new technology companies. In Denmark or Germany, for example, such schemes provide cheap loans or state guarantees for parts of realized losses on equity investment in young technology companies. Harmonizing such schemes across Europe was suggested in order to make the process of seeking such support easier and more transparent, and to favor investments in energy efficiency and renewable energy technologies by granting better conditions to small companies in that sector.

Finally, workshop participants suggested tax incentives for technology companies and their fund providers in general, and for energy efficiency and renewable energy investment in particular. Incentives for technology companies could take the form of lower taxes on gains and higher tax deductibility of losses. Incentives for investors could include allowances to defer any tax liabilities arising on the exercise of share options until the shares are sold, or to write off specific investments in energy efficiency and renewable energy technologies. However, participants cautioned that care should be taken to ensure that tax incentives do not stimulate artificial growth that may falter as soon as the incentives are removed, as happened to a certain extent in the German construction industry in the former East Germany.

The interviewees from the Commission generally agreed that the tax, legal, and administrative frameworks relating to venture capital investments in Europe need to be simplified and harmonized in order to strengthen the entire venture capital industry. However, it was questioned whether the member states would be able to come to an agreement, since this matter was the responsibility of national governments. Also, tax incentives for business angel investment were considered to be the responsibility of the governments of individual member states. Government guarantee schemes were seen as very effective by our interview partners from the Commission, but the probability of member states reaching a consensus on harmonization here was seen as being rather low. According to one interviewee, such harmonization would not be very sensible anyway, since what is regarded as an acceptable level of risk in investment depends on the cultural characteristics of different countries. However, it was also pointed out that the EU has already set up a guarantee scheme directly at the EU level – the Growth and Environment Scheme – which provides guarantees on loans that will benefit the environment. While specific tax incentives were seen as very effective in that they would give a clear signal in favour of renewable and efficient energy sources, it was again remarked that this was mainly an issue in the responsibility of national governments.

The background of global climate diplomacy

The suggestions discussed above were extracted from concrete scenario stories developed by the workshop participants on plausible development paths of innovative ecological energy technologies. These scenario stories were developed in the context of two background scenarios concerning global climate negotiations. The common element in both scenarios was the assumption that the EU had committed itself to a 15 per cent emissions reduction target for 2010 (the EU negotiation position before the Kyoto Climate Conference). The major difference between the two scenarios was in the climate policies of the other OECD countries (especially the US and Japan). In one scenario, these other players were assumed to share the EU commitments. In the other scenario, it was assumed that the US and Japan would not agree to similar targets, but the EU would keep these reduction targets unilaterally. An important finding of the workshop was that the participants saw the chances of a successful European climate policy as rather robust with regard to the outcomes of global negotiations (see Box 7.3).

Box 7.3: Business participants' views on unilateral European climate policy

One of the most striking findings of our policy exercise study, conducted just before the Kyoto Conference of the Parties to the UN Framework Convention on Climate Change, was that differences between two background scenarios concerning global climate negotiations were not expected to have grave implications for successful ecological energy investment in Europe. In the views of the workshop participants, a failure at Kyoto – i.e., no international binding commitment to reduce carbon dioxide emissions – would not necessarily have a negative effect on the investment decisions of European venture capitalists, as long as the EU committed itself to unilateral reduction goals. This was due to two counterbalancing forces: the non-participation of other OECD countries in emission reduction goals would mean smaller global markets for innovative energy-efficient technologies, but also less competition from outside Europe. This could give European companies an opportunity to take the lead and to profit from learning curves early on. So, if the EU clearly communicated its commitment to unilateral reduction targets, Europe could act successfully independently of the rest of the world.

In addition, the workshop participants recommended that if international agreements are reached, these should include "joint implementation" and similar "flexibility mechanisms," that is, mechanisms allowing countries with high pollution abatement costs to invest in countries with lower costs, and to receive credits for the resulting reductions in their own emissions. This was despite the huge practical difficulties in implementing a system of fully tradable emission allowances on a global or European scale (for experiences with a scheme of tradable emission permits developed in the US under the 1990 Clean Air Act amendments, see Pearce (1995)). While the interviewees from the Commission regarded joint implementation and the trading of carbon dioxide emission allowances as effective instruments in principle, some doubts were expressed as to the feasibility of these instruments due to the incompatibility of different national interests within Europe.

Conclusions: how much European harmonisation?

In this chapter we have discussed methods and results of a participatory process concerning options for supporting venture capital engagement in ecological energy investment as part of a European climate policy. This study included a workshop with representatives from venture capital companies and young technology firms from across Europe, and a round of subsequent interviews with representatives from the European Commission. The rationale for focusing on synergies between venture capital investment and European climate policy was that this is still an underresearched field compared to other climate policy options, and could be crucial in supporting the early stage of ecological energy innovations. Supporting venture capital engagement in ecological energy investment could lead to both greenhouse emission reductions and job creation, thus establishing synergies between environmental and employment goals in Europe. Given current constraints on public spending in Europe, encouraging private investment in ecological innovations can be expected to become increasingly important for European environmental policy.

Currently, ecological energy investment is not a focus of the European venture capital industry. Results from our study indicate that changing this would require concrete changes in policies and incentives. Venture capital and technology company representatives suggested possible options for this in discussions about scenario stories during the workshop. These measures concerned first, the market growth potential for ecological energy solutions in general, second, the ability of new companies to enter this market, and third, the feasibility of venture capital financing for such new companies. These measures were then discussed in interviews with representatives from the European Commission, from units responsible for issues of economic and financial affairs, competition, energy, environment, and research, as well as from the Forward Studies Unit. During this process, interesting points concerning the harmonization of such policy measures across Europe were raised. While there have been many debates in the literature about the roles of European and member state institutions and about the appropriate level of harmonization across Europe in general (for an overview of institutionalist approaches, emphasizing the role of European institutions, versus intergovernmentalist approaches, stressing the role of member state institutions, see Puchala (1999); for a recent discussion of the appropriate level of harmonizing corporate governance rules across Europe, see Lannoo (1999)), here we focus on differences in views between representatives of the private sector and European policy-makers concerning European harmonization of policy measures supporting venture capital investment in ecological energy technologies in particular.

Concerning many policy measures, the workshop participants from venture capital and young technology companies preferred to discuss them at the European level and saw harmonization of regulatory frameworks across EU member states as an effective support for private investment in Europe. In contrast to that, our interview partners from the European Commission – while generally seeing the policy measures suggested at the workshop as useful – were much more reserved concerning European harmonization of these measures. In some cases this seems due to negative experiences with harmonization attempts so far. Attempts at harmonization of government export credit insurance were said to have met with the resistance of national governments to let the EU touch this sensitive tool. And, despite years of negotiations, it seems to have been impossible for an agreement to be reached on a common carbon tax throughout Europe. Tax incentives were often seen to be the responsibility of national governments rather than the EU. Experiences with such difficulties in European harmonization may have led to disillusionment among European policy-makers concerning the feasibility of reaching common European solutions.

However, harmonization was sometimes not even seen as desirable by our interview partners from the Commission. Harmonizing government guarantee schemes for venture capital investment across Europe might not be sensible given different cultural norms across Europe of what levels of risk are acceptable in investments. Achieving a homogeneous level of decentralization of the energy sector across Europe might be counter to differences in traditions between member states concerning more centralized or more decentralized solutions. Also, while European harmonization of technology specific regulations was seen as useful, concerning taxation and administrative requirements for technology companies, transparency and non-discrimination were seen as more important than European harmonization by our interview partners from the Commission.

The differences in expectations for European harmonization of policy measures between the workshop participants from the private sector and our interview partners from the European Commission might in part be interpreted as a disjunction of the policy process with the realities of commercial practice. Perhaps concerning some issues, European integration of business communities has already moved further ahead than policy-makers, busy with keeping the European project going on the public policy side, have noticed. On the other hand, representatives from the private sector might underestimate the political difficulties of agreeing on common European solutions on many sensitive issues. But there may be an additional issue that neither our workshop participants from the private sector nor our interview partners from the European Commission have mentioned explicitly. While harmonizing technology-specific regulations across Europe may be essential in creating a large enough homogeneous market for new technologies, national or regional differences in tax regulations might actually be an advantage for private investment as long as trans-border investments are simplified. This would create competition between different tax regimes as private investors could shop around for the best conditions for making profitable investments. As Hans Tietmeyer pointed out when preparing to step down as president of the German Bundesbank (*International Herald Tribune* 1999), a main implication of the introduction of the Euro is just the increasing competition between the tax regulations and also welfare benefits of different EU member states. It could be an attractive option for venture capital engagement in ecological energy investment if the EU agreed on common technology specific regulations and a common push toward limiting greenhouse gas emissions by supporting private investment in new technologies, but if different national or sub-national ways to do this were thrown into competition with each other.

Finally, an interesting point came up during the workshop on harmonization on the global scale. According to workshop participants, if the EU were to introduce policies unilaterally for supporting greenhouse gas reductions by supporting technology investment, this could be at least as attractive as the harmonization of such policies between all developed economies around the globe. This was due to two counterbalancing forces: the non-participation of other OECD countries in emission reduction policies would mean smaller global markets for innovative energy-efficient technologies, but also less competition from outside, giving European businesses a competitive edge by profiting from learning curves early on. It seems that from the point of view of our workshop participants from the private sector, the size of the EU is appropriate for the successful introduction of new technologies. While the markets of individual member states might be too small to introduce new technologies successfully, the European level might be an attractive first step for such a venture before tackling global markets.

The policy exercise discussed in this chapter, involving representatives from the private sector and from public administration, is one illustration of how specific stakeholder groups can be included in participatory processes in sustainability science. Differences and similarities between such participatory procedures will depend on which groups of participants are involved. For example, collage production may be more suitable for IA

Focus Groups with citizens, while the creation of scenario-story diagrams like in the present study may be more suitable in workshop processes with business representatives. And participatory processes with different groups can be linked, as we have seen in the example of using the preference for energy reduction expressed in the citizen groups, discussed in earlier chapters, as an input to the policy exercise with representatives from business and administration, discussed in this chapter. We hope that our discussion of this policy exercise study, as well as the participatory procedures discussed in the following chapters, will be useful to others who want to explore the challenge of public participation in sustainability science. And we are eager to learn about the discoveries they will make along the way.

CHAPTER EIGHT

COOL: exploring options for carbon dioxide reduction in a participatory mode

Willemijn Tuinstra, Marleen van de Kerkhof,
Matthijs Hisschemöller, and Arthur Mol

Introduction

The ULYSSES study has been an interesting exercise, unique in its variety of research groups spread all over Europe with different research backgrounds and different foci, yet all embarking on a shared voyage. What does this experience teach us for other initiatives of participatory projects? What news do the voyagers bring to the ones ashore and what do they tell about new coasts and the adventures on their way?

We address this question from the point of view of researchers taking up a similar endeavor, though with a different starting point and looking from a different angle. The authors are involved in the Climate OptiOns for the Long term Project (COOL). The Dutch COOL project focuses on long-term (up to 2050) options to realize far-reaching carbon dioxide emission reductions.[1] Stakeholder dialogues are central to this project. As in the study discussed in the first parts of this volume, the use of knowledge and know-how of experts other than scientific experts is an important element in COOL.

In this chapter we discuss experiences from the ULYSSES project that are especially relevant for other Participatory Integrated Assessment projects like COOL. We will start with a short introduction to the COOL project in order to make clear why the ULYSSES experiences are relevant for COOL. This includes some reflection on differences and similarities between the two research efforts. Then we turn to specific experiences gained from ULYSSES, which focus on the process, the outcomes, and the multilayered purpose of the project. Within the scope of this chapter this cannot be a thorough analysis. Rather we give snap-shots of outcomes

---

[1] The COOL project is financed by the Dutch Research programme on Global Air pollution and climate change. By the time of publishing this chapter, the project has already been concluded. See for more information and final reports: http://www.nop.nl/cool

and experiences from the ULYSSES project relevant to other projects, especially the Dutch COOL project. We conclude with a short comment on the need for gaining experience with this kind of process.

Climate OptiOns for the Long term

General

Central to the COOL project is a series of so-called dialogue meetings in which stakeholders from industry and business, environmental and consumer NGOs, and unions, as well as stakeholders at different levels of government, elaborate long-term strategies for realizing 50–80 per cent carbon dioxide emission reductions by 2050 (compared to 1990 levels). It is important to note that the COOL project, unlike ULYSSES, does not involve "citizens" as such, but stakeholders giving input from their professional background. The Dialogues in the COOL project run simultaneously at three different levels: the national (Dutch) level, the European level, and the global level.

The National Dialogue includes four different sector groups: Industry and Energy, Agriculture, Traffic and Transport, and Housing. Each sector group consists of a balanced selection of stakeholders.[2] On the European level two sector groups meet: Transport and Industry/Energy. The participants have similar backgrounds to those of the participants in the National Dialogue, with the difference that they are operating on a European level. The composition of the Global Dialogue Group is somewhat different: this is one group, which includes representatives of the countries in the United Nations Framework Convention on Climate Change (UN-FCCC) process and of only a limited number of environmental and business NGOs.

The groups meet several times over a period of 14 months; the groups in the National Dialogue seven times, and the groups in the European and Global Dialogues four times. In this chapter we focus mainly on the National and European Dialogues.

Scientific input

Scientific input in the COOL dialogues is organized in various ways. Unlike in IA Focus Groups, in the COOL National and European Dialogues

---

[2] The sector Industry and Energy in the National Dialogue, for example, includes participants from, among others, the National Investment Bank, Greenpeace, Akzo Nobel, the Ministry of Economic Affairs, the Ministry of Environment, CORUS B.V., Shell International, the Centre for Church and World, and the Dutch Centre for clean technology.

computer simulations and models are not directly used during the discussions themselves. Only in the COOL Global Dialogue do the participants interactively use a computer model. In the other Dialogues a special scientific team prepares background documents and fact sheets. During each meeting, participants can formulate questions, which, if possible, are answered in the next session, taking into account different sources and pointing out the uncertainties. Also it is possible to invite special guests to the sessions to give their views on subjects on which neither the scientific team nor the participants feel that they have enough expertise. Another task of the scientific team is to do background calculations for the various steps toward the strategic visions as constructed by the participants. As in the ULYSSES research, the roles of the scientific team and the project team guiding the process are separated.

Though the processing of scientific information for stakeholders is central in all three of the COOL Dialogues, the purpose of this is not to make stakeholders familiar with climate science as such; rather, the dialogue groups generate ideas that are substantiated by scientific evidence and arguments, and they conduct a kind of extended peer review. The dialogue groups react to and evaluate the knowledge offered in terms of relevance for participants' visions and their specific information needs.

Participatory approach

In its approach to Integrated Environmental Assessment (IEA) the COOL project intends to apply and to blend both analytical methods and participatory methods (for an overview of relevant methods, see Rotmans 1998). With the need for a participatory approach some important observations can be made. First, climate change constitutes a so-called unstructured problem for public policy. Unstructured problems involve major uncertainties about what knowledge is relevant for understanding and addressing the issue, and uncertainties and conflicts about the values at stake (Hisschemöller 1993). Second, many stakeholders perceive the issue as remote in time, space, and personal experience, and hence not really as an issue of direct concern, whereas for others, the stakes can be very high, especially for those actors who are directly affected by the climate change policy. The third observation relates to differences in scale and levels of abstractness. The conceptualization of the climate problem and solutions from a global perspective do not easily match the priority given to problems and solutions at the local level. The dialogue should be designed in such a way that the participants have sufficient freedom to address their own policy questions and information needs, but at the same time should produce strategic visions that concentrate on reducing carbon dioxide emissions. In the IA Focus Groups discussed in previous chapters, the concept of urban lifestyles is used to bring the climate change problem more in line with the context of the daily life of the citizen. In the same way, in the COOL project participants are asked to connect climate policy to strategic visions for one particular sector.

In the design of the COOL Dialogues several aspects of participation play a role. Following Mayer (1997), and Mayer and Geurts (1998), we mention here a few of these aspects: mediation (What do participants know about mutual values? What level of consensus can they reach?). Coordination (What interdisciplinary knowledge should participants generate?). Coproduction (What is the relation with other policy issues or sectors? What shared responsibility can participants achieve?). And learning (Are core knowledge and attitudes changing? Are new styles and approaches to policy-making explored?). These aspects can also be found in the research discussed in the first two parts of this volume.

Differences between COOL and ULYSSES

It should be noted that there are some major differences between the ULYSSES and COOL projects, which limit the extent to which comparisons can be made and lessons drawn. One important difference has already been mentioned: ULYSSES explicitly focuses on ordinary citizens, while COOL focuses on specific stakeholder groups in certain sectors of society. Another difference is that COOL has a clear focus on the long term (2050) and a clear radical environmental goal (-80 per cent carbon dioxide emissions) determined by the project team in advance, and explored by the participants in terms of feasibility at the end of the dialogue. In ULYSSES, setting the final goal was part of the dialogue process.

Thus, ULYSSES and COOL have quite different starting points. However, the experiences from ULYSSES can be of great relevance for COOL, both in terms of process and of substance.

Learning from experiences

Process

The rationale of the ULYSSES study is described in Chapter 1 of this volume. Within the research field of Integrated Assessment (IA) there is a need to develop participatory procedures for the involvement of stakeholders, ranging from ordinary citizens to business people. Within the context of the climate change debate, the background for this need is that if an effective climate policy is to emerge, actions taking place at the level of national and international environmental policy must be combined with actions involving various kinds of stakeholders. Without integrating the points of view of citizens and other stakeholders, environmental policy runs the risk of getting stalled in the early implementation phase.

However, what is important here is not simply getting policy advice from stakeholders or consensus statements from citizens resulting from a negotiation process. Not just words count, but webs of argumentation and stakeholders' underlying assumptions (Mason and Mitroff 1981). This was a starting point for the research in ULYSSES, and it is an important point to keep in mind for research groups undertaking similar processes.

The lines of argumentation are as important as the statements or conclusions. Revealing lines of argumentation facilitates the learning of the participants from each other during the process. It also helps to clarify the context of statements and conclusions. Stakeholders need to understand each other's assumptions (Mason and Mitroff 1981). In the discussions in the different stakeholder groups in the COOL project much attention is given to working modes that help to reveal the different lines of argumentation. Final strategic visions are a clear end product of the COOL Dialogues, but they will be more relevant if they clearly show the different lines of argumentation and the mutual learning processes that have led to their formulation. Stakeholder dialogue is a form of problem structuring, that is, the identification, confrontation, and – where possible – integration of the most divergent views with respect to a given problem situation (Hisschemöller 1993). To a certain extent, conflict can be productive, as – if it is managed properly – it can highlight the pros and cons of different options and the underlying argumentation structure. As also stated several times in the preceding chapters, this kind of setting of a group discussion is meant to support debates instead of settling them.

Substantive outcome: citizen reports and strategic visions

For outsiders curious about the outcome of such an exploratory study like ULYSSES, an obvious question is: "So what did those citizens come up with in the end?" In Chapter 6 the research team reports on the different kinds of output from the groups, ranging from citizen reports to logbooks and video-tapes.

Each of these outputs has a substantive content. Though the research team stresses that the main goal was to advance the research agenda of Participatory Integrated Assessment, they also express the hope that the indicative findings regarding citizens' informed opinions and recommendations on addressing climate change and urban sustainability are of use for both the research and the policy community. And indeed, in the end also the substantive outcomes appeared to matter. Participation, process, and form have to be related to the substantive results.

Outcomes from the citizen reports

For the COOL project, we feel that the overview and observations with regard to the citizen reports are interesting for two different reasons. First, the series of questions dealt with in the IA Focus Group citizen reports (see the list in Chapter 6, p. 129) show some similarities to the questions that are asked in the different steps of the COOL process leading up to the final strategic visions. For example, within the European component of the COOL project, the questions to be addressed in the strategic visions are:

(a) How will Europe, and the selected sectors in particular, look in 2050, assuming that the 80 per cent target has been achieved?
(b) Which steps have to be taken in order to reach 80 per cent reduction of carbon dioxide emissions?
(c) Where and when should responses be taken and by whom?
(d) What barriers are expected to these actions?

These questions are explored in COOL with a "backcasting" methodology briefly discussed in Box 8.1.

Second, even though the substantive outcomes of the citizen reports from the IA Focus Groups have to be seen in their context and to be treated with care, it is interesting to look on what they really say. The proposals of the citizens are in fact quite sophisticated. Even if this didn't come as a surprise to the ULYSSES research team, for others it is an interesting result. The citizens' proposals are, for example, quite comparable to the initial proposals formulated by the "expert" stakeholders taking part in the COOL Dialogues.

For example, the suggestion from the Venice citizens (Group B, 2 June 1997, see Chapter 6) to increase dissemination of information in order to bring about awareness and responsibility is very much in line with the suggested long-term information plan suggested by participants in the second COOL Europe workshop. Also, the plea for establishing common objectives to be attained by setting well-defined steps can be linked directly to the request of industry stakeholders in COOL to governments to be clear and consistent in their goals and standards. If there is no clear and consistent policy, it is difficult for stakeholders to act and take decisions, especially regarding long-term and strategic choices.

From this point of view it is also interesting to see what the citizens in the IA Focus Groups see as barriers to action. Lack of action from government is mentioned but also power relations: economic interests

Box 8.1: "Backcasting" methodology applied in the COOL project

Within the COOL project, the methodology of backcasting has been operationalized in five main steps, illustrated in the following figure and briefly explained below.

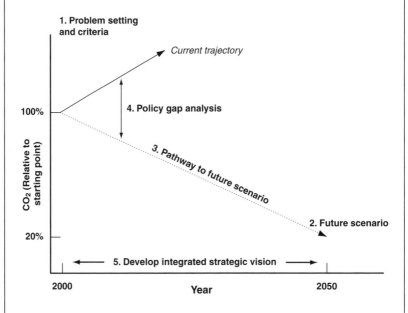

Step 1 – Define the problem and set the criteria for a solution (a reduction in greenhouse gas emissions and 80 per cent carbon dioxide emission reduction between 1990 and 2050 for the OECD countries, respectively). *Step 2* – Develop an "image of the future," an image of the social system or sector in 2050 that meets the requirements set by the criteria. *Step 3* – Path analysis: an analysis is made of the pathway from the image of 2050 back to today to identify the transformations that are necessary, the lead-time for different options that can contribute to such transformations (e.g., rate of development and diffusion of fuel cell technology), the crucial actors and conditions that make such options work, and the starting time to make these options contribute to the final image. *Step 4* is a comparison of current trends – not only in greenhouse gas emissions, but also in energy production and use, transport demand and supply, agricultural production and consumption – and the desirable trends according to the path analysis. This gap

analysis provides us with ideas on the necessary policies for the coming years to close this gap and set in motion the required social transformations. Finally, *Step 5* entails the formulation of an integrated strategic vision, in which the outcomes of the former four steps are integrated into one document. That document brings together the possible options and necessary measures to be taken, the time paths for these options and measures, the conditions that support these options measures, and the coalition of actors that are crucial for implementing these options and measures.

and lobbies. Some of the stakeholders in COOL represent certain economic interests and lobbies. In some cases, the COOL participants perceive the same barriers as the ULYSSES participants, in other cases the COOL participants are more optimistic about opportunities. For example, the COOL participants are far more enthusiastic about the possibilities for more cooperation instead of competition between transport companies and between companies and government in order to achieve a European-wide logistical information system for transport that would add to more sustainable transport planning.

In analyzing the expectations and behavior of the citizens themselves, the barriers for action mentioned are induced consumption needs and the expectation that most people are not prepared to decrease living standards. At the same time from the IA Focus Group collages discussed in Chapter 4, the conclusion is drawn that for the participants, strong reductions of energy use are more desirable than business-as-usual and that the precautionary principle should be applied. Participants in the COOL process expressed the need to know more about the view of consumers on the climate problem, their ideas on actions to be taken and their perception of the need for behavioral change. In this respect, the IA Focus Group citizen reports form interesting illustration material for the discussions in COOL. To some extent, the differences in group composition make the two projects complementary.

Outcomes from the stakeholder dialogue on venture capital
and climate policy

Other substantive information that is relevant for the COOL Dialogues are findings from the stakeholder dialogue concerning venture capital and climate policy (see Chapter 7).

This specific stakeholder dialogue is even more like the COOL Dialogues than is the case for the IA Focus Groups with citizens, also concerning the design of the process.[3] Proposals like increases in energy prices, changes in tax exemptions, government guarantee schemes and subsidies, as well as a plea for stronger harmonization return in the COOL Europe discussions as well. Of special interest to COOL is the comparison given in Chapter 7 between the outcomes of the stakeholder dialogue and the interviews with members of the European Commission. The EU seems to be much more reserved about the possibilities for the harmonization of policy measures than the participants in the stakeholder dialogue.

Directly of relevance for the COOL Dialogues is also the statement that policy measures are needed to provide targeted support for venture capital engagement in ecological energy investments. The question of whether this should be on the European or at the member state level has been a point of consideration within COOL as well.

Among the COOL participants there is the idea that governments should be urged to fund research and facilitate breakthroughs in technology development. In this respect the recommendations of the citizens and other stakeholders in the research discussed earlier in this volume are similar: the EU and national governments should be clear in communicating their commitment to reduction targets and act accordingly and consistently.

Multilayered purpose projects: participants and ownership

The research discussed earlier in this volume is an example of a study with a multilayered purpose. Several groups have been involved in the study, each with its own goal: the participants, the research team, the funding agency, local groups which were involved etc. In fact, Participatory Integrated Assessment projects are always multilayered. A long list of addressees and objectives can be formulated, often not completely without internal contradictions. What is the main product? The process, the outcome, the networks, the lessons that the research team has learned? Who is the main user? The participants, the funding agency, the policymakers, your fellow researchers? All users will push for the output of the project that they defined as the most important for themselves. A research team taking up such a project has to keep many balls in the air at the same time. Following the ULYSSES experience, we will examine one of those "juggling-balls" a little more closely: the role of the participants and their ownership of the process (see Box 8.2).

---

[3] There is one participant in the COOL process who also participated as stakeholder in the ULYSSES stakeholder dialogue on venture capital.

Box 8.2: The role of the participants and their ownership of the process

From the experiences in Venice and St Helens as described in Chapter 2 of this volume we learn that it is very important for the participants to have insight into the conditions and the scope of their personal and group involvement in the process. Important issues mentioned in this respect are: Context and objectives (Why are we meeting? What are the practical objectives and rules? Who is behind the meetings?); Knowledge (What kind of information is being provided to us? How do we discuss the topics? What kind of information do we provide?); Assessments (How do we, and others, interpret and assess knowledge? What will be done with the assessments?).

Not only is it motivating for the participants themselves to know what they can expect and what they can gain and contribute. It is also useful, not to say essential, for the process itself when the participants "own" the process and have a commitment toward it and toward its end product. The more the participants get the opportunity to define for themselves the objectives of their meetings, the relevant issues, the relevant policy arenas etc. the more they feel responsible for the process and for the end product. Of course, the meetings and discussions have to remain within the scope of the project: it is a challenge for the research team to keep the discussion to the point and at the same time not to steer too much and smother creativity. The ULYSSES study has shown that it is possible to bring this "ownership" about: both in "research" or "policy for real" settings. For future projects this is an important lesson. Within the National Dialogue of the COOL project one way of trying to facilitate "ownership" is by having a participant instead of a project team member chairing the meetings. Another way is by inviting participants to bring topics of interest to themselves to the table and to contribute major expert input in the dialogue on specific topics. The ownership in the COOL process is especially important, because of the ambition that the strategic visions produced by the participants should have an effect on the policymaking process.

Closing remarks

In this chapter, snap-shots have been shown of relevant outcomes and experiences from the ULYSSES project for other projects, especially the Dutch COOL project. These outcomes and experiences concern both process (the importance of revealing lines of argumentation, the importance of mutual learning and of ownership), and substance (the importance of dissemination of information, the need for international harmonization of policy). There might be some skeptics who will say those are only trivialities or things you could have known beforehand. However, the proof of the pudding is in the eating, and while eating, the pudding might be different than originally expected. Columbus was quite sure that he knew another route to India and that was the reason that he set sail to go there. On the way he discovered America. The ULYSSES voyagers might have found some things they had expected on their way, but also they have discovered many unexpected shores and strange animals. In the end the most important thing is that an example is given and experiences have been gained. It is a motivation for other groups to experiment as well. At the same time it is important to note that though one should certainly learn from experiences in other projects (and we know now that America exists), Participatory Integrated Assessment is still a matter of learning by doing. Constantly changing internal developments and external conditions force you to change the voyage. Depending on the passengers embarking on your voyage, you have to adjust your program. Depending on the weather, you have to change your course. Even if your colleagues told you several times how to find your way in New York, you will still reach your destination faster once you have actually been there. For each project the contexts have to be explored again and the researchers themselves have to go through a learning experience too. Though this is not easy, it is exciting!

CHAPTER NINE

Expert stakeholder participation in the Thames region

Thomas E. Downing, Karen Bakker, Kate Lonsdale,
Neil Summerton, Erik Swyngedouw, and
Consuelo Giansante

Introduction

Social and institutional adaptation to climate change impacts must take account of present coping ability and how stakeholders and institutions are likely to evolve over the next few decades. Motivating effective adaptation requires participation; sustainability science in general, and integrated assessments in particular, must blend the formalisms of models with knowledge of institutional change. The ULYSSES project pioneered methods of public participation in integrated environmental assessment, with a focus on climate change and urban greenhouse gas emissions. Citizen Integrated Assessment (IA) Focus Groups were developed and tested in seven cities in Europe. Furthermore, a stakeholder dialogue was conducted with sub-sets of experts, concerning venture capital investment and climate policy.

This chapter relates the experiences of the Social and Institutional Responses to Climatic Change and Climatic Hazards (SIRCH) project to these earlier experiences. The SIRCH project benefited from the examples set by the ULYSSES team. The following section summarizes our stakeholder analysis, using drought management in the Thames region as an example. An outline of scenarios of future drought risk and the analytical methods being developed illustrates the relevance of the research discussed in the first two parts of the present volume to our analyses.

The SIRCH project evaluated capacity to adapt to climate change, and the adaptive processes likely to be employed by stakeholders.[1] The project

[1] The SIRCH project was funded by the European Union, Contract No. ENV4 – CT97 – 0447. The Environmental Change Institute, Oxford University, was the project coordinator. Similar exercises of scenario building and evaluation were being carried out in the other case study regions. Further details: working papers on institutions (Bakker *et al.* 1999), demography (Pedregal Mateos 1999), technology (Riesco Chueca 1999),

includes case studies of climatic hazards in southern England (drought and flood), The Netherlands (flood), and southern Spain (drought).

An earlier EU project (Downing, Olsthoorn, and Tol 1999) reviewed prospective impacts of climate change in Europe, including subsidence, drought, floods, windstorms, and heat stress. That project adopted a conventional climate change impact assessment, with a linear construction of: climate change scenario → first-order impacts → adaptation measures → socio-economic impact → policy implications. At the conclusion of the project, this "climate scenario-driven" construction of climate change impact assessment was felt to be unsatisfactory. It presumes that we know much more about future climates, and especially extreme events, than current models are able to deliver. As a result, the entire chain of assessment is built on a shaky foundation.

However, many researchers are convinced that climate change will have significant impacts, and indeed that the distribution and intensity of climatic hazards is already showing the first signs of global warming. In such a case, adaptation to climate change will hinge critically on our ability to cope with changing risks of climatic hazards. It is the prospects for coping, as processes of stakeholder-institutional adaptation, that are the subject of the SIRCH project.

Two climatic hazards that have widespread implications for spatial policy are drought and floods. Both involve many stakeholders in negotiated constructions of the risk and risk reduction measures. Both tend to have poor institutional mechanisms for responding to changing risk, partly reflecting the diversity of roles and jurisdictions.

The adaptation challenge can be viewed as the adequacy of coping with present risks. Hurricane Mitch, the Mozambique floods, the winter floods in Britain in 2000/01 and even the French winter windstorms of 2000 suggest that this is a formidable challenge. Climate change presents a further challenge, of coping with changing risks as they unfold over the time scale of the next few decades and longer. To address this challenge requires a research methodology that focuses specifically on the processes of stakeholder and institutional adaptation.

To do this, the SIRCH methodology follows an inverse approach. The SIRCH methodology can be portrayed, somewhat idealistically, as the difference between ecological modernism and a hybrid political ecology (Table 9.1). The emphasis is on characterizing the nexus of present

stakeholders (Giansante 2000), new institutional economics (Calatrava, Garrido, and Iglesias 1999), and background material to each case study (Bakker *et al.* 2000; Tol *et al.* 1999). Contact the lead author for the final report. Some of these issues will be explored in a related EU project, Freshwater Integrated Resource Management with Agents, see www.cpm.mmu.ac.uk/firma.

Table 9.1 *Two approaches to climate impact assessment*

	Conventional climate change impact assessment	Adaptation as social and institutional learning
Intellectual tradition	Rational choice and ecological modernism	Political ecology with hybrid, participatory methods; new institutional–stakeholder analysis
Climate change	External, real risk, probabilistic estimates of mean changes and climatic hazards required in order to plan specific adaptation measures	Risk is socially constructed – negotiated between stakeholders; future of climate hazards is highly uncertain, especially at the scale customarily required for decision analysis; awareness of climate change is linked to signal extreme events – knowledge of future risk is uneven
Impacts	Linked impacts models are required to establish sensitivity to climatic variations and evaluate specific adaptation measures	Multiple stakeholders have competing (and competitive) objectives, with different interpretations of impacts, thresholds for concerns, and planning horizons and means
Adaptation	Focus on near-term measures identified by experts (e.g., water-saving technology?)	Need for long-term strategies (monitoring, decision-making, financing); options are proposed through political and regulatory processes
Policy evaluation	Decision support systems required to translate climate change impacts into management strategies for coping with present and near-future climatic risks	Stakeholders use different means of evaluation, and do not agree over methods for appraising long-term futures; some stakeholders are not entrained in decision-making at this time-scale and are powerless
Decision-making	Managers need to be aware of climate change as an issue, and adopt long-term planning frameworks; requires external support, education, and training	Institutions are continually changing (e.g., regulatory regimes); adaptation evolves in a hierarchy of decisions that matches the geographic and temporal scale of climate change itself
Methodology	Linked models; single or tractable number of stakeholders who agree to evaluation criteria	Representation of multiple stakeholders in deliberative processes of long-term futures with different levels of adaptation, means for identifying critical pathways, and decision nodes

stakeholder-institutional-resource relationships. This contrasts with conventional climate change impact assessment, the linear model referred to above. In the main, the emphasis is on scenarios of change that challenge present resource management, rather than prediction of socio-economic-political conditions and their susceptibility to climate change. Thus, we see adaptation to climate change, given the deep uncertainty, as essentially a process of stakeholder learning and institutional development, rather than evaluation of specific measures and risk assessment.

There are similarities and distinctions between the SIRCH project and the research discussed in the first two parts of this volume. Both are examples of participatory processes of stakeholder engagement in integrated assessment (or our wider label of political ecology as distinct from classical climate change adaptation studies). SIRCH is closer to the venture capital panels (Chapter 7) than to the IA Focus Groups with citizens, in that the stakeholders represent a specific sector rather than citizens in general. Box 9.1 compares expert-stakeholder and citizen participation.

Box 9.1: Expert-stakeholder and citizen participation

Participatory Integrated Assessment differs somewhat in goals and means for expert stakeholders and citizen panels.

- Expert stakeholders are likely to seek solutions to current problems, whereas general awareness of environmental issues is usually the focus for a citizen panel.
- The analyst is an expert for citizens, but may be more of a generalist (or concerned with integration) for expert stakeholders who have a wealth of specialist knowledge.
- Expert stakeholders are familiar with formal modeling, and often desire their development for specific problems; citizens are more likely to be interested in argumentative approaches with varying enthusiasm for formal models.

The stakeholders in the SIRCH project are part of a regulatory regime where decision-making is a mixture of cooperation (e.g., drinking water standards) and competition (e.g., between water companies and the economic regulator). This is "real world" decision-making – climate change is already part of the rules and political discourse. In contrast, the panels discussed in the first parts of this book appear to be more open-ended. Either citizens are asked to consider climate change, with no real decisions at stake, or stakeholder panels are making choices but in a framework that is only emerging at the national and EU levels. Global change is only partly a process of public engagement (or individual beliefs and actions). Many decisions, and indeed the frameworks for action, stem from action at a more corporate level.

The distinction between adaptation to climate impacts (in SIRCH) and mitigation of greenhouse gas emissions (in earlier parts of the present volume) is less important.

Both approaches have used a mix of qualitative and quantitative methods. In the SIRCH case, the analytical models are new, tailored to the local issues and conditions. Scenarios and model results focus on *institutional* change, rather than perceptions, and are local rather than global. Bridging the expert-model formalism of policy issues and the "real world" politics of decision-making is a challenge (see Chapter 5).

Stakeholder analysis

The key stakeholders for water resource management in the Thames region are:

- Water service companies (WSCo) – commercial enterprises with a natural monopoly (at present) to provide water to domestic, corporate, and municipal users.
- Environment Agency (EA) – quasi-government organization that issues water abstraction licenses and regulates on behalf of the aquatic environment (pollution standards, drinking water quality, low flows).
- Office of Water Services (Ofwat) – the economic regulator, set up on privatization of the water industry in 1989 to stimulate competition and set both prices for water and allowed capital expenditure.
- Department of the Environment, Food and Rural Affairs (DEFRA) – oversees both the EA and Ofwat, political representation in setting policy.
- Local authorities – planning and service levels of government, with little direct representation in water issues other than planning approval for new development and major infrastructure.
- Consumers – represented in terms of service standards (e.g., billing disputes), but generally not directly involved in water resource decisions. There are few active non-governmental organizations (NGOs) which represent consumer interests in water use, although national NGOs take an interest in specific issues (such as wetlands).

Having identified the stakeholders, the next task is to understand their positions, motivations, and relationships with each other. The SIRCH project has utilized a variety of qualitative methods to do this, including in-depth interviews, document analysis, and participant observation.

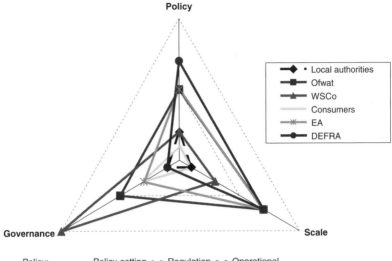

Policy: Policy-setting <--> Regulation <--> Operational
Scale: National <--> Regional <--> Local
Governance: Market <--> Mixed <--> Command

Figure 9.1 Stakeholder mapping in the Thames region

A graphical way to map stakeholders is shown in Figure 9.1. From our qualitative analysis, three dimensions appear to be critical. In this example, the ratings are subjective – by the project team and not the stakeholders themselves. They are intended to show the ordinal differentiation of stakeholder action rather than absolute ratings of observable indices.

Policy refers to the level of decision-making. The government (DEFRA) has the highest level of responsibility – to set the overall policy framework and intervene in policy failures. Regulators interpret and apply that framework, while operational stakeholders (e.g., water companies) work within the guidelines set out by the policy regulatory process. Notably, consumers generally are not involved in policy setting. Of course there is a concerted attempt by those who are regulated to influence the policy process itself, beyond the normal rules of consultation.

The scale of operation spans the national (and some companies are international) to the very local end user. Consumers rarely present a regional lobby (except in times of crisis). In contrast, the major policy decisions are implemented at the local level, through regional offices (e.g., the EA has a strong network of regional centers).

Governance, the decision-making environment, ranges from market/profit maximization to a command economy. WSCos are private enterprises (with shareholders) that operate under corporate rules and mandates. The economic regulator (Ofwat) is charged with stimulating a competitive market (using price cap regulation). Consumers have mixed economic motivations – less than a third in the Thames region are metered; the remainder pay a flat monthly rate for their water. The government is traditionally based on a command economy. For instance, abstraction licenses are granted based on a balance of expected demand and environmental considerations; they are not allocated based on explicit market mechanisms (e.g., WSCos' willingness to pay for the water).

Notable in the diagram is the overlap between the stakeholder ratings, particularly between DETR, Ofwat, and the EA – they all have similar frames of reference. In contrast, the WSCo are at odds with the regulatory bodies. And the local authorities and consumers have restricted levels of engagement.

Scenarios and analysis of institutional risk

The Thames case study in the SIRCH project has developed an analysis based on comparison of drought management for the present and three scenarios of future institutional arrangements, with and without climate change (shown schematically in Table 9.2). The focus of analysis for the present risk is the current round of drought contingency plans in the current regulatory regime. The second stage adds scenarios of climate change, especially a drought episode that would be the drought of record for design purposes. The final stage explores drought management against very different institutional settings (summarized below).

Three models were developed. A dynamic simulation model tracked the balance between water supply and demand, using conventional forecasts of the micro-components of consumer demand (e.g., bathing, toilets, washing clothes, garden watering) (see Downing 2002). The scope for cooperation between regulators and water companies was explored in a game theoretic model. Agent-based social simulation looked at the behavior of consumers, particularly how they might respond to signals from water companies, regulators, public bodies, and their own neighbors (see Downing, Moss, and Pahl-Wostl 2001).

Our approach to developing scenarios is somewhat distinct from approaches common in climate impact assessment:[2]

---

[2] Scenarios used in the UK have been developed by the Department of Transport and Industry Foresight panel (www.foresight.gov.uk), IPCC (www.rivm.ni/env/int/ipcc), the UK Climate Impacts Programme (www.ukcip.org), and by the Environment Agency in their Water Resources for the Future: A Water Resources Strategy for England and Wales (www.environment-agency.gov.uk).

Table 9.2 *Analysis of drought risk scenarios*

	Institutions	Drought Risk	Analysis
Present	Present configuration of stakeholders Conventional wisdom of trend projection	Present distribution of drought risk Historical analogue (e.g., 1976/77)	Models: • dynamic simulation of demand • game theory of regulation • agent-based social simulation of consumers Qualitative: • stakeholder profiles of drought impacts/coping
Including: climate change	• Present/trend projection	Scenarios of changed drought risk based on mean climate change and potential variability	As above
Including: institutional change	Additional scenarios of institutional change: • economic growth • environmental stewardship	Climate change scenarios and plausible future "drought of record"	As above, with evaluation of institutional changes

- The scenarios focused on a specific issue–institutional capacity to manage future drought risk. That is, they were bottom-up analytical devices rather than global, alternative futures. They were not intended to span a range of all possible futures.
- The scenarios were constructed by an expert group of stakeholders, by invitation – not a public exercise – drawing upon an established community of water resource managers and regulators who are accustomed to working with each other at various levels.
- The process was participatory. The project facilitators provided an outline of several scenarios, while the story-lines and details were developed in small working groups.
- The scenarios were part of a two-shot exercise. The first workshop designed the scenarios. The second analyzed them, reporting on a variety of models (dynamic simulation, game theory, and agent-based social simulation) and using participatory methods.

Three scenarios were developed:

- trend projection and conventional wisdom
- economic growth and market enterprise
- regulation and environmental stewardship

The planning horizon for each scenario is 2050. Water companies and the economic regulator plan initially to 2016 and the EA to 2025; although both include longer views at some levels.

We had willing attendance from the major stakeholders. In part, this was because the workshop was easily contained in a day (10a.m. to 4p.m.) and held in the attractive setting of an Oxford college, with a formal lunch. The schedule provided ample time for side discussions (while the facilitators wrote up the first working groups). In contrast, the meeting on venture capital (see Chapter 7) included an overnight stay that allowed reflection on the earlier discussions.

The mode of framing the scenarios began with a plenary discussion of scenarios and broad agreement on three scenarios to take forward. The first round of working groups provided storylines for each scenario. A storyline is a short history of the main features of the scenario with consideration given to changes in the driving forces of society. It can be a text or a collection of observations. The results of this were reported back in a plenary session by a rapporteur from each group, and copies distributed over lunch.

A second round of working groups divided the participants broadly according to expertise – resources, stakeholders, and institutions. In this session each storyline was translated into more quantitative indicators (where possible). Suggestions for indicators were given to each group although it was acknowledged that they might not be adequate to capture all of the relevant institutional changes.

Throughout, participants were encouraged to be controversial. Other than the trend projection, the scenarios were intended to be plausible, but extreme views of the future. The scenarios are not best guesses or predictions. Nor are they necessarily desirable, or policy recommendations. They simply provide quite different backdrops for evaluating the risk of drought and potential strategies to cope with climate change.

Thus, the scenarios entail a clear proviso – it is not a consensus view of what the future should be or what policy is required at present to cope with climate change. Participants did not necessarily represent the views of their own agencies or companies. The workshop was conducted under the Chatham House rule – where findings can be reported but not attributed to any individual.

Preparation for the workshop was quite detailed. The team of facilitators (two for each working group) met regularly to agree on objectives, review scenario approaches in other exercises, decide on introductory material to be distributed before the workshop, identify a participant list, and think about the expected results (and potential problems).

Water regulation is a highly political process. The workshop itself could not be scheduled before January 2000, after the round of negotiations on allowed capital expenditure and water charges. This is a mandatory process between the economic and environmental regulators (Ofwat and the EA respectively) and the water companies. We wanted to take an independent view of the future, focussing on long-term regulatory issues rather than trying to influence the regulators' decisions. It was also unlikely that all the stakeholders would agree to the process in the midst of the negotiations – partly due to time pressures. In the event, we had representatives from each of the main stakeholders.

The storylines for each scenario are presented below. The scenarios have been reviewed by the participants, but not altered or amended.

Trend projection and conventional wisdom

The experience of the last ten years is projected forward, with increased wealth and consumer demand in a mixed regulatory regime

The trend projection is a rough outline of what are considered likely developments in water resources and management. To some extent, it is the reference, or baseline, scenario against which the two more extreme scenarios should be compared.

Economic growth continues, with a concentration along the corridor from London to the west. Regional growth is not controlled at a national level. The existing mode of regulation (carrots and sticks) continues. Demand is subject to modest improvements in efficiency. Leakage control reaches the economic level of leakage. Present limits to per capita consumption are only temporary, with bounce back in ten years as incomes increase. Tariff structures are similar to at present and growth in metering does not have a dramatic effect on price and demand. The price cut in 2000 is temporary and prices rise to pay for conventional resource development.

Society is more concerned about the environment. Climate change results in wetter winters and drier summers – highlighting the changing climate to consumers. However, water availability does not constrain housing development. Water quality is improved, with no consumer hysteria over effluent reuse. Modest improvements in sustainable catchments continue. Customer expectations increase, placing a high value on uninterrupted availability during drought – stand pipes and rationing are not allowed.

There is a reduction in abstraction for industrial use. Water resources planning maintains public water supply as a priority. There are more surface reservoirs, along with aquifer storage and recovery.

Economic growth and market enterprise

High economic growth increases wealth, raises expectations, elevates demand for water, increases willingness to pay for water-related amenities, and also creates conflicts between water users

The South-East experiences high growth due to inward migration and natural increase, well above currently projected rates of increase. High-rise affluent urbanites have second homes in the country, or new estates on the fringes of metropolitan areas. The resulting high demand puts pressure on resources and supply systems. Marginal costs rise, encouraging the prioritization of water use efficiency – not only conservation, but also gray water and fit-for-use supplies. In areas of localized affluence, consumers demand dual supply: gray water in taps, bottled water for drinking. Efficiency offsets demand to some degree, but structural deficits persist, as overall demand remains high due to increasing population and changing per capita consumption, related to increasing affluence and changing lifestyles.

Deregulation occurs at the national scale. EU support is confined to free market mechanisms. If the EU's policies constrain regional growth,

Britain may leave the EU. The water industry fragments and specializes as network functions are divided between different companies (e.g., suppliers and distributors, along the lines of the gas industry). Companies, in a fragmented industry, compete to supply consumers on the basis of quality as well as price. Metering and cost-reflective pricing are the results of higher costs and resulting pressures for efficiency, resulting from competition for all aspects of the water supply cycle (including water abstraction rights and control of resources). Market forces are the method of developing the environment, leading to the creation of private, high-cost conservation zones, and conversely zones where the environment is sacrificed. But, water conflicts are common.

Environmental stewardship and regulation

A high general awareness of environmental issues, increased wealth and a more egalitarian society leads to a balance between water use and the environment

Society has a high general awareness of environmental issues, and this drives policy. High environmental standards are sought, with less concern for individuals and more for the common good. People are relatively affluent and well educated, able to afford high environmental values. Resources are more equally distributed across the population.

Informed customers (who have high expectations) are willing to pay for "environmental friendliness." Water is considered a scarce resource to be valued. Metering and water recycling are accepted as well as variable tariffs. The general public participates more in water management and consequently feels a greater degree of commitment to the outcome of any decisions made. Regulation is used less due to an increase in voluntary action. There are more holistic, long-term approaches to water management with the focus on sustainability rather than preservation. Governmental control is less overall, when compared to the present day, but a strong framework is still in place. In business, competition exists, but is virtuous. Companies compete to have the best green credentials and all firms are concerned about their environmental reputation and efficiency.

Closing remarks

Concerning the SIRCH scenarios, the differences between the two outlier scenarios are clear, with each extending elements of the present trend toward more extreme conditions. Regarding drought risk, the likelihood and effects of periodic water scarcity, and institutions that manage the risk, the key differences appear to be:

- Role of government and regulators in setting markets for water during periods of enhanced scarcity. Will spot markets emerge spontaneously, or will they be regulated?
- Willingness of consumers to balance their own demand and the environment, as reflected in voluntary choices, acceptance of regulation, or accepting higher tariffs.
- Locus of risk management – shared among all users, off-loaded onto the environment, taken as higher prices and shared among water providers?
- Expectations of levels of service and responses to drought shortages.
- Locus of adaptation to changing drought risk – consumers (e.g., through higher prices and efficiency incentives), corporate (supply enhancement and network expansion), or regulators (imposed balancing).

The process of stakeholder participation seems to have been successful. The mood of the scenarios workshop was engaging, with lots of creative discussion and stimulation about alternative futures. Some felt we should have provided more guidelines – but the facilitators felt that we had a fair balance between presenting a challenge and forcing the participants to follow (i.e., downscale) predetermined scenarios. Several participants were involved in parallel scenario exercises, and most were familiar with the similar efforts – so we did not have to spend too much time on the background to scenarios as tools for policy analysis.

This paper noted differences and similarities between the SIRCH work and the research on public participation conducted in the ULYSSES project. The key points are summarized in Box 9.2.

Box 9.2: Differences and similarities between SIRCH and ULYSSES

The approach reported here differs from the participatory processes with citizens and experts discussed in the first two parts of this volume, while the overall goals of the two approaches are complementary. Three main points are worth exploring.

- First, the SIRCH project brought together stakeholders who compete in an existing regulatory framework. The work reported earlier involved citizens or groups with common interests, such as venture capital. The participatory modes and techniques are likely to differ as a result.

- Second, the SIRCH project developed models to use in the analysis. In the work discussed in earlier chapters, models that had already been developed were employed. Doubtless, this created some difficulties, as models are never as transparent and portable as they might seem, especially to their creators. The SIRCH models were focused on issues of common concern among the stakeholders, and developed with a reasonable level of interchange between stakeholders and the rest of the project team. Still, there are major questions about how to derive insight from the models and relate the formalisms of models to the discourses of institutional change.
- Finally, notwithstanding these differences, the two research efforts have much in common, not least the central ambition of seeking new modes of science–policy interfaces and effective participation in sustainability science.

CHAPTER TEN

On the art of scenario development

Chris Anastasi

Background

The only relevant discussions about the future are those where we succeed in shifting the question from whether something will happen to what would we do if it did happen.

(Arie de Geus, Former Head of Group Planning, Shell International)

In a global environment of rapid economic, technological, and social change, scenario analysis is increasingly being seen as a key aid to the decision-making process in many organizations. A study of this relatively young methodology shows a wide spectrum of views on many of the fundamentals involved and with major differences in the development process used. A key issue in scenario development is to find the right balance between formal models with quantitative information and narrative elements that address "soft" issues like social values. Also, the key dissemination process is still inadequate in many cases, and there is a danger that if the technique is not used in an effective manner, confidence will be eroded and widespread use of a valuable aid will be curtailed.

As the world became a less certain place in the late 1960s and early 1970s, organizations began experimenting with scenario analysis as a method of gaining insights into the way the world might evolve. This method took root when the large oil price rises in the 1970s ensured the world had undergone a fundamental change, the scale of which shook the confidence of governments, policy-makers and private industry to plan effectively. The 1980s saw many new attempts at scenario analysis, with the methodology extended into new areas, encouraging improvements in the development and dissemination processes. Today there is recognition that scenario analysis is one of the few tools available for unraveling the secrets of the future.

The term scenario means different things to different people and this can be confusing to those not familiar with the methodology. Most people would agree to the following: scenarios are not forecasts; scenarios recognize that our ability to predict the future course of events is limited;

and they are particularly useful for investigating the uncertainty of the future. In particular, scenario analysis provides valuable insights into how the future might unfold, and in this way aids the decision-making process. The following points capture the essence of the analysis:

- a scenario is an archetypal image of the future based on an interpretation of the present
- it is an internally consistent story exploring a path into the future
- it must be plausible, recognizable, and challenging

Clearly it is important that scenarios are internally *consistent*, both qualitatively and quantitatively, if they are to be accepted. They must also be *plausible* and *recognizable*, since this will ensure credibility and encourage their use. And most important of all, the scenarios must *challenge* conventional thinking, since this is the one way in which new insights about the future can be gained.

The basis of scenario analysis then lies in surfacing weak signals that herald changes in society, sometimes fundamental in nature, be they political, economic, or social. Often it requires a unique combination of elements to initiate the onset of transitions. Scenario analysis, by addressing such combinations, is one of the few methodologies that offers the opportunity to prepare us for transitions, including the especially challenging transition toward sustainability.

Scenario methods

Although there have been many scenarios published over the years, the most popular are those based on modeling studies at the national, regional, and global levels (e.g., Alcamo 1994), global scenarios with strong narrative components (e.g., Kassler 1994), and scenarios which address single issues such as energy (e.g., World Energy Outlook 1995), technology (e.g., Eckersley and Jeans 1995), and climate change (e.g., Intergovernmental Panel on Climate Change 1996b); focused scenarios which concentrate on a particular geographical area have enjoyed less exposure. Each approach has strengths and weaknesses but there are compelling arguments for more widespread use of focused scenarios since these offer solutions to some of the problems associated with the first three approaches.

While this chapter refers mainly to a fairly limited part of the literature on scenario building, selected for its specific relevance for the scenario studies chosen to illustrate the chapter's main points, there is a wealth of literature on scenarios available for the interested reader. A good starting point are the papers, and the references cited therein, contained in a recent issue of the journal *Energy Policy* (volume 29, issue 14). That issue demonstrates clearly that scenario analyses currently play a key role in technology strategy and policy development. In the studies discussed there, scenario analysis was used to illustrate potential environmental benefits of for example carbon permit trading, and new policies and investments that support new technology development (Brown *et al.* 2001; Koomey *et al.* 2001; Hadley and Short 2001).

Scenario analysis has also been applied to other sustainability issues – for example, a study that challenged the proposed harmonization of community-level regulations that govern greenhouse gas emissions trading in Europe. This study came to the conclusion that uncoordinated efforts may not negatively impact industrial competitiveness nor necessarily induce industries to relocate to more favorable locales (Viguier 2001). In another recent example, a scenario study explored the role that the US agricultural industry can play in reducing greenhouse gas emissions, under the constraints of a scenario that includes overall higher energy prices brought about by an implementation of the Kyoto Protocol (Konyar 2001).

In the following, different types of scenario studies and their strengths and weaknesses are discussed in more depth. These are modeling studies, global scenarios, "single issue" scenarios, and focused scenarios.

Modelling studies

The essence of this modeling approach is shown in Figure 10.1. The key drivers in such studies are the socio-economic indicators that include, for

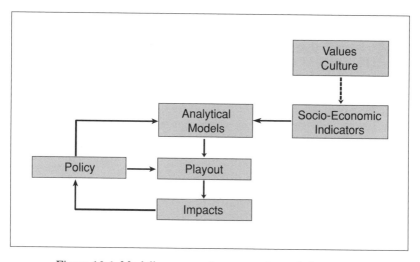

Figure 10.1 Modeling approach to scenario analysis

example, GDP, population growth and demographics, natural resources and their rates of exploitation. These are input into models which describe, through mathematical formulae, the linkages and elasticities between key variables such as GDP and energy use, resource demand and price, and so on. Models can describe, in numerical terms, environmental impacts associated with scenarios, and it is possible to assess potential policy actions on the impacts, so long as the policy actions are similarly described in numerical terms.

There are important inadequacies in this approach. Models can describe national, regional, and global conditions but clearly as the scale increases, the ability to provide detail at the lowest level decreases, and this creates a tension between the needs associated with different scales. There has been a tendency to work at the larger scales so that global interactions can be more easily accommodated, and where inaccuracies in the raw data are lost in the aggregate; unfortunately, this tends to be at the expense of national distinctiveness, the natural domain of most policy-makers.

Another problem relates to the *consistency* criterion highlighted above, which is ensured in only a few models where interactions can be fully accounted for. Also, it is becoming apparent that models addressing the same problems tend not to agree in important details, even when the underlying principles of the analytical method employed are similar.

It has been possible for models to capture some of the societal trends observed in the past such as the increased demand for individual mobility, the description of domestic energy demand, and even changing employment patterns, activities that can be coded into a model with some degree of confidence. Addressing the same issues for the next generation is much more problematic because of the large structural changes observed over the last decade, that continue in many parts of the world today. Also, models have been unable to incorporate "softer" societal issues, captured in terms such as "values" or "culture," which are expected to be fundamental drivers in shaping the future, just as they have been in the past. These have been addressed effectively by other approaches such as the IA Focus Group work described in earlier chapters on citizens' perspectives, using narrative techniques of collage production, conversations, and citizens' reports.

Global scenarios

An influential global scenario approach is one that has a strong narrative component associated with it, typified by the Shell approach (Kassler 1994). Here "weak" signals of the present are interpreted in global terms

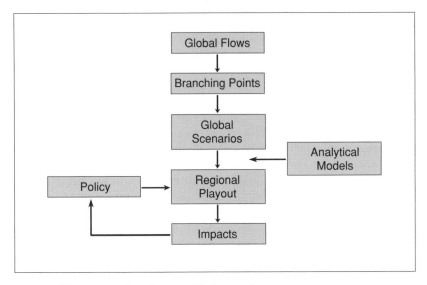

Figure 10.2 Developing global scenarios

and branching points are sought that describe the dominant themes. In the past, branching points may have emphasized differences in, for example, political systems, treatment of environment, and more recently, economic philosophy.

In a relatively few studies, the scenarios have been rich in several domains, presented in a way which is internally consistent, and thus making them more attractive to a wide constituency. Crucially, these scenarios also have the capacity to engage the policy-maker in a manner models do not, perhaps because the latter are viewed as "black boxes" with little transparency for many would-be users. And, most importantly, these kinds of scenarios can provide a common "language" for a meaningful discussion of the future.

The individual steps involved in developing global scenarios of this kind are shown in Figure 10.2. The most effective scenarios are those that have been developed by a group of individuals with different, yet complementary experiences. This is very important in the process as it not only allows many constituencies to be represented, but also makes possible beneficial, synergistic interaction between participants; in this way there is every opportunity for the development of scenarios rich in breadth and depth. This approach requires significant resources not always available in many organizations.

The important social dimension that is often lacking in the modeling approach can be captured in the global scenario approach described here, albeit in a qualitative way, through the strong narrative component that forms the dominant part of the study. Nevertheless, models do have an important underpinning role by quantifying the dynamics described in the scenario narratives and providing valuable outputs; in this way, models can provide not only a *consistency* check, but also provide additional insights, and this raises confidence in the overall analysis.

An important advantage of global scenarios is that they essentially provide a common framework for a variety of issues to be discussed. However, the scenarios described on a global scale may not be *recognizable* or *relevant* in some regions or countries, and may even be seen as "straitjackets" or otherwise confining and restrictive. At best, they may simply not be used in these cases; at worst, any criticism voiced serves to undermine their value in other areas.

The importance of the social dimension, captured in variables such as governance, education, and awareness, is illustrated in a workshop that addressed environment issues in the Latin America region for the period to 2020 (UNEP 1997). In all, almost seventy individual issues that were relevant to the environment debate in this region surfaced, the essence of which was captured in the thirteen potential scenario variables shown in

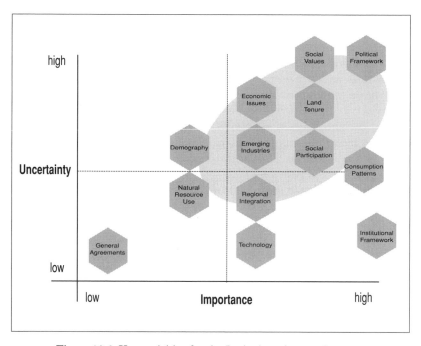

Figure 10.3 Key variables for the Latin American region

Figure 10.3. These variables spanned a wide cross-section of concerns, confirming the truly multivariable nature of environmental problems.

What is also obvious from this figure is the importance placed on "soft" issues such as social values and social participation, along with land tenure issues, an important problem in Latin America but less so elsewhere in the world. The fact that these variables were also deemed to be highly uncertain in the time frame considered makes them important variables around which scenarios for these regions need to be developed. These comments are also true for other "soft" issues such as the political and institutional framework that were ranked more important than the more traditional economic and technology issues, or emerging industry and consumption patterns.

Single issue scenarios

It has been popular to develop scenarios, global or otherwise, where the emphasis has been on single issues such as energy, technology, or a particular environmental issue such as climate change. The reasons for this approach may be the focus of the organization involved, a lack of resources or capacity, or a combination of these. Some are straightforward modeling exercises while others have a narrative approach. In either case, the limitations are obvious: there are key linkages of the kind outlined above that are not necessarily included in the work and this makes the study less useful than it needs to be for a meaningful analysis.

Figure 10.4 compares a small group of scenarios in which energy is the key issue addressed: IPCC (IPCC 1996a); SEI/Greenpeace (Stockholm Environment Institute 1993); IEA (International Energy Agency 1995); WEC (World Energy Council 1993); the OECD (OECD 1997); CPB (Central Planning Bureau 1992); Shell International Petroleum Company (SIPC) (Kassler 1994).

The *Process* axis stretches between those scenarios that have been designed to perform a specific function (e.g., the original IPCC scenarios which explored ways in which carbon dioxide emissions could be doubled by a specific future time), to those that suggest possible futures based on prevailing weak signals.

The *Nature* axis varies from those scenarios that largely address a single issue (like energy) with less attention given to the possible evolution of other, related issues (such as political, economic, and social dynamics), to those scenarios that attempt to explore possible interactions between key issues.

It is clear from this simple matrix that, with an odd exception, scenario exercises tend to reside in the bottom, left-hand quadrant of this

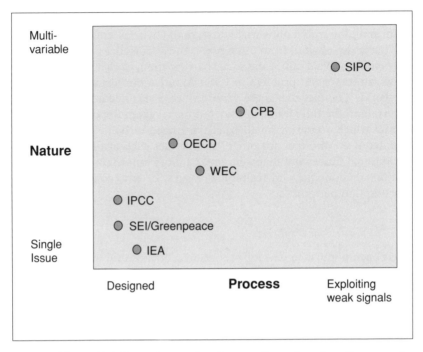

Figure 10.4 Scenario overview (see text for explanation of acronyms)

matrix. Unfortunately, these scenarios are incomplete, with the key consistency criterion largely left unaddressed, and this tends to limit their usefulness.

Focused scenarios

One way of addressing some of the concerns with the global scenarios highlighted above is to construct focused scenarios. By focused is meant constructing scenarios for a particular region (or subregion, country, or corporation), so that the needs specific to that region can be more accurately represented. However, it is also important that the global trends, and the ways in which these are adopted in the region are also recognized in the exercise, providing a common, overarching backdrop. Figure 10.5 summarizes a process for developing such scenarios.

The "global flows" component includes the liberalization process that has had such a profound effect on many economies and stimulated international trade, globalization of key industries such as communications, and increasing international technology transfer which has the capacity for releasing economic potential.

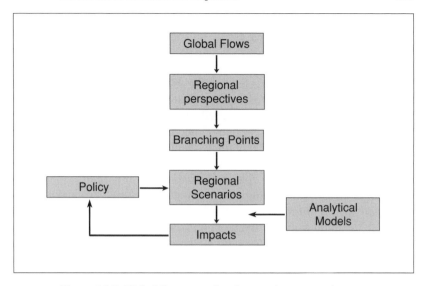

Figure 10.5 Global flows – regional scenarios approach

Clearly each region (or subregion) will adopt these global flows to a lesser or greater degree dependent on their circumstances. They might even distort or bias the global flows thus providing an important feedback mechanism; foreign direct investment in China, for example, has dominated this part of the global flows in recent years. In this way a regional perspective of the global flows becomes apparent. Similarly, the branching points for the scenarios now become region specific rather than global. This offers the best opportunity for the scenarios to satisfy the *plausible* and *recognizable* criteria highlighted above, while regional models can provide the quantification needed to underpin the scenarios and at the same time aid consistency. This approach has proved both popular and effective, marrying global trends and regional focus in an optimal fashion.

Scenario process and dissemination

As indicated earlier, with a few notable exceptions, scenarios have been developed by small "core" groups of experts, particularly when they have been model based. Unfortunately this tends to produce scenarios lacking in "richness," a quality that becomes evident as more people become involved, each contributing their expertise and knowledge to the process. Sharing of the scenarios with interested groups at an early stage of development also solicits useful comment and content, and makes the scenarios more robust, easing their acceptance once completed. The "richness" of scenarios could be increased further by including the views of ordinary citizens, as explored in earlier chapters of this volume.

Another major limitation relates to the dissemination process. In some cases, the scenarios have been developed almost as an academic exercise with the dissemination process limited to a book or the publishing of key findings in learned journals, supplemented by an occasional presentation by the authors. Policy-makers, for example, must extract the relevant aspects of the analysis pertinent to their needs in the absence of any support. This is a relatively "passive" dissemination process.

In progressive organizations where scenarios are developed the dissemination process is much more "active." In addition to the usual package of material highlighted above, members of the scenario team run workshops for different stakeholders. Here, the scenario "stories" are first presented, followed by a workshop in which expert facilitators solicit stakeholder response through a clearly defined process. Policy-makers interested in the environment, for example, are able to assess policy actions in the context of the possible futures they are exposed to. In this way they are able to check the robustness of existing policy, or policies being developed; they are also able to consider policy action over the longer term, "safe" in the visions of the future presented.

A wide cross-section of stakeholders may be involved in this process: policy-makers, economists, industrialists, NGOs, politicians, as well as representatives of the media. In this way, the scenarios provide a vehicle for constructive dialogue and interaction, and at the same time raise awareness of different stakeholder needs. Crucially, the ULYSSES project has explored opportunities and problems of disseminating scenarios by confronting ordinary citizens with scenarios developed by experts.

It is possible to compare the performance of the small group of scenario exercises introduced earlier on a matrix which addresses the "process" and "dissemination" dimensions (see Figure 10.6). Once again, most of the scenario exercises reside in the bottom left-hand quadrant of the matrix; this means that the scenarios tend to be less robust and rich than they need to be, and the value associated with an active dissemination process is largely missed.

Conclusions on common lessons

There is little doubt the scenario approach provides a powerful method for addressing the uncertainties of the future. Although this approach has been successfully used in the energy sector (and by association, in

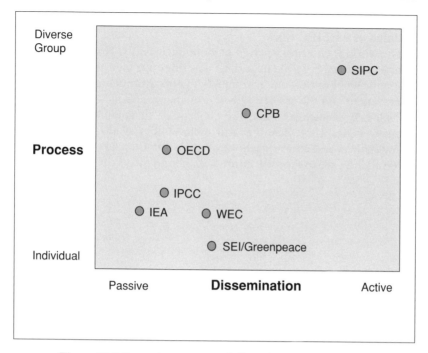

Figure 10.6 Scenario process and dissemination (see p. 207 for explanation of acronyms)

the climate change debate) its potential use in other sectors has hardly been exploited.

The research discussed in the first two parts of the present volume, and the reflections described in this chapter, start from the same basic assumption: that analytical models are necessary but not sufficient for preparing us for the future. An understanding of "soft" issues like different perspectives and values are essential for unraveling possible futures. Those scenarios that have a strong narrative, as well as quantitative component, are able to engage key stakeholders, while focused scenarios address national/regional concerns and, at the same time, take account of prevailing global dynamics.

While the research described in earlier chapters was not about developing stringent scenarios, it has used citizens' exposure to model scenarios for exploring the difficult, "soft" issues. This research has also shown that citizens see it as more natural to consider multiple linked issues than to restrict considerations to a single isolated issue. Policy-makers need to take into account the views of citizens, and the results suggest that future scenario work should explore a rich texture of interconnections in the tradition of the SIPC work.

The world is entering a period of great uncertainty. Not only are there significant changes within developed countries but the emergence of new economic and political powers offers both opportunities and threats. The environment and the associated issues of energy and technology are presenting new challenges while the concept of sustainable development is finally taking root. The scenario methodology is an essential tool if policy-makers and other stakeholders, from commercial organizations to governments, are to face the future with confidence.

PART FOUR

Future perspectives

INTRODUCTION

This final part of the present volume looks at the research described in the earlier parts, especially the work on IA Focus Group procedures, from a bird's-eye perspective, and explores its meaning for the future development of integrated assessment and sustainability science. In Chapter 11, van Asselt and Rotmans discuss the role of this research for the development of a broader research program of integrated assessment. As an example, they describe how this research has helped them build a bridge between earlier work on integrated modeling and uncertainty, and more recent research on "integrated visions for a sustainable Europe" that combines stakeholder participation with modeling work. While their work, like the bulk of the research on public participation in sustainability science discussed in this volume, has been conducted in Europe, in Chapter 12 Ramakrishna discusses what role citizens of developing countries can play in sustainability debates. He explores similarities and differences between the research discussed throughout this volume and experiences in the developing world, and from this draws conclusions on how increasing public participation could support understanding and collective action toward sustainability, particularly in developing countries. Finally, in the concluding Chapter 13, Stoll-Kleemann, O'Riordan and Burns assess the general potential of increasing the role of citizens in shaping a sustainable future. They argue that interactive, multilevel governance is essential in tackling the sustainability challenge, and that the experiences discussed in this book can help us understand how this might be achieved. Overall, the chapters of this final part of the present volume discuss three major challenges that sustainability science has to meet in the future: bridging views of experts with those of laypersons, integrating developing as well as developed country perspectives, and supporting interactive governance for sustainable futures. The aim of this book has been to explore how public participation can be integrated into sustainability science in order to succeed in meeting such challenges.

CHAPTER ELEVEN

From projects to program in integrated assessment research

Marjolein B. A. van Asselt and Jan Rotmans

ULYSSES and Integrated Assessment

It is frequently argued that Integrated Assessment (IA) should be an international, multi-institute program, in which projects are covering for each other. In the current chapter, the research described in the first two parts of this volume is discussed from such a broad point of view. To that end, the authors explore if, and if so how, this research built upon previous IA projects and whether it provided input for subsequent IA projects. In doing so, its value for Integrated Assessment beyond the study's main products and insights is explored.

Apart from being a project that addressed the climatic change issue from the perspective of citizens, the ULYSSES project was explicitly designed as an Integrated Assessment (IA) project. For decades, scientists have been working with decision-makers to address local and regional problems in a more or less integrative manner, especially in the field of environmental policy, most of them without calling it "Integrated Assessment." Although the term IA dates back to the 1980s, it is only since the late 1990s that IA has been recognized as a kind of profession and as a specific branch of scientific research. For that reason, it was not at all trivial that the project explicitly aimed to develop new IA methodologies.

When this study was designed, modelers, mainly natural scientists and economists, dominated IA. Modeling was considered as the way to do IA. Papers reviewing IA in the mid and late 1990s described and categorized IA Models (IAMs), usually without even referring to other non-modeling, social-scientific methods (see, e.g., Weyant *et al.* 1996). It is therefore significant that primarily social scientists were involved in the ULYSSES project and that it explicitly aimed to use and further develop participatory methods from social sciences in IA.

The idea of using participatory methods in IA as such was not new. In the late seventies, Holling (1978) proposed the idea of using participatory approaches in assessment efforts. Brewer (1986) repeated and rephrased this plea some ten years later. Toth (1988a; and 1995) and Parson (1996) advanced the idea of combining IA models with simulation-gaming approaches in policy exercises in the late 1980s and early 1990s. Experiences with policy exercises in IA are discussed in Parson (1997) and Toth and Hizsnyik (1998). Cohen (1977) and his colleagues were among the first to set up stakeholder processes in an IA study on the Mackenzie Basin. However, in hindsight, these efforts probably did not get the attention they deserved. Referring to the success of the RAINS model (Hordijk 1991), some IA practitioners began to realize that co-design by the targeted users (especially decision-makers) could be an interesting approach to advance the use of models (see e.g., Rotmans 1994; Alcamo, Kreileman, and Leemans 1996). However, participation and participatory methods were not intrinsically valued by the IA community in the mid-1990s.

The research discussed in the first two parts of this volume was the very first IA study that aimed to set up similar participatory processes all over Europe with the aim of developing a tested procedure for IA. Such a large-scale participatory IA project in the field of climate change was unprecedented. In view of the dominant perspective, it was highly ambitious to propose to use IA models in participatory processes. Although it was the aim of the study to use participatory methods and models in a complementary manner, it was clear from the research design that participatory methods were the leading assessment methodology and that IA models were "just" tools in this process.

Next to that, it was remarkable to involve citizens as targeted participants.[1] The few previous participatory efforts in Europe were all focussed on involving governmental decision-makers. It was the explicit aim of this study to complement the expert knowledge embedded in IA models with lay knowledge. In the context of IA, the idea of involving stakeholders in general, and citizens in particular, was new and controversial. By going beyond the realm of the professionals, the project had an innovative potential from the beginning. In sum, the unique features of the study were:

- the dominance of social science
- the focus on citizens
- the size and coverage of the project

As becomes clear from the current book, this endeavor resulted in a wealth of empirical experience and exploratory, instructive insights on participation as assessment methodology. It clearly advanced the concept

---

[1] Although ULYSSES also involved some focus groups with regional decision-makers and venture capitalists, citizens were the key target group. The large majority of the focus groups conducted in the context of ULYSSES involved citizens.

of IA Focus Groups. We would like to argue in this chapter that doing justice to the study implies discussing its value for IA beyond its main products and insights. We, therefore, aim to evaluate its impact on the IA community. We hope to make clear that whatever the evaluation of its specific output, this study anyway has to be considered as a milestone in the young history of IA.

It is argued that IA should be conceived as an international multi-institute research program (Wilbanks and Kates 1999). Such a perspective implies that IA practitioners are in a way "covering for each other"[2] in their respective projects. In other words, each single IA project can be considered as contributing to the larger research program. In practice, this means that it is interesting to evaluate how a particular IA project made use of previous projects and how it covered for succeeding projects. In this chapter, we will discuss the study described in the first two parts of this volume from such a program point of view. To that end, we will explore how it made use of RIVM's[3] research program, Global Dynamics and Sustainable Development (phase 1992–96), also known as the TARGETS project, and how it provided stepping stones for the subsequent VISIONS project (1998–2001). In this way, we hope to convincingly argue that it contributed significantly to the international multi-institute research program of IA.

From TARGETS to ULYSSES

In 1992, the project "Global Dynamics and Sustainable Development" was launched at RIVM in the Netherlands. The development of the IA model TARGETS (Rotmans 1994; Rotmans and de Vries 1997), which stands for Tool to Assess Regional and Global Environmental and Health Targets for Sustainability, was central to the project. For that reason, the project is quite often referred to as the TARGETS project. The philosophy and aims underlying the project, the details of the TARGETS model and the ultimate assessment of global change are comprehensively described in Rotmans and de Vries (1997), Schellnhuber (1998), and Rotmans and van Asselt (1999). In this chapter, we will therefore limit ourselves to touching upon those aspects relevant to the research discussed in earlier parts of this book.

The TARGETS project was designed as an integrated assessment of global change taking plural social and cultural perspectives into account.

[2] Remark from Steve Schneider at Matrix workshop: Scaling issues in Integrated Assessment, Mechelen, The Netherlands, 12–19 July 2000.
[3] RIVM is the Dutch Institute for Public Health and the Environment, Bilthoven, the Netherlands (http://www.rivm.nl).

The aim of the assessment was to address the question: "Can we provide a future world population with enough food, clean water and energy to guarantee a healthy life, while safeguarding our natural resource base?" To that end, the TARGETS model was built to enable IA analysts to evaluate a number of global environmental, social, and economic consequences of several types of human activities simultaneously. Systems theory provided the main building blocks for the conceptual framework. At the highest level of aggregation, the TARGETS model comprises a human and environmental system. Following a modular approach, the TARGETS model consists of a population and health sub-model, an energy sub-model, an economic module, a biophysics sub-model, a land/soil sub-model, and a water sub-model. Interactions and feedback loops between the sub-models are taken into account in each time step of the simulation period. The time horizon spans two centuries (1900–2100).

A crucial feature of the TARGETS model is the incorporation of multiple model routes as a method to assess uncertainty and its consequences in terms of robustness of the policy conclusions (van Asselt and Rotmans 1996; 1997; 2002; van Asselt, Beusen, and Hilderink 1996; Rotmans and van Asselt 1999; van Asselt 2000). These are "colored" interpretations of the uncertainties prevalent in the model. The model routes are fleshed out according to three perspectives associated with cultural theory, that is, the hierarchist, the egalitarian, and the individualist (see Box 11.1). The freedom of interpretation is bounded by two criteria: (1) the range of freedom is determined by the variety of quantitative and qualitative estimates found in scientific literature, and (2) the historical trajectories (generally from 1900 till present) generated by each model route have to represent the observed time-series. The model routes were used as building blocks for performing scenario experiments in a systematic way. If policy preferences (management style) and the social, economic, and environmental processes (world view) are in accordance with one perspective, this is called a "utopia." Mismatches are called "dystopias."

The philosophy underlying the multiple model route approach complied with the explicit ambition of the research discussed in this volume to address uncertainty (see Pahl-Wostl *et al.* 1998; Kasemir *et al.* 1999b). This research and the TARGETS project shared the conviction that multiple perspectives are legitimate and that as a consequence IA studies should involve different perspectives. Where the TARGETS model addressed the issue within the modeling "paradigm," the ULYSSES project explored how participatory processes could serve to articulate and integrate multiple perspectives in the assessment effort. In that sense the two projects reinforced each other's message. Both research efforts contributed to setting the issue of pluralism on the IA agenda, without closing the debate or offering the ultimate strategy for dealing with pluralism in IA efforts. The two approaches can thus be considered as complementary, although they were not explicitly designed that way.

Box 11.1: Cultural Theory's typology of perspectives

Cultural Theory describes four, and at times even five, perspectives, that is, hierarchist, egalitarian, individualist, fatalist, and hermit. The first three perspectives are also referred to as "active perspectives," because they share an action-oriented world view and management style, although they differ fundamentally with regard to the type of action and the effectiveness thereof. Because the TARGETS model envisioned policy action, the fatalist and the hermit were not of primary interest. For simplicity reasons, those two were not included in the perspective-based model route application to the TARGETS model.

Egalitarians hold that all humans are born "good," but that they are highly malleable. Just as human nature can be "corrupted" by bad influences, it can be positively guided by an intimate relationship with nature and other people. Self-realization lies in spiritual growth rather than in the consumption of goods. The egalitarian world view implies a risk-averse attitude. The associated management style can therefore be characterized as preventive. With regard to the capitalistic economic system, drastic structural, social, cultural, and institutional changes are advocated. The egalitarian has it that nature is very fragile. Small disturbances may have catastrophic results. Any human-made change is likely to be detrimental to the environmental system. Nature is in a delicate balance. Activities that are to a greater or lesser extent likely to harm the environment should be abandoned.

For *individualists*, human nature is based on self-seeking behavior. Human beings are considered to be rational self-conscious agents seeking to fulfil their ever-increasing materialistic needs. Individualists hold that changes in principle provide opportunities for human ingenuity that will be revealed through market mechanisms. The individualist can be characterized as risk seeking. Eventual highly unlikely negative consequences of human activities will be resolved by technological solutions. The management style of the individualist can therefore be described as adaptive. Seen from an individualist perspective, nature is very robust. Anthropogenic perturbations, even if they are large, will do no more than result in mild and harmless disruptions. The individualist considers humans the center of the universe, while nature is seen as providing resources that are there to be exploited.

Hierarchists consider humans to be born sinful, but that they can and should be educated by good institutions. The role of management is to prevent serious problems by careful control, that is, by keeping the system within its limits. This management style of control can be associated with a risk-accepting attitude. Hierarchists believe that nature is robust within certain limits. Nature is able to cope with small disturbances. However, as soon as a threshold is passed, anthropogenic disturbances pose a threat to the functioning of nature. The hierarchist can be associated with an attitude towards the relationship between man and nature in which the mutual dependency between humans and nature is stressed. A balance between human and environmental values has to be ensured.

Key sources on Cultural Theory are: Douglas (1972; 1982), Rayner (1984; 1991; 1992), Schwarz and Thompson (1990), and Thompson, Ellis, and Wildavsky (1990). Some recent papers on Cultural Theory that are interesting in the present context are: Pendergraft (1998), Proctor (1998), and O'Riordan *et al.* (1999). See also van Asselt *et al.* (1996; 1997).

One of the aims of the TARGETS project was to facilitate debates in the decision-making community. For that reason, the initial idea was to develop a policy exercise in which the TARGETS model could be used as a tool. Although designs for policy exercises have been tested with draft versions of TARGETS as well as with sub-models (de Vries, Fiddaman, and Janssen 1993; de Vries 1995) policy exercises with the TARGETS model were never carried out with decision-makers. It was furthermore the ambition that policy analysts at ministries and international organizations, such as the EU and UN, could use the model in their daily practice. Therefore, emphasis was put on the development of a user-friendly interface. To that end, software (referred to as "M") was developed that enabled the configuration of the model presentation (so-called "views") to be changed in a relatively easy manner, in terms of language used, variables chosen, naming of the variables, and additional text boxes. Furthermore, a hypertext library summarizing expert knowledge with regard to the sustainability issues covered in the model as well as on-line instructions for model use was integrated with the TARGETS model's graphical user-interface on a CD-ROM (Hilderink *et al.* 1998).

TARGETS was the first IA model to be made available in that accessible and user-friendly way.

Taking the above into account, in a certain way the research discussed in the first two parts of this book can be seen as a natural follow-up of the TARGETS project. It focussed on using IAMs as assessment tools in participatory processes, while the TARGETS model had been explicitly designed so as to enable users to interactively work with the model themselves. From that point of view, it is not surprising that the TARGETS model was selected as one of the computer models to be used in the participatory process with citizens. The study served to a greater or lesser extent as a platform for addressing relevant questions with regard to the TARGETS model that were not covered within the TARGETS project itself. In a certain way, the study described in this volume tested the usability of the TARGETS model in a specific environment (i.e., IA Focus Groups with citizens), thereby performing a particular "quality test" (see Rotmans and van Asselt 2002; van Asselt 2000; van Asselt and Rotmans 2002).

On the other hand, the TARGETS model was an expert model, not developed for use by citizens. None of the global IA models used in the research discussed in this volume had been designed for use by laypeople. It is then not surprising that these tools were found not to be sufficiently user friendly to be assessed in an IA Focus Group with citizens. This is not meant to trivialize the study's endeavor; it was legitimate and useful to explore the extent and the ways in which existing IA models could be used in participatory processes with citizens. In doing so, it was possible to explore what design criteria a next generation of IA models should satisfy in order to be useful in participatory IA. The experiences reported in this volume "fuel" the IA research agenda with design criteria for the next generation of IA models and computer tools (compare Chapter 5):

- focus on the region the participants are living in, with global information in the background
- time horizon of about one generation (twenty to twenty-five years)
- qualitative information as well as quantitative information
- a broad variety of regional policy options
- back-casting option
- user friendliness: interactive, multimedia (sounds, graphics, animations, video clips), SimCity-like, different levels (beginners, advanced, experts)
- model presentations should be simple, explaining a few modeled key processes carefully

The study emphasized the limits to current IA models in view of participatory processes involving citizens. By doing so, its output stimulates a new mode of IA modeling. On the other hand, the experiences reported also provide food for thought and inspiration for those who want to set up policy exercises or other stakeholder processes around existing IA models with participants other than citizens groups.

We conclude that the ULYSSES study on the one hand built upon the TARGETS project. On the other hand, it evidently advanced issues that were first addressed in the TARGETS project, i.e. pluralism and user friendliness aimed at enabling users other than the modelers themselves to work with the models.

Intermediate station: ULYSSES

An important spin-off associated with the ULYSSES project is that it served as an intermediary platform to involve social scientists in the IA community. Participatory methods are a form of social scientific research methodology.[4] Focus groups, for example, have been applied in market research since the seventies (Cox, Higginbotham, and Burton 1976), while consensus conferences were used in technology assessment (Grin, van de Graaf, and Hoppe 1997; and Joss and Durant 1995). Gaming approaches have been prominently in use for training purposes (e.g., military and business games) since the early seventies (Hausrath 1971). Teaching and training games for environmental management have been around since the 1980s (Meadows 1985). For this reason, it turned out to be not too difficult to get enough social scientists experienced in participation interested in a participatory endeavor that aimed to assess citizens' views on the climate change issue.

From discussions at project meetings it became clear that most of the partners understood the idea of participation mainly as a way to democratize science and to empower citizens, rather than just as a means to improve the quality of IAs. Climate change decisions imply that citizens must either accept the undesired consequences, or they must rearrange their lifestyles accepting substitutes for their usual habits. It was argued that people and communities have a right to participate in decisions that affect their lives, property, and things they value. The idea of IA focus groups was advocated as a way to involve citizens more directly in the formulation of climate policy.

---

[4] See for recent overviews of participatory methods: Coenen, Huitema and O'Toole (1998); Dürrenberger *et al.* (1997); Grin, van de Graaf and Hoppe (1997); Joss and Durant (1995); Renn, Webler and Wiedemann (1995); van Asselt and Rijkens-Klomp (2002). See also: http://www.iadb.org/ exr/english/policies/participate/ and http://www.worldbank.org/html/edi/sourcebook/

This difference in ambitions and principles led to debates among the partners in the study. From the broader program point of view these debates were crucial, because they highlighted fundamental differences in paradigms between IA modelers and social scientists. Both via working papers and presentations, and via intense exchanges in the new European Forum for Integrated Environmental Assessment (EFIEA),[5] these debates reached the community outside the project team and made more interdisciplinary-oriented IA practitioners aware of the large challenges associated with reconciling modeling-oriented IA with participatory IA. In that sense, although the study was mainly a social science project, through actively using IA models in the focus groups it stimulated real communication between social scientists and modelers. It probably served as a catalyst within the IA community. Although the natural scientists and economists are, numerically speaking, still dominating the IA community,[6] the social scientists who through this endeavor joined the community are now taken more seriously. This is not at all a minor change. The presence of some highly respected social scientists in the IA community will stimulate interest among other, especially young, social scientists in IA. It is interesting to see how this experience directly and indirectly seems to inspire more and more social scientists to explicitly consider their research as IA endeavours.

It seems legitimate to conclude that the research agenda of the IA community has changed irreversibly due to this study. As argued before, "participation" was a minor issue, if an issue at all, when the study kicked off. However, over its course, the conviction has grown within the IA community that participation of non-scientists in the assessment process is important (see, e.g., Cohen 1997; Rotmans and van Asselt 1996; Funtowicz and Ravetz 1994b; Jäger 1998; Kasemir et al. 1999b; Parson 1997; Tol and Vellinga 1998; Toth and Hizsnyik 1998). There is now broad agreement that integration of non-scientific knowledge with values and preferences through social discourse will improve the quality of IA. Societal actors can indicate what is desirable and acceptable, and what is not. They can also provide relevant knowledge that is not held by the "experts." Participatory methods enable IA practitioners to have access to practical, local knowledge and experience, and to sketch a wider range of perspectives and options. In the last couple of years, IA is increasingly described as a cyclic and participatory process with two pillars:

---

[5] See http://www.vu.nl/ivm/research/efiea/

[6] As is, for example, clear from the background of scholars attending the last EFIEA workshop on Scaling Issues in Integrated Assessment (http://www.icis.unimaas.nl/matrix/): eight social scientists out of forty-three participants.

(1) the participation of scientists in the form of interdisciplinary research
(2) the participation of societal actors, such as the policy community, the business community, non-governmental organizations (NGOs), and citizens

In this transition from pure modeling-oriented IA to IA as a cyclic and participatory process, the ULYSSES project discussed in the first two parts of this volume played a pioneering role.

From ULYSSES to VISIONS

The VISIONS project (Rotmans *et al.*, 2000; 2001) was, like the ULYSSES study, an IA project under the auspices of the European Union's "DG Research and Development" (formerly known as DGXII – Fourth Framework Program, Environment and Climate, Theme 4, Human Dimensions of Environmental Change). The ultimate ambition was to assist the process of policy making for sustainable development in Europe. The main objective of VISIONS was to create a set of alternative scenarios for future sustainable development paths, up to 2020 and 2050 for Europe as a whole and for three regions in Europe: Greater Manchester (UK), Venice (Italy), and the Green Heart (Netherlands). The selected regions served as examples of different types of European issues that are relevant in the context of sustainable development. The European and regional scenarios were developed employing participatory methods. The scenarios were linked to create integrated visions for Europe addressing both European and regional outlooks and interests (see Figure 11.1). The visions are qualitative narratives about the future,

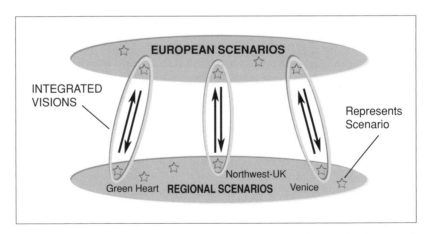

Figure 11.1 VISIONS: European and regional scenarios integrated into visions.

blended with quantitative ingredients (e.g., historical data and results of model simulations).

The VISIONS project was explicitly designed as building upon ULYSSES in a number of ways. It is to be doubted whether without this earlier project as "role model," the VISIONS project would have been so explicitly participatory. To guarantee that VISIONS would benefit from the lessons learned from this earlier study, researchers who participated in that endeavor were involved in the VISIONS project with the explicit task of bringing in their experiences from this earlier work (especially Carlo Jaeger, Bernd Kasemir, and Jerry Ravetz) (Rotmans and van Asselt 2002). Next to that, two of the regional case studies, that is, Venice and North-West UK, built upon the participatory processes set in motion through the research discussed in this volume. The key researchers in those regional case studies (Venice: Silvio Funtowicz and Ângela Guimarães Pereira; North-West UK: Joe Ravetz and Clair Gough) were all involved in this earlier study. The advantage is that the material collected about citizens' views on the future can be re-used in the scenario development and that the contacts and networks established before can be utilized. So the VISIONS project developed from the study discussed in this volume through using insights, output, and evolved networks, the latter both in terms of stakeholder contacts and established research collaboration.

On the other hand, the VISIONS project also built upon this earlier research by being complementary. It was an explicit choice that the targeted participants of the VISIONS project would be people from the business sector, politicians, and representatives from NGOs. In other words, the VISIONS project was focused on institutionalized stakeholders. Although citizens were not actors targeted specifically in the VISIONS project, they cannot be ignored. Especially in Venice and the Green Heart regional scenario development citizens and their views were explicitly incorporated. In Venice, a couple of citizens were interviewed and the Venice focus groups also involved citizens (Funtowicz and Guimarães Pereira 1999). Some citizens participated in the Green Heart scenario workshops (van Asselt and Greeuw 1999). Next to that, in the context of the VISIONS project a background study on regional identity has been carried out using the Green Heart as a case study (van 't Klooster, van Asselt and Koenis 2002). This study involved a survey among inhabitants of the Green Heart. This regional identity research was used to enrich the scenarios. In this way, citizens' ideas on their region were integrated in the assessment of the future.

Building upon a decade of experiences with IAs, it is clear that the issues IA aims to address are far too complex and too diverse to be dealt with by only one, unique approach. Multiple approaches are needed, employing combinations of tools and methods. The simultaneous and complementary use of various methods can improve the quality and adequacy, because each method has its own strengths and weaknesses. Although IA Focus Groups were the main assessment methodology in the research discussed in earlier parts of this volume, the clear ambition was to explore how IA models and other ICT tools could be used in participatory processes. This research effort thereby illustrated the fact that it is a major methodological challenge for IA to take advantage of the existence of multiple methods.[7] The VISIONS project aimed to address this challenge by using both participatory methods and models to develop scenarios. The participatory processes provided the basis for the scenario narratives. Existing models were used to explore the sketched futures in terms of quantitative trends for particular variables, such as demography and economic development. For the Green Heart case, a spatially explicit cellular automata model (RIVM 2000) was developed, which was used to explore spatial patterns that can be plausibly associated with the scenario narratives.

The VISIONS project was also complementary to the study discussed in this volume in the sense that the research team involved both modelers and social scientists in about equal numbers. This means that constructive discussion about the complementary value of models and participatory tools has taken place within the IA project itself. On the other hand, it is legitimate to assume that a successful IA project dominated by social scientists was a necessary condition to allow a more multidisciplinary IA project team. Also, due to the earlier study, social scientists became more familiar with models, from which the discussions in the VISIONS project benefited.

Conclusions

We have argued that the research discussed in this volume has significantly contributed to the field of IA. In this chapter, we have illustrated that, on the one hand, this research built upon and made use of previous IA endeavors, while, on the other, it evidently influenced the IA research agenda, thereby setting the scene for successive IA endeavors. We conclude that the ULYSSES study considerably influenced the research agenda of the IA community. Box 11.2 summarizes the main points of that influence.

---

[7] See, for example, Rothman and Robinson (1997) for pleas to integrate participatory methods and modelling.

Box 11.2: Major contributions of ULYSSES to the IA research agenda

We conclude that the study discussed in the first two parts of this volume had a major influence on the overall research agenda of the IA research community, by

- highlighting the intrinsic value of participation of stakeholders in IA
- furthering participatory methods as tools for IA
- drawing design criteria for IA models for participatory processes
- reinforcing the notion that multiple perspectives are legitimate and that as a consequence any IA study should involve different perspectives
- indicating the challenge of using multiple methods in a complementary way in an IA endeavor ('IA toolkit')

Many chapters in the two final parts of the present volume discuss recent IA projects that were to a greater or lesser extent developed from the ULYSSES experience. Without these "heirs" it is to be doubted whether in the long run this study would have been regarded as a milestone. The COOL project (Chapter 8), the SIRCH project (Chapter 9), the East Anglia endeavor (Chapter 13) and the VISIONS project (this chapter) reinforce the significance of participation as a vital dimension of IA and advance the use of participatory methods as tools for performing IA. Although an international, multi-institute IA research program was never formally designed, institutionalized, and financed, the evolving web of complementary projects furthering synergy indicates that it seems legitimate to conclude that such a program in which IA projects are covering for each other through furthering long-term strategic research questions is emerging. It is a challenge for the growing IA community to use this recognition of such a broad common research program explicitly in the design and evaluation of particular IA projects.

CHAPTER TWELVE

Citizen participation and developing country agendas

Kilaparti Ramakrishna

Introduction

This chapter seeks to provide a blueprint for carrying out the type of analysis that underpinned many of the earlier chapters in this book with reference to developing countries. In addressing the role that citizens can play in sustainability debates, it discusses the roles played both domestically and internationally by civil society representatives, the scientific community, and governmental representatives in developing countries.

A couple of disclaimers at the outset. Material in this chapter is not the result of any long-term assessment like that which has underpinned the content of many of the chapters in this book. (It does, however, draw on over two decades of the author's experience in dealing with these issues.) As is clear, many of the book's chapters present an interesting set of observations culled from a project that spanned several countries and hundreds of individuals. It contains important lessons for all those interested in public participation in sustainability science albeit largely with a "European" perspective.

The first question addressed here in this regard is the feasibility of this approach for developing countries. This includes expectations as to the potential outcome and of course the usefulness of the results in making better connections between the general public, the scholarly community and the policy-makers in the developing world. Once these connections are made, it can be expected that they will help negotiators to be better prepared in including views of their countries' general public and scholarly community when adopting international agreements, and when preparing their domestic implementation.

However attractive this proposition is, there is no short cut to reaching that goal. It is necessary to undertake several steps and foremost among them is to address the issue of the compatibility of "public" as opposed to "scholarly" views on sustainability science. The question is not whether they are or should be compatible but whether there is a useful way of ensuring dialogues between these types of views? This volume explores procedures for such dialogues.

As far as the developing countries are concerned, several issues present themselves. First there is the definitional question of how one might arrive at either the public or scholarly opinion on anything. Then there is the question of assumptions made: (a) that there is a "gap" between these two views; (b) that it can be "bridged," with correct emphasis on certain elements that go into the process undertaken. But any attempt at "bridging" the gap between the public and scholarly views on sustainability requires the definition and better understanding of processes involved in attaching these labels. And what happens if they are not bridged? At least in the European context, this group of questions has been addressed in a variety of ways throughout the book.

The purpose of this chapter is to assess what role, if any, citizens in developing countries have played in decision-making for sustainable development. First of all one needs to consider whether non-governmental organizations (NGOs) are sufficiently representative of the public at large. Acknowledging that the answer is generally in the affirmative, to what extent can this be generalized across 134 countries that are members of the so-called Group of 77? What has been the interface between scholarly institutions and the public in this group of countries? Could one envisage a project of the kind initiated for Europe and reported in this volume to yield approximately similar results if carried out in the developing countries? How much of what is learned in this book, the results of research in several European countries, has application among the developing countries? Are these results "transferable?" Should they be?

Though the words used may be different and approaches adopted seldom have the feel of the one taken in this book, many individuals, institutions, and to some extent even governmental agencies in developing countries are looking at how one might increase public participation in decision-making on sustainability. This chapter attempts to review those and point out the similarities and differences and suggest a way forward for better understanding and collective action in the goal of increasing public participation and sustainable development. Since the present volume takes the issue of global warming as a point of departure, the rest of the analysis with reference to what one might expect in the developing world is looked at through this prism.

This chapter first looks at the role of NGOs generally and with special reference to climate change both in the industrialized and developing countries. It then looks at how the scholarly community was engaged in the developing countries and the influence they were able to have on developing country environmental policy formulation. Such an analysis is not complete without an understanding of how the policy-makers deal with these issues at the international level within the Group of 77 and in their interactions with the industrialized world. Finally, the chapter addresses some of the policy issues emanating from this analysis that are of relevance to this volume.

The non-governmental level

The advent of non-governmental organizations

Barring some conservation organizations such as the IUCN and WWF, environmental NGOs as we know them now are of relatively recent origin.[1] The early examples came from the United States with the establishment of the Environmental Defense Fund in 1967 and the Natural Resources Defense Council in 1970. The Earth Day campaign, begun in 1970, clearly launched the environmental movement in the United States. Realizing the important work these groups could accomplish in the US, the head of the preparations leading to the organization of the first global conference on environment, Mr Maurice Strong, identified citizen action as vital for any successful intervention in addressing the enormity of global environmental problems.

The first United Nations Conference on Human Environment (UNCHE) in 1972 thus created the United Nations Environment Program (UNEP) as well as the Environmental Liaison Center International (ELCI) in Nairobi. One of the central purposes of ELCI (with help from UNEP) was to help create and support environmental organizations in the developing world and build appropriate connections with their counterparts in the industrialized world.[2]

Greenpeace International (GPI) and Friends of the Earth International (FOEI), which started in 1971 in industrialized countries, have spread their work in the world with GPI operating in thirty-nine countries and FOEI in sixty-six countries, and thirteen affiliate groups. The two conservation organizations referred to earlier (IUCN and WWF) have broadened their scope considerably and include aspects currently dealt with by other environmental organizations since the early 1970s. IUCN brings

[1] Information on some key networks and NGOs relevant for the discussion in this section can be found at: CAN (www.climatenetwork.org), Earth Day Network (www.earthday.org), ED (www.environmentaldefense.org), FOEI (www.foei.org) GPI (www.greenpeace.org), IUCN (www.iucn.org), NRDC (www.nrdc.org), WWF (www.panda.org).

[2] For further information, see: UNCHE (Stockholm 1972) – (www.unep.org/Documents/Default.asp?DocumentID = 97), ELCI (www.elci.org).

together 78 states, 112 governmental agencies and 735 non-governmental organizations with 35 affiliates, whereas the WWF is active in some 100 countries.

When looking at the developing world a couple of decades ago, it was not just the case that there were no NGOs for the protection of the environment, but often there were no governmental agencies either specifically for that purpose. The efforts of the organizations mentioned above with roots firmly set in the industrialized world, and work carried out by UNEP and ELCI, accomplished the twin jobs of creating both environmental ministries/administrative agencies and other governmental structures, as well as a range of NGOs outside the governments. The growth has been so healthy in the world as a whole that the recent edition of the Yearbook of International Organizations (Union of International Associations 2001) listed as many as 25,504 NGOs as "active."

Interactions at the non-governmental level and questions of sustainability

NGOs have transformed global environmental dialogue in ways that few predicted. NGOs from the developing countries joined in this venture in a remarkable fashion. It is important to note at the outset that NGOs have been part of the UN system since its inception, but they have focused primarily on civil, political, and economic aspects. With the UN Conference on Human Environment in 1972 a new group called environmental NGOs or ENGOs came into existence. With the UN Conference on Environment and Development (UNCED) in Rio in 1992, the term has been broadened to include the entire civil society comprising the scientific community, the business community, women, youth, religious and indigenous groups, etc.[3] While this addition brought issues of concern to civil society to the attention of the global community, in some cases it also made it harder to reach agreement on what the civil society contribution to the management of an issue might be.

If we, for the time being, limit our consideration only to ENGOs, it must be pointed out that the participation of ENGOs has not been of the same intensity for each of the global environmental issues. While this is true of NGOs whether they are from industrialized or developing countries, there are several differences between them. (Parenthetically, though, it is worth pointing out that the question of whether NGOs really represent public views adequately is open to debate – in developed

---

[3] For UNCED (Rio de Janeiro 1992) documents, see www.un.org/esa/sustdev/agreed. htm).

as well as in developing countries – and that accountability of NGOs toward the public is not a fully solved problem.) By and large, environmental NGOs in the industrialized countries are firmly in support of protecting the environment. In contrast, many NGOs from the developing countries make a distinction between issues where the country they are coming from is responsible, and issues where the responsibility lies firmly with the industrialized countries. In the first case, they are unceasing in their criticism of their government, through taking various agencies of the government to court, launching intense public campaigns, or using the full potential of the scientific community and the media to articulate their viewpoint. In the second case, when they participate in international meetings they sometimes act as an extension of government delegations, espousing the same positions with reference to equity, fairness, and concerns about sustainability.

One particular innovation, initially introduced by a few ENGOs from the industrialized countries but then further developed together with ENGOs from developing countries, helps cast some useful light on how ENGOs formulate their positions domestically and internationally. This innovation, started in 1989, is called the Climate Action Network (CAN). The idea was to bring together grass roots activists, lobbyists, and members of the scientific community who are experts in climate change science and policy. It became a prominent body for advancing well-informed positions and has also been a key source of specific policies in official declarations.

One interesting aspect of this development was the fact that when CAN was formally launched, it had very few members from the developing world. Those that joined did not have a well-articulated position on what their particular role might be and it is fair to say that the public in those countries knew little about climate change issues. Now with a membership of 328 organizations from 81 countries, some of the most powerful ideas to shape the international agreements, both the 1992 Framework Convention on Climate Change and its 1997 Kyoto Protocol, came from the developing country members of CAN.

CAN members played a prominent role in the IPCC, in large part because governmental delegations from developing countries were small and not well versed in the details of the science, impacts, and policy issues associated with global warming. In the three IPCC assessments released in 1990, 1995, and 2000,[4] there is a very perceptible difference from one assessment to the next in the structure of the teams that were responsible for producing the assessments, contributions from the scientific

---

[4] IPCC 1990; IPCC 1996a; IPCC 2001.

community from the developing countries, and even the emphasis on certain key issues.

One example illustrates the contributions of developing countries in the IPCC and climate change debate. With the increase of developing country scientists in IPCC came more vigorous participation by negotiators from developing countries in formal sessions of the UNFCCC. Equity concerns have been predominant in many of the arguments advanced by these negotiators. But when an attempt was made by developing countries to introduce equity considerations in IPCC assessment, there was a significant uproar from their northern counterparts. In the end, however, the Third Assessment Report of IPCC included a cross-cutting chapter on equity, sustainability, and development.

This success illustrates the fact that there is a connection between what the civil society saw as issues of concern and those that were identified and articulated by the scientific community and governmental representatives. But the next steps are going to be even harder and are discussed later in the present chapter.

The intergovernmental level

Interactions within the Group of 77 and questions of sustainability

Before we look at whether a study similar to the one discussed in the first two parts of this volume could be carried out in the developing world, we must realize the large number of members of that group and both the similarities and the differences that exist between them. The Group of 77 was created in 1964 with the primary function being articulation and promotion of their collective economic interests in the international arena.[5] Thirty-some years later, after a near-doubling of its membership from 77 to 134 developing countries, the challenge of preserving its strength in numbers while capitalizing on the diversity (cultural, religious, economic, and geographic) within the group has remained acute. Members of the Group of 77 recognize that the primary purpose of the Group is to negotiate global development matters on behalf of its membership. While attempts have been made from time to time to enlarge the scope of these activities to reflect changing times, they have not always succeeded in shaping their operations to ensure that the coalitional strength was put to its best use.

Such changes are often unsuccessful in large part because the kind of unity that can be expected from a close knit number of countries that share a common geography, economic base etc. is lacking within the Group.

---

[5] For more information on the G77, see (www.g77.org).

A look at the number of recommendations that have been made from time to time and their scant support illustrate the point further. The recommendations also include providing support to individual or sub-groups of member countries negotiating in pursuit of their own agendas. The idea behind this is to ensure that interests of small countries do not fall by the way side. It is then imperative that the leadership of Group of 77 take those interests, however defined, either at national and/or at a regional level where appropriate, into global forums. It is obvious that for the Group of 77 to be relevant to the changing times, its leaders must be sensitive to, and capitalize on, the diversity of interests within the Group of 77. Despite the diverse membership, the economic and development issues that can be advanced by cooperative action continue to be common among the Group of 77 members.

A clear transparent process of identifying and promoting priority issues, including the identification of selection criteria, has not yet been developed within the Group of 77. But none of these issues are new to the leadership and every once in a while they do address them. They agree that acting as a group they could stress issues on which difficult conflicts exist within and without and which could be better addressed if significant capacity building activity is carried out for the membership of the Group of 77. They also agree that stressing cross-sectoral concerns (like technology transfer and capacity building) rather than single-treaty or single-issue concerns might be a better strategy. They might thus be able to identify issues on which there is an unusual or immediate opportunity for the Group of 77 to have an impact (i.e. issues on which negotiations are about to commence or other global meetings are about to be held).

One particular item of interest for this volume is the recognition by the Group of 77 leadership that it needs to build and maintain a network of qualified research centers. The primary tasks of these centers should be (1) to undertake background technical and policy research on issues of concern to the membership in order to clarify the Group of 77's views on key issues; (2) to brief members (on request) on technical aspects of issues under discussion; (3) to develop supporting technical and policy material to assist the Group of 77 in its negotiations with the OECD countries and other negotiating partners; and (4) to foster public, private, and stakeholder awareness on issues of relevance to the Group of 77. While this list is not explicit about sustainability science as it is defined in this volume, given the interest of the membership about sustainable development one cannot but see a clear nexus between the issues identified above and the core concerns of this volume.

In order to develop core negotiating objectives and strategies the Group of 77 should, in its internal dealings, pay close attention to the differences in views among its members on key issues of concern. One key step in this direction might be to invest in the preparation of written "needs assessments" on selected issues. The Group of 77 should ensure that adequate time is set aside to explore and reconcile (to the greatest extent possible) differences in views and conflicting interests among its members on key issues facing the membership. The Group of 77 should understand the views, concerns and goals of "the other side" on as many issues on its negotiation agenda as is possible. And the Group of 77 should develop response strategies that address all such sets of interests.

This detailed description of current thinking among the Group of 77 membership is furnished only to show the ground to be covered in taking it in any different, however useful, direction. If there is one topic on which the Group of 77 worked outside of the economic/development set of issues with great success, it is the climate change issue. When UNEP and WMO decided to establish the Intergovernmental Panel on Climate Change (IPCC), the executive heads of these two organizations thought it best to limit the membership of IPCC to thirty countries. The formula they advanced would include countries whose greenhouse gas emissions are the cause of the current concern (large industrialized countries), countries that are likely to add significant greenhouse gas emissions in the near future (large developing countries), and countries that are likely to suffer most damage if no action is taken to reduce greenhouse gas emissions (small island nations, etc.). But as soon as the idea was advanced, the entire membership of Group of 77 rose up and denounced the core–periphery concept and wanted to be full members of IPCC! A great departure indeed from a time when the prevailing norm was that developing countries could not be interested in anything but development assistance issues and such.

When we look at the evolving positions within the global climate change debate, it is clear that there were times when national interests sometimes came rather close to splintering the Group of 77 coalition. This was in large part because small island nations saw their future as inextricably tied to averting the cascading effects of global warming, while the OPEC countries demanded compensation for any losses that they might suffer through policies that may impinge on their oil export revenues. African nations are concerned that any benefits that might accrue in an eventual climate agreement would disproportionately favor large developing countries, ignoring the interests of Africa, and so on. In the end, however, the Group of 77 members always managed to stay together as a group. Could this group take on sustainability issues successfully without fully heeding many of the recommendations that emanated from their own meetings? That seems hardly likely.

*Interactions at the general intergovernmental level and
questions of sustainability*

What the developing countries do as a group is always within the context
of what goes on within the global arena. The world community witnessed
a remarkable number of meetings over the past decade where its quest
for sustainability was paramount. Most of the multilateral environmental agreements (MEAs) pay homage to the sustainability concept even
though no specific operational aspects are included in the resulting text.
A legitimate question is if countries in fact would like to attain sustainability, couldn't they work more consciously and more systematically toward
it? Granted countries are abstract entities, but what about the negotiators? Is it their fault, or are they constrained by the circumstances within
which the negotiations are conducted, or is it simply a question of lack
of ability? What is worse is that sometimes even the modest gains made
in one MEA are not automatically advanced in another. Don't the negotiators who are familiar with the way things operate know what they
need to do to ensure that there is gradual progress made from one to the
next?

To answer such questions, we first need to understand the asymmetric
relationship between the industrialized and developing country negotiators. Second, we need to realize the fact that the kind of interagency
coordination that is oftentimes found in the industrialized countries is
seldom seen in most developing countries. Third, even if a negotiator
makes a very conscientious effort at improving the synergies between different MEAs to promote sustainability, it is not given that she or he would
be able to realize such linkages (largely because the way delegations are
composed in the national capitals has little to do with the connections
that exist between different issues). Fourth, the sheer magnitude of developing a framework for sustainability through international agreements
increases the institutional inertia. This challenge is akin to combining
all of the desperate issues dealt with in the international state system in
one negotiation, and therefore a lot harder than working on one isolated
issue at a time. All this of course does not take into account whether the
negotiators from the developing countries even have the capacity to make
those connections.

Capacity building is the buzzword these days. Ranging from the Millennium Summit of the United Nations to the recently concluded Ministerial
Session of the World Trade Organization to a range of MEAs, this issue
has been identified by all as the most pressing one to be dealt with. If
one were to take just the capacity building needs identified in the context
of climate change, a recent bottom-up needs assessment of thirty-three

developing countries carried out by the UNITAR and the Consortium for North–South Dialogue on Climate Change (UNITAR and Consortium for North–South Dialogue on Climate Change 2001) includes the following:

Screening and selecting: mitigation measures, adaptation measures; designing and implementing: awareness building programs, joint ventures, mitigation measures, adaptation measures; compiling GHG inventories; preparing vulnerability studies; development, transfer and adaptation of technology; planning and establishment of research and systematic observation systems; analyzing regulatory issues; planning and introduction of early warning systems and gaining experience in international negotiations.

If one were to carry out similar studies of other MEAs since the early 1990s, similar lists specific to the subject area of the agreement could be advanced. Common to all of them however will be the desire of the negotiators to build capacity among negotiators to do a "better job."

Building capacity of negotiators is vitally needed but that is by no means an answer to the issue we are trying to grapple with here. What is the role of negotiators? Is it that they, acting as a group, agree on ways to address pressing global problems quicker or should they be better at furthering their national interest? How is national interest defined? Where does sustainability figure in all this? As soon as we go down this route, efforts at coordination at the national level, even in defining the national interest, become the area of focus. The classical approach to negotiations is that a negotiator's principal function is to advance the national interest. Could one assume that the national interest is in negotiating an agreement that would further sustainable development?

Let us assume that the capacity building exercise is hugely successful. Obviously the recipient of it can use it in whatever forum she or he would like to use it. But the trouble is the commonly held view that for negotiations to be successful they should be "focused." In other words, anything that is seen as extraneous to the issue, whether it be global warming or biological diversity or any of the other myriad issues, should be respectfully deferred until some other appropriate fora and time. This often means ignoring other issues, however central they might be to several countries. This is true not only of the agreements entered into at the Rio Summit in 1992 but also before and since. The only compromise for negotiators seems to be to adopt general principles, or mention such concerns in the introductory paragraphs or a stated objective, all of which are hortatory but devoid of any operational significance. This approach has resulted in adopting scores of MEAs in the past decade but has done precious little to advance the larger goal of attaining sustainability.

Recognizing this, a number of efforts have tried to explore synergies between different MEAs and make the most of the interlinkages that exist between them. A UNEP sponsored multi-year study resulted in a publication *Protecting Our Planet: Securing Our Future* (UNEP, US NASA, and the World Bank 1998). UNDP likewise carried out similar studies on synergies that exist between different MEAs (UNDP 1997). More recently the UNU had taken up the task through a series of thoughtful publications (UNU, GEIC, and IAS 1998; UNU *et al.* 2001) with a view to making specific recommendations to the World Summit on Sustainable Development (WSSD) in Johannesburg in 2002.[6] However, unless a conscious effort is made to link issues of equity and sustainability as central themes for the consideration of the world community, the goal of adequately addressing them will not be met. The WSSD affords us all an ideal opportunity to advance this issue.

Conclusion and a way forward

It is not in the least bit the intention of this chapter to suggest that similar studies to the one carried out in this volume for Europe are not warranted for developing countries. But the model, however attractive, needs to be reworked to reflect the particular circumstances of the diverse membership of the Group of 77. It is important to fashion a system that increases the confidence of people with respect to the scientific inquiry carried out and the bonafides of the same. It is important to ensure that questions of relevance to developing countries are identified after a needs assessment carried out by developing countries themselves. The intense attention currently being paid to the support of capacity building exercises for developing countries provides an ideal opportunity for connecting NGOs, the scientific community, and governmental representatives. In embarking on this route, it is not enough that we recognize that the model that worked in Europe may not work in developing countries, but that we recognize that there is no single model which works across all of the developing countries either. With transparency and wide inclusiveness as the operating principles, initiating the kind of exercise carried out in this volume across a selection of developing countries could, in addition to increasing the legitimacy of the exercise, yield extremely valuable lessons indeed.

[6] See WSSD (www.johannesburgsummit.org).

CHAPTER THIRTEEN

Linking the citizen to governance for sustainable climate futures

Susanne Stoll-Kleemann, Tim O'Riordan, and Tom R. Burns

The coupling of humans and nature

It is now apparent that climate is no longer a natural phenomenon. Indeed, there is no such thing as a single climate future. We have begun to recognize that the climate that will embrace our grandchildren will largely be determined by how we behave, how we run our democracies, how we value the morality of fairness, and how we relate our everyday actions to how we feel about the impact of future climates on our grandchildren's neighbors. What is particularly significant about this state of affairs is that the decisions we take, individually and collectively in the next two decades, will have a huge affect on the nature of climate a century hence. The profound truth is that we cannot escape our responsibilities for shaping future climates, by leaving it to future generations to determine.

The purpose of this chapter is to examine the implications of this perspective for further research and active policy design aimed at linking citizens to new vistas of governance. That governance will involve many centers of power at every conceivable scale. It will be determined by partnerships with business and civil society through innovative formal and informal arrangements. It will require a participatory form of democracy whose early manifestations are beginning to appear. The implications for both theory and methodology, as well as for climate change research are considerable. At the very least, research will become an active ingredient in this new pattern of governance. Possibly even more dramatic is that the fruits of this research will, in their own way, help determine the very nature of citizenship and of democracy as this new polycentered nature of participatory governance continues to take shape.

Philosophers and policy-makers have long struggled over what precisely is the relationship between humans and nature. The Greeks, and many thinkers afterwards, concentrated on the separate ego, that identifiable distinctiveness that is human consciousness. Others, as ably summarized by the American philosopher Richard Tarnas (1993, pp. 352–359) believe that nature only has meaning through human consciousness. When humans engage with the world, so nature reveals its treasures and its tribulations.

When it comes to climate, a fresh revelation on this ever-mysterious revelation is emerging. The American writer Bill McKibben (1990) mused:

We have changed the atmosphere, and thus we are changing the weather. By changing the weather, we make every spot on earth man-made and artificial. We have deprived nature of its independence, and that is fatal to its meaning. Nature's independence is its meaning; without it there is nothing but us.

To some extent, McKibben is right. There is no climate of any future year that is purely "natural." The forces of human-caused climate change have ensured that all climates from now on, at any scale of occurrence, are a product of both a highly complex and dynamic set of physical and biological forces as well as of human consciousness and, therefore, human interference.

A study of climate futures in eastern England, as published by Lorenzoni and her colleagues (2000) shows that the climate of 2055 and beyond will be very different, depending on the character of political economies of the planet over the forthcoming twenty-five years. More to the point, each form of political economy will dictate the character and effectiveness of climate change mitigation policies and adaptation strategies. The very nature of governance, therefore, not only shapes how society perceives and judges climate change. It also determines the acceptability of the policies and consuming behaviors of those societies. In short, there is an inescapable linkage between forms of governance, human behavior, and societal morality which combine to create the climates of the future. To return to the East Anglian example, the temperature in 2055 could range from 2.3 degrees warmer than today to 1.2 degrees warmer. Precipitation could be 7 per cent lower in the summer, or as much as 15 per cent lower, with a corresponding elevation of precipitation for the winter. Sea levels may be 20 cm higher, or, possibly 50 cm higher with much more extreme stormy weather conditions. So, even over a modest time period that is not longer than the period since the end of the second world war, the climates of this gentle part of the world could be dramatically different. It almost goes without saying that even in East Anglia there will be gainers and losers who will differ in their social and economic membership as well as in their responses, depending on the form of political economy they share, and hence which climate scenario actually encompasses them. Yet the irony is that these different groupings of interests cannot in themselves change the outcome. What they do in the face of these uncertainties,

and to some extent their sense of impotence, becomes a significant issue of their economic behavior and their social morality in the coming
decade.

At this point it is perhaps worth commenting that, as climate scenarios
are targeted more and more at the local scale, so the pattern of beneficiaries and those afflicted becomes clearer. Lorenzoni *et al.* (2000) found
that the very presentation of climate probabilities for fifty years hence trig-
gered very different responses from stakeholders who realized that they
had so much to gain or lose. This finding suggests that "citizens" are by
no means homogenous in their approach to climate change futures, or
to climate change mitigation policies and adaptation strategies. Hence at
the local scale of climate forecasting, it is less likely that a democratic
consensus can be reached over how serious climate change is as a social,
economic, or even moral issue.

The ULYSSES project was pioneering in assisting a cross-section of
citizens throughout Europe to address their possible role in shaping future
climates. By presenting a variety of climate futures, validated by experts,
it introduced a process whereby citizens could begin to realize their own
responsibilities for creating, and indeed possibly choosing, the climates of
the future. Of course, it is never as simple as that, for the obvious reason
that no single individual has any control over the convoluted dynamics
and contours of human intervention and associated "learning." So the
potential value of this study was in part to create the basis for a "moral
framework" for climate futures that at least allowed ordinary citizens,
meeting in small interactive discussion groups, to address their individual
and collective responsibilities.

In actuality, this "moral framework" was not created. This was not the
purpose of the original IA Focus Group formats. What these particular
focus groups did achieve was a fruitful learning experience concerning
possible future climate states, and the revelation on the part of a wide
cross-section of citizens, that they could engage with these images. In
so doing they were able to construct their own interpretations of two
very different future energy scenarios. They were also able to generate a
coherent set of discourses, or common realms of meaning, around these
images. These discussions in turn led to a rich assemblage of reactions
as to how and why citizens should relate to climate/energy futures, what
their responsibilities ought to be, how others should behave, who should
act, how effective government is in dealing with such matters, and how
the comforts of material consumption should be interpreted.

So the strength of this study was to enable citizens to search beyond
their own outlooks, so as to engage in meaningful dialogues with others
over the causes and consequences of climate change. In so doing they

could re-interpret the meanings attributed to such concepts as "victim," "blame," "effectiveness of action," "responsibility," "denial," and "trust" when formulating how they should behave, how they should judge their lifestyles, and how they should engage in the mysterious process of governance. These are the ideals attached to the research discussed in the first two parts of the present volume, so we now explore how these ideals can be taken further in future research of this kind.

Taking the research onward

In order to take this research onward we have to meet a couple of challenges, which are summarized in Box 13.1 and explained in more detail in the following paragraphs.

Box 13.1: Challenges for public participation in sustainability science

The following major challenges will have to be met, if we want to take the research on public participation in sustainability science forward:

- *Clarifying scenarios* for climate futures, so that they are meaningful for citizens
- *Enriching the visualizations* by including exercises in "story-telling" about climate futures and personal responsibilities
- *Opening up new opportunities for schools* by using sustainability and climate change topics for inter-curricular education
- *Setting up creative partnerships with businesses*, who want to enter into dialogues on sustainability with their customers
- *Extending research methodologies* by providing room for both "hard data" and intuition to play a role in participatory procedures

Clarifying the scenarios

In ULYSSES, CLEAR, and the East Anglian study, it became apparent that citizens do not always feel comfortable with the style of scenario presentation that is popular with experts. Graphs, statistics, and models generally do not slip easily into the mind of the lay observer. There is a real danger that what is taken as a meaningful interpretation of uncertainty by experts is not judged so by citizens unfamiliar with these styles of presentation.

We need to think long and hard about how to improve the images of climate futures so that such visions are genuinely meaningful to participants. By "meaningful" we seek to make the case for a more participant-based dialogue about how all kinds of images might be generated and interpreted. In other words, we are arguing for a much more interactive relationship between the generation of images by experts, and the appropriate methods of presenting these images for different groups in society. For example, cultural theory (O'Riordan and Jordan 1999), for all its faults, does tell us that identical images of climate futures are interpreted very differently depending upon people's outlooks, the social solidarities with which they engage, and their sense of trust and judgments about fairness, notably in the conduct of business and government. There is certainly a case to be made for analyzing how different groups in society relate to various means of displaying uncertainty in climate futures. What emerges from the research already done in this area, is that attitudes to trust and effectiveness of governance, reliability of science, judgments about handling ambiguity all need to be fully addressed before any images of possible climate futures are prepared.

We have already noted that climate change is by no means perceived in the same way by different stakeholders. In the East Anglian study the tourist industry senses an advantage, while farmers dependent on spray irrigation are distinctly nervous. Images of climate change may therefore have to be created in a slightly different manner in order to allow each category of stakeholder to see more clearly how different interests in society are affected, in relation to their own preferences or anxieties. So we call for a period of reflective research on the interrelationships between social solidarities and meanings attached to scientific policy-related images.

We believe this research should be highly participatory and interactive, engaging "experts" with representatives of many different civic interests in a highly imaginative and constructive manner. In essence we are suggesting that an active, lay, engaged cross-section of citizens can actually help shape the very character of the images on which the research is targeted.

Enriching the visualizations

People like to play with visual images. The visualization can be as much a game, and therefore a rich learning experience, as it is "serious." We need to move away from the curve of temperature or sea level rise to much more dramatic forms of expression. What we have in mind here are ways of combining understanding of uncertainty with the sense of responsibility for any climate future, regardless of that uncertainty. Emphasizing uncertainty in visualizations can create relatively easy ways for avoiding responsibility. For example, if cherished lifestyles such as driving a car and keeping warm and flying to exotic holiday locations, appear to be threatened by climate change mitigation strategies, then playing up the uncertainty can be one of the ruses for denying the dissonance that this conflict can create. The trick therefore, is to find a means of visualization that allows uncertainty to be addressed, and both appreciated and understood, without enabling it to cause any participant to hide behind the cloak of uncertainty and deny a sense of civic responsibility.

We feel this approach can best be taken by a number of innovative measures. One might be to combine socially active citizens with climate scientists and policy practitioners so that collectively they can address this issue and search for commonly agreed solutions. Another might be to innovate with the practice of "story-telling." This would mean encouraging participants from a variety of ages and social settings to devise their own ways of creating narratives, or painting pictures, or acting out role playing, or interacting with sophisticated simulations. In such ways, participants themselves can devise what they regard as the most "authentic" means of creating meaningful messages about climate futures and personal responsibility. The trick here is to keep these action groups of innovative visualization methodologies similar in age, social disposition, and political power. However, when it comes to targeting gainers and losers it would be wise deliberately to place them together in more interactive groups to combine story-telling with more traditional focus group approaches.

Story-telling is a novel art form. The roles can be played by citizens themselves, either based on prompts by facilitators, or simply in free flow dialogue. Story-telling is particularly pertinent for discontinuous simulations of climate futures, such as can be found in sudden ice melt, or thermo-haline collapse. This is so because no one can possibly predict how society, in its various interest configurations, might react to the suddenness of so-called "side-swipes" of altered nature. Story-telling can enable participants to overwrite ambiguity, and to explore creatively how to form alliances with all manner of gainers and losers. This approach may help policy-makers to identify precursor policy options through sensing the acceptability or intolerance of citizens' views in the face of discontinuing uncertainty.

Opening up new opportunities for schools

Sustainability and climate change is a perfect intercurricular topic. It spans science and the arts, social change and citizenship, analysis and ethical judgment. With the advent of viewer-friendly computer packages, it is now possible for youngsters to embark creatively on visualizations, story-telling and role playing. Above all, there is a real opportunity to introduce them to different concepts of citizenship and democracy. A task for the research community beyond the work discussed in earlier chapters of this volume is therefore to design this broadened methodology for the classroom, hopefully in collaboration with business sponsorship and government (national and local) assistance.

There is also another option. This is to create a sense of real responsibility in pupils by enabling them to design energy-saving and low-carbon futures for their school. With assistance from local business, and the local authorities, it may be possible for groups of pupils, acting across the curriculum, to design and help implement a low-carbon audit and budget for the school, along, possibly, with some sort of energy-from-waste scheme. Pupil assessment would be based on their initiative, and their capacity to put their ideas into practical effect. This would also involve pupils working as teams, monitoring their individual responsibilities, and being graded on their individual and collective contributions. The protocols for such assessment schemes will require careful thought. The aim, essentially, is to encourage teamwork and citizenship. This surely is the way forward for education for sustainability.

Combined with enriched visualizations, it should be possible for pupils to understand how difficult (or, at times, how easy) it can be to prepare and execute such an audit, why it is necessary for their school, and what might be the influence on future climate if every school followed their example. In addition they would learn about how difficult it is to join up budgets across governmental scales, and the public to private sectors. Furthermore, they would learn a lot about the politics and economics of energy prices, and the implications of a carbon tax for creating pools of money to finance such low carbon initiatives (see O'Riordan 1997, for further discussion). So the school of the future would be both a learning and active agent in the transition to more sustainable climate futures. Some of the carbon tax revenue, plus the expenditure saved by the pupils' initiative should be invested in projects of value to the pupils themselves.

Partnerships with business

The business community is slowly beginning to wake up to their sustainability responsibilities. This invariably is taking time, as businesses peer through the contradictions that envelop the notion of sustainability and see a vista that is not always immediately pleasing (see e.g., Elkington 1999, for a review). So business is proceeding cautiously; the bigger players first, but the small and medium sector some distance behind. The drivers toward environmental management systems, to greater accountability to consumer requirements, to the increasingly watchful eyes of the market analysts, and to the need to retain a good reputation image, have coalesced to create a number of new business-based initiatives. These include corporate social reporting, new ethical positioning, changing the culture of the corporation, and generating new business ventures around sustainability options (see Welford 2000).

In this mobile arena, there is scope for a number of creative partnerships with business, arising out of the ULYSSES ideals. There is a possibility, for instance, of providing a visualization center in one petrol station in every city. This could be used as a learning center for car drivers to understand the climate change contribution of the automobile, and to evaluate a number of locally generated options to reduce car usage. If community empowerment arrives at the sub-city level, as is being proposed for the "new look" sustainability strategies for cities and towns (see, for example, Department of the Environment, Transport, and the Regions 1998), then it may be possible for such activities to be part of a more deliberative civic process regarding the future of transport and mobility in low carbon futures.

Extending methodology

All these proposals, if put into action, will require a fresh approach to methodology. The key will lie in the creative mixing of quantitative and qualitative approaches, the introduction of intuition and empathetic feelings into the research agenda, and the role of research generally as an active ingredient in policy design and citizen learning.

Quantitative and qualitative approaches can operate in a number of ways. One is to track the "mind set" of a given individual through a range of responses to social, political, and ethical pathways to climate futures. Multilevel modeling (see Langford, Bentham, and McDonald 1998) provides a basis for this. Another is to enable participants to rank options based on "hard data" and subsequently to discuss the implications for specified different groups in society. This analytical-judgmental linkage, set in a political-stakeholder interest framework, is potentially very revolutionary in awareness raising. A third approach is to use a more interactive methodology to break down the "third dimension" power stranglehold. The notion of "third dimension" was introduced by the British sociologist Steven Lukes (1978). Lukes claimed that the "real interests" of citizens are being deliberately obscured by elites and controlling agencies, who manipulate information and preferences. Accordingly, individuals are shielded from realizing their own essential values and inner power to change their worlds. But because they are manipulated into thinking that their worlds, as shaped by these dominant interests, are satisfactory, they are unable to realize the hidden conflicts that contradict their actions set against their inner moral framework. Thus even images of dangerous climate futures may not dissuade them from abandoning a carbon-rich and comfortable lifestyle. This theme is given a detailed airing from a socio-psychological perspective by Stoll-Kleemann *et al.* (2001). Citizens can create an imaginative array of reasons why they should not change their consumer behavior, even when it clearly contradicts their outlook on climate change and moral norms. A richer methodology should be able to explore this fascinating interface between the worlds of socio-psychology and political power (or disempowerment).

Intuitive approaches deserve a special mention. By "intuition" we mean sensing the inner being of a participant or respondent, derived through creating a real sense of trust and openness, thereby exposing true feelings about how various "others" are judged, and how moral norms are violated or remain in contradiction. Treated sensitively, and always coupled to reliable data about personal outlook, sense of self-esteem and the influences of social networks, this approach can enable the many ambiguities in social and private behavior, in the face of deep underlying anxieties over climate change implications for future peoples, to be delicately and sensitively explored. For loser–beneficiary dialogues, such an approach could be particularly illuminating.

Engaging in interactive governance

Government is becoming governance as the twenty-first century dawns. Governance is the process of conducting government through many centers of action, at a huge variety of geographical scales, and via partnerships of formal and informal democracy (Burns 1999; Burns *et al.* 2000). Pierre and Stoker (2000) summarize these changes:

> multi-level governance emphasizes negotiated arrangements between clusters of actors at different levels. Such negotiated arrangements are created not because the levels of governments are hierarchical or "nested"... but precisely because much of the contemporary governance defies hierarchical orders.

Multilevel governance operates through open and accommodating structures, creating effective partnerships at the intergovernmental level (at all scales) and also with the private and voluntary sectors.

Such a perspective allows for a more deliberative and participatory democracy. Civil society is already mobilized (see Rosenau 1992;

O'Riordan 2000), but not always constructively. Local governance in the UK is now geared to more formal patterns of civil empowerment (Department of the Environment, Transport and the Regions 1998). What all this means will depend on how the patterns of formal and informal governance plays out. There are as many prognoses as commentators. One perspective on the chances and dangers along this way is given in Box 13.2 below.

Box 13.2: Opportunities and risks of interactive governance on climate futures

For the purposes of this chapter, we foresee a period of considerable social mobilization of groups seeking to promote or resist climate change mitigation policies such as tough regulation, carbon or energy levies and various incentives for low carbon technologies and economies. Such mobilization could, if left unaided, create prolonged dispute during transitional political intervention in social behavior and economic choices. Such discontent could weaken the resolve of governments and businesses, even if working in creative partnerships, to maintain prolonged policy commitments for serious reduction of greenhouse gas emissions. On the other hand, a society made more aware of its responsibilities, and the implications of its actions and consumer preferences, could be creatively mobilized toward consensus through demonstrably fair means of compensating losers and penalizing gainers. Such a delicate combination of outcomes can only come through participatory forgiveness and mutual trust. The research discussed in the first two parts of this book provides a glimpse of how this might be achieved.

For the aftermath of this research effort, therefore, the prospects of a more poly-centric and participatory democracy may provide the opportunities and the accommodative political framework for a more imaginative and empowering approach to citizenship in the coming decades. We foresee that the scope and opportunities for many of the suggestions made in this chapter will be much greater than in the past. There has never been a more propitious time to realize and extend the vision of public participation in sustainability science discussed in this volume.

References

Alcamo, J. (ed.) (1994). *IMAGE 2.0: Integrated Modelling of Global Climate Change*. Kluwer, London.

Alcamo, J., E. Kreileman, and R. Leemans (1996). "Global models meet global policy. How can global and regional modellers connect with environmental policy makers? What has hindered them? What has helped?" *Global Environmental Change* 6(4), pp. 255–259.

Alexander, J. C., and P. Smith (1996). "Social science and salvation: risk society as mythical discourse." *Zeitschrift für Soziologie* 25, pp. 251–262.

Andriessen, D. G. (1995). "Policy simulation and crisis management: the harsh winter scenario," in D. Crookall and K. Arai (eds.), *Simulation and Gaming Across Disciplines and Cultures: ISAGA at a Watershed*. Sage, Thousand Oaks, CA, pp. 101–110.

Annan, K. A. (2000). "Sustaining the earth in the new millenium: the UN secretary-general speaks out," *Environment* 42(8), pp. 20–30.

Bailey, P. D. (1997). "Integrated environmental assessment: a new methodology for environmental policy?" *Environmental Impact Assessment Review* 17, pp. 221–226.

Bailey, P., S. Yealey, and J. Forrester (1999). "Involving the public in local air pollution assessment: a citizen participation case study," *International Journal of Environment and Pollution* 11(3), pp. 290–303.

Bakker, K., L. del Moral, T. E. Downing, C. Giansante, A. Garrido, E. Iglesias, B. Pedregal, P. Riesco, and SIRCH team (1999). *A Framework for Institutional Analysis*. SIRCH Working Paper. 3. University of Oxford, Environmental Change Institute, Oxford.

Bakker, K., T. E. Downing, J. Handmer, E. Crook, and E. Penning-Rowswell (2000). *Hydrological Risk in the Thames Valley*. Flood Hazard Research Centre, Middlesex.

Bauman, Z. (1991). *Modernity and Ambivalence*. Polity Press, Cambridge.

(1998). *Globalization – The Human Consequences*. Polity Press, Cambridge.

Beck, U. (1992). *Risk Society: Towards a New Modernity*. Sage, London.

(1994). "The reinvention of politics: towards a theory of reflexive modernization," in U. Beck, A. Giddens, and S. Lash (eds.), *Reflexive Modernization. Politics, Tradition and Aesthetics in the Modern Social Order*. Polity Press, Cambridge, pp. 1–55.

Beck, U., A. Giddens, and S. Lash (1994). *Reflexive Modernization – Politics, Tradition and Aesthetics in the Modern Social Order*. Polity Press, Cambridge.

Bell, A. (1994). "Climate and opinion: public and media discourse on the global environment," *Discourse and Society* 5(1), pp. 33–64.

Bohman, J., and W. Rehg (1997). *Essays on Reason and Politics – Deliberative Democracy*. MIT Press, Cambridge, MA.

Bostrom, A., G. Morgan, B. Fischoff, and D. Read (1994). "What do people know about global climate change? Part 1: Mental models," *Risk Analysis* 14(6), pp. 959–970.

Brand, K.-W. (1997). "Environmental consciousness and behaviour: the greening of lifestyles," in M. Redclift and G. Woodgate (eds.), *The International Handbook of Environmental Sociology*. Edward Elgar, Cheltenham, pp. 204–217.

Brandom, R. B. (1998). *Making it Explicit: Reasoning, Representing and Discursive Commitment*. Harvard University Press, Cambridge, MA.

Brewer, G. D. (1986). "Methods for synthesis: policy exercises," in W. C. Clark and R. E. Munn (eds.), *Sustainable Development of the Biosphere*. Cambridge University Press, pp. 455–475.

Brooks, M. (1999). "Live and let live," *New Scientist*, 3 July, pp. 33–36.

Brown, M. A., M. D. Levine, W. Short, and J. G. Koomey (2001). "Scenarios for a clean energy future," *Energy Policy* 29(14), pp. 1179–1196.

Burgess, J., C. Harrison, and P. Filius (1995). *Making the Abstract Real: A Cross-Cultural Study of Public Understanding of Global Environmental Change*. University College London, London.

Burgess, J., M. Limb, and C.M. Harrison (1988). "Exploring environmental values through the medium of small groups: 1. Theory and practice," *Environment and Planning A* 20, pp. 309–326.

Burns, T. R. (1999). "The evolution of parliaments and societies in Europe: challenges and prospects," *European Journal of Social Theory* 2(2), pp. 167–194.

Burns, T. R., and R. Ueberhorst (1988). *Creative Democracy: Systematic Conflict Resolution and Policymaking in a World of High Science and Technology*. Praeger, New York.

Burns, T. R., C. C. Jaeger, M. Kamali, A. Liberatore, Y. Meny, and P. Nanz (2000). *The Future of Parliamentary Democracy: Transition and Challenge in European Governance*. The Italian Parliament, Rome.

Buttel, F. H., and P. J. Taylor (1992). "Environmental sociology and global environmental change: a critical assessment," *Society and Natural Resources* 5, pp. 211–230.

Byers, P. Y., and J. R. Wilcox (1991). "Focus groups: a qualitative opportunity for researchers," *Journal of Business Communication* 28(1), pp. 63–78.

Calatrava, J., A. Garrido, and E. Iglesias (1999). *Economics Applied to Drought Planning and Management for Drought Mitigation*. Polytechnical University of Madrid, Madrid.

Castells, M. (1996). *The Rise of the Network Society*. Blackwell, Oxford.

    (1997). *The Power of Identity*. Blackwell, Oxford.

Casti, J. L. (1986). "On system complexity: identification, measurement, and management," in J. L. Casti and A. Karlqvist (eds.), *Complexity, Language, and Life: Mathematical Approaches*. Springer, Berlin, pp. 146–173.

Cebon, P., H. C. Davies, D. M. Imboden, and C. C. Jaeger (eds.) (1998). *Views from the Alps. Towards Regional Assessments of Climate Change*. MIT Press, Cambridge, MA.

Central Planning Bureau (1992). *Scanning the Future: A Long-Term Scenario Study of the World Economy 1990–2015*. Central Planning Bureau of the Netherlands.

Clark, W. C., and N. M. Dickson (1998). *The Global Environmental Assessment Project: Overview for 1998*. GEA Working Paper, June. John F. Kennedy School of Government, Harvard University, Cambridge, MA.

Coenen, F. H. J. M., D. Huitema, and L. J. O. J. O'Toole (1998). *Participation and the Quality of Environmental Decision Making*. Kluwer Academic Publishers, Dordrecht.

Cohen, J. E. (1977). "Mathematical models of schistosomiasis," *Annual Review of Ecology and Systematics* 8, pp. 209–233.

Cohen, S. J. (1997). "Scientist–stakeholder collaboration in integrated assessment of climate change: lessons from a case study of Northwest Canada," *Environmental Modelling and Assessment* 2(4), pp. 281–293.

Conner, J., K. Richardson, and N. Fenton (1991). *Nuclear Reactions*. John Libby, London.

Coote, A., and J. Lenaghan (1997). *Citizens' Juries: Theory into Practice*. Institute for Public Policy Research, London.

Cox, K. K., J. B. Higginbotham, and J. Burton (1976). "Application of focus group interviews in marketing," *Journal of Marketing* 40, pp. 77–80.

Crenshaw, E. M., and J. C. Jenkings (1996). "Social structure and global climate change: sociological proposition concerning the greenhouse effect," *Sociological Focus* 29(4), pp. 341–358.

Dahinden, U. (1998). "Umweltpolitik zwischen Technokratie und Demokratie (Environmental policy between technocracy and democracy)." Ph.D. dissertation. Faculty of Social Sciences and History, Darmstadt University of Technology, Darmstadt.

Darier, É. (1997). *Ulysses Manchester IA Focus Group 1 – Process Description and Preliminary Observations*. Internal report. CSEC, Lancaster University, Lancaster.

Darier, É., C. Gough, B. De Marchi, S. O. Funtowicz, R. Grove-White, D. Kitchener, A. Pereira, and B. Wynne (1999). "Between democracy and expertise? Citizens' participation and environmental Integrated Assessment in Venice (Italy) and St. Helens (UK)," *Journal of Environmental Policy and Planning* 1(2), pp. 103–121.

Darier, É., and D. Kitchener (1997). "Transcripts and Notes of the St. Helens Citizens' Panels" (manuscript). CSEC / Lancaster University, Lancaster.

Darier, É., and R. Schüle (1999). " 'Think Globally, Act Locally'? Climate change and public participation in Manchester and Frankfurt," *Local Environment* 4(3), pp. 317–330.

De Marchi, B., and S. O. Funtowicz (1997). *Proposta per un modulo comunicativo sperimentale sul rischio chimico a Porto Marghera*. Quaderno 97-6. Institute of International Sociology of Gorizia, Mass Emergencies Programme, Gorizia.

De Marchi, B., S. O. Funtowicz, S. Lo Cascio, and G. Munda (2000). *Ecological Economics* 14, pp. 267–282.

De Marchi, B., S. O. Funtowicz, C. Gough, Â. Guimarães Pereira, and E. Rota (1998). *The ULYSSES Voyage: The ULYSSES Project at the JRC*. EUR 17760EN. Joint Research Centre, European Commission, Ispra.

de Vries, H. J. M. (1995). *SusClime*. Globo Report Series. 11. National Institute of Public Health and Environmental Protection (RIVM), Bilthoven.

de Vries, H. J. M., T. Fiddaman, and R. Janssen (1993). *Strategic Planning Exercise about Global Warming*. 461502001. National Institute of Public Health and Environmental Protection (RIVM), Bilthoven.

Department of the Environment, Transport, and the Regions. (1998). *Modern Local Government in Touch with People*. Department of the Environment, Transport, and the Regions, London.

Doble, J. (1995). "Public opinion about issues characterized by technological complexity and scientific uncertainty," *Public Understanding of Science* 4, pp. 95–118.

Douglas, M. (1972). "Environments at Risk," in J. Benthall (ed.), *Ecology: The Shaping Enquiry*. Longman, London, pp. 129–145.

Douglas, M. (ed.) (1982). *Essays in the Sociology of Perception*. Routledge and Kegan Paul, London.

Douglas, M., and A. Wildavsky (1982). *Risk and Culture. An Essay on the Selection of Technical and Environmental Dangers*. University of California Press, Berkeley, CA.

Dowlatabadi, H., and M. G. Morgan (1994). "A model framework for integrated studies of the climate problem," *Energy Policy* 22(3), pp. 209–221.

Downing, T. E. (2002). "Impacts of climate change on domestic demand for water in southern England," *Water Policy* (forthcoming).

Downing, T. E., S. Moss, and C. Pahl-Wostl (2001). "Understanding climate policy using participatory agent-based social simulation," in S. Moss and P. Davidsson (eds.), *Multi-agent Based Simulation: Second International Workshop (MABS 2000)*. *Lecture Notes in Computer Science*. Springer, Heidelberg, pp. 198–213.

Downing, T. E., A. A. Olsthoorn, and R. S. J. Tol (eds.) (1999). *Climate, Change and Risk*. Routledge, London.

Dunlap, R. E. (1998). "Lay perceptions of global risk. Public views of global warming in cross-national context," *International Sociology* 13(4), pp. 473–498.

Dunlap, R. E., and W. R. J. Catton (1994). "Struggling with human exemptionalism: the rise, decline and revitalization of environmental sociology," *American Sociologist* 25(1), pp. 5–29.

Dunlap, R. E., and A. G. Mertig (1996). "Weltweites Umweltbewusstsein. Zu den Ursachen und Konsequenzen von Umwelteinstellungen in der Bevölkerung," in A. Diekmann and C. C. Jaeger (eds.), *Kölner Zeitschrift für Soziologie und Sozialpsychologie*. Westdeutscher Verlag, Opladen, pp. 193–218.

——— (1997). "Global environmental concern: an anomaly for postmaterialism," *Social Science Quarterly* 78(1), pp. 24–29.

Dunlap, R. E., G. H. Gallup, and A. M. Gallup (1993a). *Health of the Planet: Results of a 1992 International Environmental Opinion Survey of Citizens in 24 Nations*. The George H. Gallup International Institute, Princeton, NJ.

——— (1993b). "Of global concern," *Environment* November 1993, pp. 6–15, 33–39.

Dürrenberger, G., J. Behringer, U. Dahinden, Å. Gerger, B. Kasemir, C. Querol, R. Schüle, D. Tàbara, F. Toth, M. B. A. van Asselt, D. Vassilarou, N. Willi, and C. C. Jaeger (1997). *Focus Groups in Integrated Assessment: A Manual for a Participatory Tool*. ULYSSES WP-97-2. Center for Interdisciplinary Studies in Technology, Darmstadt University of Technology, Darmstadt.

Dyson, E. (1999). "Losing touch with reality," *The Guardian*, 4 March, Online Supplement, p. 11. London.

Eckersley, R., and K. Jeans (eds.) (1995). *Challenge to Change: Australia in 2020*. CSIRO Publishing, Victoria.

Elkington, J. (1999). *Cannibals With Forks: The Triple Bottom Line of 21st Century Business*. Touchstone Press, London.

Ellis, J. J. (2000). *Founding Brothers. The Revolutionary Generation*. Knopf, New York.

European Commission (1993). *White Paper: Growth, Competitiveness, Employment: The Challenges and Ways Forward into the 21st Century*. CEC, Brussels.

(1998). *The Competitiveness of European Industry*. Office for Official Publications of the European Communities, Luxembourg.

European Communities (1994). *Potential Benefits of Integration of Environmental and Economic Policies*. Graham and Trotman, London.

EVCA (1996). *White Paper*. European Venture Capital Association (EVCA), Brussels.

(1997). *The EVCA Yearbook 1997: A Survey of Venture Capital and Private Equity Capital in Europe*. European Venture Capital Association (EVCA), Brussels.

Exner, J. E. (1993). *The Rorschach: A Comprehensive System*. John Wiley & Sons, Hoboken, NJ.

Fiorino, D. J. (1990). "Citizen participation and environmental risks: a survey of institutional mechanisms," *Science, Technology & Human Values* 15, pp. 226–243.

Forrester, J. (1999). "The logistics of public participation in environmental assessment," *International Journal of Environment and Pollution* 11(3), pp. 316–330.

Foucault, M. (1981). "Omnes et Singulatim: towards a criticism of 'political reason,'" *The Tanner Lectures on Human Values*. University of Utah Press, Salt Lake City, and Cambridge University Press, pp. 223–254.

(1991). "Governmentality," in G. Burchell, C. Gordon, and P. Miller (eds.), *The Foucault Effect*. Harvester Wheatsheaf, Hemel Hempstead, pp. 87–104.

Fukuyama, F. (1996). *Trust: The Social Virtues and the Creation of Prosperity*. Free Press, New York.

(1999). *The Great Disruption: Human Nature and the Reconstitution of Social Order*. Free Press, New York.

Funtowicz, S. O., and Â. Guimarães Pereira (1999). *VISIONS Report: Venice 2050*. Joint Research Centre, Ispra, Italy.

Funtowicz, S. O., and J. R. Ravetz (1990). *Uncertainty and Quality in Science for Policy*. Kluwer, Dordrecht.

(1991). "A new scientific methodology for global environmental issues," in R. Constanza (ed.), *Ecological Economics*. Columbia University, New York, pp. 137–152.

(1992). "Three types of risk assessment and the emergence of post-normal science," in S. Krimsky and D. Golding (eds.). *Social Theories of Risk*. Praeger Publishers, Westport, pp. 251–273.

(1993). "Science for the post-normal age," *Futures* 25(7), pp. 739–755.

(1994a). "Emergent complex systems," *Futures* 26(6), pp. 568–582.

(1994b). "The worth of a songbird: ecological economics as a post-normal science," *Ecological Economics* 10, pp. 197–207.

(1997). "The poetry of thermodynamics," *Futures* 29(9), pp. 791–810.

Gallie, W. B. (1956). "Essentially contested concepts," *Proceedings of the Aristotelian Society* 56, pp. 167–198.

Giansante, C. E. A. (2000). *Adaptive Responses to Hydrological Risk: An Analysis of Stakeholders*. University of Seville, Seville.

Gieser, L., and M. L. Stein (eds.) (1999). *Evocative Images: The Thematic Apperception Test and the Art of Projection*. American Psychological Association, Washington, DC.

Goss, J. D., and T. R. Leinbach (1996). "Focus groups as alternative research practice: Experience with transmigrants in Indonesia," *Area* 28(2), pp. 115–123.

Grin, J., H. van de Graaf, and R. Hoppe (1997). *Technology Assessment Through Interaction: A Guide*. SDU, The Hague.

Grove-White, R., P. Macnaghten, S. Mayer, and B. Wynne (1997). *Uncertain World – Genetically Modified Organisms, Food and Public Attitudes in Britain*. Lancaster University, Lancaster.

Guimarães Pereira, Â., C. Gough, and B. De Marchi (1999). "Computers, citizens and climate change – the art of communicating technical issues," *International Journal of Environment and Pollution* 11(3), pp. 266–289.

Gundersen, A. G. (1995). *The Environmental Promise of Democratic Deliberation*. University of Wisconsin Press, Madison, WI.

Gutman, A., and D. Thompson (1996). *Democracy and Disagreement*. Harvard University Press, Cambridge, MA.

Habermas, J. (1981). *The Theory of Communicative Action: Reason and the Rationalization of Society*. Beacon Press, Boston, MA.

Hadley, S. W., and W. Short (2001). "Electricity sector analysis in the clean energy futures study" *Energy Policy* 29(14), pp. 1285–1298.

Haigh, N. (1998). "Roundtable: challenges and opportunities for IEA – science-policy interactions from a policy perspective," *Environmental Modeling and Assessment* 3(3), pp. 135–142.

Hannigan, J. A. (1995). *Environmental Sociology: A Social Constructionist Approach*. Routledge, London.

Harrison, C. M., J. Burgess, and P. Filius (1996). "Rationalizing environmental responsibilities – a comparison of lay publics in the UK and the Netherlands," *Global Environmental Change* 6(3), pp. 215–234.

Hausrath, A. (1971). *Venture Simulation in War, Business and Poltitics*. McGraw-Hill, New York.

Held, D. (1987). *Models of Democray*. Basil Blackwell, Oxford.

(1995). *Democracy and the Global Order: From the Modern State to Cosmopolitan Governance*. Polity Press, Cambridge.

Hilderink, H. B. M., E. Mosselman, A. H. W. Beusen, M. B. A. van Asselt, M. G. J. den Elzen, P. J. F. de Vink, and J. Rotmans (1998). *TARGETS CD*. Baltzer Science Publishers, Bussum.

Hisschemöller, M. (1993). *De democratie van problemen. De relatie tussen de inhoud van beleidsproblemen en methoden van politieke besluitvorming*. VU Boekhandel, Amsterdam.

Holling, C. S. (ed.) (1978). *Adaptive Environmental Assessment and Management*. Wiley, London.

Hordijk, L. (1991). *An Integrated Assessment Model for Acidification in Europe*. Free University of Amsterdam, Amsterdam.

Hourcade, J.-C. (1993). "Modelling long-run scenarios. Methodology lessons from a prospective study on a low CO2 intensive country," *Energy Policy* 21, pp. 309–326.

Imboden, D., and C. C. Jaeger (1999). "Towards a sustainable energy future," in OECD (ed.), *Energy: The Next Fifty Years*. OECD, Paris, pp. 63–94.

International Energy Agency (1995). *World Energy Outlook*. International Energy Agency, Paris.

International Herald Tribune (1999). "Tietmeyer's parting advice to Europe," *International Herald Tribune*, 23 August, p. 1 & 5.

IPCC (1990). *First Assessment Report*. (vol. 1). Intergovernmental Panel on Climate Change, Cambridge University Press, Cambridge.

(1996a). *Climate Change 1995: The Science of Climate Change. Technical Summary of Working Group I Report*. Intergovernmental Panel on Climate Change, Cambridge University Press, Cambridge.

(1996b). "Global Environmental Change Report 2. IPCC Second Assessment Report: A Review," March. Intergovernmental Panel on Climate Change, Geneva, pp. 1–8.

(2001). *Third Assessment Report of the Intergovernmental Panel on Climate Change*. Intergovernmental Panel on Climate Change, Cambridge University Press, Cambridge.

Irwin, A., and B. Wynne (1996). *Misunderstanding Science? The Public Reconstruction of Science and Technology*. Cambridge University Press, Cambridge.

Jaeger, C. C. (1998). "Risk management and Integrated Assessment," *Environmental Modeling and Assessment* 3, pp. 211–225.

Jaeger, C. C., R. Schüle, and B. Kasemir (1999). "Focus groups in Integrated Assessment: a micro-cosmos for reflexive modernization," *Innovation* 12(2), pp. 195–219.

Jaeger, C. C., G. Dürrenberger, H. Kastenholz, and B. Truffer (1993). "Determinants of environmental action with regard to climatic change," *Climatic Change* 23, pp. 193–211.

(1998). "Decision analysis and rational action," in S. Rayner and E. L. Malone (eds.), *Human Choice and Climate Change. The Tools for Policy Analysis*. Battelle Press, Columbus, OH, pp. 141–215.

Jaeger, C. C., O. Renn, E. A. Rosa, and T. Webler (2001). *Risk, Uncertainty, and Rational Action*. Earthscan, London.

Jaeger, C. C., T. Barker, O. Edenhofer, S. Faucheux, J.-C. Hourcade, B. Kasemir, M. O'Connor, M. Parry, I. Peters, J. R. Ravetz, and J. Rotmans (1997a).

"Procedural leadership in climate policy: a European task," *Global Environmental Change* 7(3), pp. 195–203.

Jaeger, C. C., S. O. Funtowicz, B. Wynne, S. Giner, Å. Gerger, M. Giaoutzi, F. Toth, J. Jäger, J. R. Ravetz, and G. Dürrenberger (1997b). *Preliminary Report on Urban Sustainability: Annex 1 to ULYSSES Progress Report – May 1996 to April 1997*. University of Technology, Darmstadt.

Jaeger, C. C., M. Chadwick, B. Wynne, S. O. Funtowicz, M. Giaoutzi, S. Giner, F. Toth, J. Jäger, G. Dürrenberger, J. R. Ravetz, and C. Casilli (1995). *ULYSSES: Urban Lifestyles, Sustainability and Integrated Environmental Assessment. A RTD proposal for Framework Programme IV (EC), Environment and Climate*. University of Technology, Darmstadt.

Jäger, J. (1998). "Current thinking on using scientific findings in environmental policy making," *Environmental Modeling and Assessment* 3(3), pp. 145–153.

Jasanoff, S. (1990). *The Fifth Branch: Science Advisers as Policy Makers*. Harvard University Press, Cambridge, MA.

Jasanoff, S., and B. Wynne (1998). "Science and decisionmaking," in S. Rayner and E.L. Malone (eds.), *Human Choice and Climate Change*. Vol. 1: *The Societal Framework*. Battelle Press, Columbus, OH, pp. 1–87.

Jasanoff, S., G. E. Markle, J. C. Petersen, and T. Pinch (1995). *Handbook of Science and Technology Studies*. Sage, Thousand Oaks, CA.

Joldersma, C., J. L. Geurts, J. Vermaas, and G. Heyne (1995). "A policy exercise for the Dutch health care system for the elderly," in D. Crookall and K. Arai (eds.), *Simulation and Gaming across Disciplines and Cultures: ISAGA at a Watershed*. Sage, Thousand Oaks, CA, pp. 111–121.

Joss, S., and J. Durant (eds.) (1995). *Public Participation in Science: The Role of Consensus Conferences in Europe*. Trustees of the Science Museum, London.

Karl, T., N. Nicholls, and A. Ghazi (eds.) (1999). *Weather and Climate Extremes: Changes, Variations, and a Perspective from the Insurance Industry*. Kluwer Academic Publishers, Dordrecht.

Kasemir, B., D. Schibli, S. Stoll, and C. C. Jaeger (2000). "Involving the public in climate and energy decisions," *Environment* 42(3), pp. 32–42.

Kasemir, B., M. B. A. van Asselt, G. Dürrenberger, and C. C. Jaeger (1999b). "Integrated Assessment of sustainable development: Multiple Perspectives in Interaction," *International Journal of Environment and Pollution* 11(4), pp. 407–425.

Kasemir, B., J. Behringer, B. De Marchi, C. Deuker, G. Dürrenberger, S. O. Funtowicz, Å. Gerger, M. Giaoutzi, Y. Haffner, M. Nilsson, C. Querol, R. Schüle, D. Tàbara, M. B. A. van Asselt, D. Vassilarou, N. Willi, and C. C. Jaeger (1997). *Focus Groups in Integrated Assesment: The ULYSSES Pilot Experience*. ULYSSES WP-97-4, Center for Interdisciplinary Studies in Technology, Darmstadt University of Technology, Darmstadt.

Kasemir, B., U. Dahinden, A. Gerger, R. Schüle, D. Tàbara, and C. C. Jaeger (1999a). *Fear, Hope and Ambiguity: Citizens' Perspectives on Climate Change and Energy Use*. ULYSSES WP-99-1. Center for Interdisciplinary Studies in Technology, Darmstadt University of Technology, Darmstadt.

Kassler, P. (1994). *Energy for Development*. Shell Selected Paper, Shell International Petroleum Company, London.

Kates, R. W., W. C. Clark, R. Corell, J. M. Hall, C. C. Jaeger, I. Lowe, J. J. McCarthy, H. J. Schellnhuber, B. Bolin, N. M. Dickson, S. Faucheux, G. C. Gallopin, A. Gruebler, B. Huntley, J. Jäger, N. S. Jodha, R. E. Kasperson, A. Mabogunje, P. Matson, H. Mooney, B. Moore III, T. O'Riordan, and U. Svedin (2001). "Sustainability science," *Science* 292, pp. 641–642.

Kelly, M. (1994). *Critique and Power: Recasting the Foucault/Habermas Debate.* MIT Press, Cambridge, MA.

Kempton, W. (1991). "Lay perspectives on global climate change," *Global Environmental Change* 1(3), pp. 183–208.

(1997). "How the public views climate change," *Environment* November 1997, pp. 12–21.

Kempton, W., and P. P. Craig (1993). "European perspectives on global climate change," *Environment* 35(3), pp. 16–45.

Kitchener, D., and É. Darier (1998a). "ULYSSES St. Helens Citizens Panel – Process Description and Preliminary Observations" (unpublished report). Centre for the Study of Environmental Change, Lancaster University, Lancaster.

(1998b). "ULYSSES St. Helens Joint Citizens/Policy-makers Panel – Process Description and Preliminary Observation" (unpublished report). Centre for the Study of Environmental Change, Lancaster University, Lancaster.

Klabbers, J. H. G., C. Bernabo, M. Hisschemöller, and B. Moomaw (1996). "Climate change policy development: enhancing the science/policy dialogue" in F. Watts and A. Garcia Carbonell (eds.), *Simulation Now! Learning through Experience: The Challenge of Change.* Diputacio de Valencia, Valencia, pp. 285–297.

Klabbers, J. H. G., R. J. Swart, A. P. Van Ulden, and P. Vellinga (1995). "Climate policy: management of organized complexity through gaming," in D. Crookall and K. Arai (eds.). *Simulation and Gaming across Disciplines and Cultures: ISAGA at a Watershed.* Sage, Thousand Oaks, CA, pp. 122–133.

Kleindorfer, P. R., H. C. Kunreuther, and P. J. H. Schoemaker (1993). *Decision Sciences: An Integrative Perspective.* Cambridge University Press, Cambridge.

Knoepfel, I., J. E. Salt, A. Bode, and W. Jakobi (1999). *The Kyoto Protocol and Beyond: Potential Implications for the Insurance Industry.* UNEP Insurance Industry Initiative, Geneva.

Konyar, K. (2001). "Assessing the role of US agriculture in reducing greenhouse gas emissions and generating additional environmental benefits," *Ecological Economics* 38(1), pp. 85–103.

Koomey, J. G., C. A. Webber, C. S. Atkinson, and A. Nicholls (2001). "Addressing energy-related challenges for the US buildings sector: results from the clean energy futures study," *Energy Policy* 29(14), pp. 1209–1221.

Kreps, D. M. (1988). *Notes on the Theory of Choice.* Westview Press, Boulder, CO.

Kristeva, J. (1977). *Polylogue.* Seuil, Paris.

Krueger, R. A. (1988). *Focus Groups. A Practical Guide for Applied Research.* Sage, Newbury Park, CA.

Kuhn, T. S. (1962). *The Structure of Scientific Revolutions.* University of Chicago Press, Chicago, IL.

Kuper, R. (1997). "Deliberating waste: the Hertfordshire Citizens' Jury," *Local Environment* 2(2), pp. 139–153.

Lafferty, W. M., and J. Meadowcroft (1996). *Democracy and the Environment – Problems and Prospects*. Edward Elgar, Cheltenham.

Laird, F. N. (1993). "Participatory analysis, democracy and technological decision making," *Science, Technology and Human Values* 18(3), pp. 341–361.

Lakoff, G., and M. Johnson (1980). *Metaphors We Live By*. University of Chicago Press, Chicago, IL.

Langford, I. H., C. G. Bentham, and A. L. McDonald (1998). "Multi-level modelling and geography aggregated health data: a case study on malignant melanoma mortality and UV radiation in the European Community" *Statistics in Medicine* 70(1), pp. 41–58.

Lannoo, K. (1999). "A European perspective on corporate governance," *Journal of Common Market Studies* 37(2), pp. 269–294.

Lilienfeld, S. O., J. M. Wood, and H. N. Garb (2000). "The scientific status of projective techniques," *Psychological Science in the Public Interest* 1(2), pp. 27–66.

(2001). "What's wrong with this picture?" *Scientific American*, May, pp. 81–87.

Löfstedt, R. E. (1992). "Lay perspectives concerning global climate change in Sweden," *Energy and Environment* 3(2), pp. 161–175.

(1993). "Lay perspectives concerning global climate change in Austria," *Energy and Environment* 4, pp. 140–154.

Lorenzoni, I., A. Jordan, T. O'Riordan, R. K. Turner, M. Hulme (2000). "A co-evolutionary approach to climate change impact assessment – Part II: A scenario-based case study in East Anglia (UK)", *Global Environmental Change Part A*, 10 (2), pp. 145–155.

Luke, T. (1999). "Environmentality as green governmentality" in É. Darier (ed.), *Discourses of the Environment*. Blackwell, Oxford.

Lukes, S. (1978). *Power: A Radical View*. Macmillan, London.

Luks, F. (1999). "Post-normal science and the rhetoric of inquiry: deconstructing normal science?" *Futures* 31(7), pp. 705–719.

Macnaghten, P., R. Grove-White, M. Jacobs, and B. Wynne (1995). *Public Perceptions and Sustainability in Lancashire – Indicators, Institutions, Participation*. Lancashire County Council, Lancashire.

Magalhaes, A. R. (1998). "Planning for Sustainable Development in the Context of Global Change," *Global Environmental Change* 8(1), pp. 1–10.

Mason, R. O., and I. I. Mitroff (1981). *Challenging Strategic Planning Assumptions. Theory, Cases and Techniques*, Wiley, New York.

Mayer, I. (1997). "Debating technologies. A methodological contribution to the design and evaluation of participatory policy analysis," Tilburg University Press, Tilburg.

Mayer, I., and J. Geurts (1998). "De instrumentele mogelijkheden van de argumentatieve beleidsanalyse: participatieve methoden" in R. Hoppe and A. Peterse (eds.), *Bouwstenen voor argumentatieve beleidsanalyse*. Elsevier, The Hague, pp. 187–204.

Mazur, A. (1998). "Global environmental change in the news," *International Sociology* 13(4), pp. 457–472.

McGranahan, G., and Å. Gerger (1999). "Participation and environmental assessment in northern and southern cities, with examples from Stockholm and Jakarta," *International Journal of Environment and Pollution* 11(3), pp. 373–394.

McKibben, W. (1990.) *The End of Nature*. Viking Press, New York.

Meadows, D. H. (1985). *User's Manual for STRATEGEM-1. A Microcomputer Based Management Training Game on Energy-Environment Interactions*. Resource Policy Center, Hanover, NH.

Meadows, D. H., D. L. Meadows, J. Randers, and W.W. Behrens (1972). *The Limits to Growth*. Universe Books, New York.

Mermet, L. (1992). "Policy exercises on global environmental problems," in D. Crookall and K. Arai (eds.), *Global Interdependence: Simulation and Gaming Perspectives*. Springer Verlag, Tokyo, pp. 216–222.

Merton, R. K. (1987). "The focussed interview and focus groups: continuities and discontinuities," *Public Opinion Quarterly* 51(4), pp. 550–566.

Merton, R. K., and P. L. Kendall (1946). "The focused interview," *American Journal of Sociology* 51, pp. 541–557.

Misztal, B. A. (1996). *Trust in Modern Society*. Polity Press, Cambridge.

Morgan, G. M., and H. Dowlatabadi (1996). "Learning from Integrated Assessment of climatic change," *Climatic Change* 34(3–4), pp. 337–368.

Morgan, D. L., and R. A. Krueger (1998a). *The Focus Group Kit (Volume 1–6)*. Sage, London.

(1998b). *The Focus Group Kit: Developing Questions for Focus Groups*. Sage, Thousand Oaks, CA.

(1998c). *The Focus Group Kit: Involving Community Members in Focus Groups*. Sage, Thousand Oaks, CA.

(1998d). *The Focus Group Kit: The Focus Group Guidebook*. Sage, Thousand Oaks, CA.

Morgan, M. G., T. Smuts, H. Dowlatabadi, B. Fischhoff, L. Lave, and E. Rubin (1994). *Brochure: Global Warming and Climate Change*. Carnegie Mellon University, Pittsburgh, PA.

Moss, R. H. (1995). "Avoiding 'dangerous' interference in the climate system. The roles of values, science and policy," *Global Environmental Change* 5(1), pp. 3–6.

Murray, G. C. (1998). "A policy response to regional disparities in the supply of risk capital to new technology-based firms in the European Union: the European Seed Capital Fund Scheme," *Regional Studies* 32(5), pp. 405–419.

National Research Council, Board on Sustainable Development, Policy Division (ed.) (1999). *Our Common Journey: A Transition Toward Sustainability*. National Academic Press, Washington, DC.

Nilsson, M. (1997). *Work Package: Using PoleStar in ULYSSES*. Stockholm Environment Institute, Stockholm.

(1998). *Computer Tool Experiences in ULYSSES*. Stockholm Environment Institute, Stockholm.

Nordhaus, W. D. (1994). "Expert opinion on climatic change," *American Scientist* 82 (January–February), pp. 45–51.

O'Connor, M. (1999). "Dialogue and debate in a post-normal practice of science," *Futures* 31, pp. 671–687.

OECD (1997). *The World in 2020. Towards a New Global Age*. OECD, Paris.

O'Riordan, T. (ed.) (1997). *Ecotaxation*. Earthscan Publications, London.

  (2000). *Globalism, Localism and Identity: Fresh Perspectives on the Sustainability Transition in Europe*. Earthscan Publications, London.

O'Riordan, T., and J. Jäger (1996). "Beyond climate change science and politics," in T. O'Riordan and J. Jäger (eds.), *Politics of Climate Change. A European Perspective*. Routledge, London and New York, pp. 346–360.

O'Riordan, T., and A. Jordan (1999). "Institutions, climate change and cultural theory: Towards a common analytical framework," *Global Environmental Change* 9(2), pp. 81–93.

Osborne, M. J., and A. Rubinstein (1994). *A Course in Game Theory*. MIT Press, Cambridge, MA.

Pahl-Wostl, C., C. C. Jaeger, S. Rayner, C. Schaer, M. B. A. van Asselt, D. Imboden, and A. Vckovski (1998). "Regional Integrated Assessment of climate change and the problem of indeterminacy," in P. Cebon, H. C. Davies, D. M. Imboden, and C. C. Jaeger (eds.), *Views from the Alps. Towards Regional Assessments of Climate Change*. MIT Press, Cambridge, MA, pp. 435–497.

Pahl-Wostl, C., C. Schlumpf, A. Schönborn, M. Büssenschütt, and J. Burse (2000). "Models at the interface between science and society: Impacts and Options," *Integrated Assessment* 1, pp. 267–280.

Palerm, J. R. (2000). "An empirical-theoretical analysis framework for public participation in environmental impact assessment," *Journal of Environmental Planning and Management* 43(5), pp. 581–600.

Parson, E. A. (1995). "Integrated assessment and environmental policy-making – in pursuit of usefulness," *Energy Policy* 23(4–5), pp. 463–475.

  (1996). *A Global Climate Change Policy Exercise: Result of a Test Run, July 27–29, 1995*. WP-96-90, Working paper. International Institute for Applied Systems Analysis (IIASA), Laxenburg, Austria.

  (1997). "Informing global environmental policy making: a plea for new methods of assessment and synthesis," *Environmental Modeling and Assessment* 2, pp. 267–279.

Parson, T. (1937). *The Structure of Social Action*. McGraw-Hill, New York.

Pearce, D. (1995). "Joint implementation: a general overview," in C. J. Jepma (ed.), *The Feasibility of Joint Implementation*. Kluwer, Dordrecht, pp. 15–31.

Pedregal Mateos, B. (1999). *Adaptive Responses to Hydrological Risk: A Demographic Perspective*. University of Seville, Seville.

Pendergraft, C. A. (1998). "Human Dimensions of Climate Change: Cultural Theory and Collective Action," *Climatic Change* 39, pp. 643–666.

Perhac Jr., R. M. (1998). "Comparative risk assessment: where does the public fit in?" *Science, Technology & Human Values* 23(2), pp. 221–241.

Pierre, J., and G. Stoker (2000). "The restructuring of British polity: towards multi-level governance," in P. Dunleavy (ed.). *Developments in British Politics*. Macmillan, Basingstoke, pp. 29–46.

Proctor, J. D. (1998). "The meaning of global environmental change: retheorizing culture in human dimensions research," *Global Environmental Change* 8(3), pp. 227–248.

Puchala, D. J. (1999). "Institutionalism, intergovernmentalism and European integration: a review article," *Journal of Common Market Studies* 37(2), pp. 317–331.

Querol, C., Å. Gerger, B. Kasemir, and D. Tàbara (1999). *Citizens' Recommendations for Addressing Climate Change. A Participatory Integrated Assessment Exercise in Europe.* ULYSSES WP-99-4. Center for Interdisciplinary Studies in Technology, Darmstadt University of Technology, Darmstadt.

Raskin, P., C. Heaps, J. Sieber, and G. Pontius (1996). *Polestar System Manual.* Stockholm Environment Institute, Stockholm.

Ravetz, J. R. (1971). *Scientific Knowledge and its Social Problems.* Oxford University Press, Oxford.

(1994/5). "Economics as an elite folk-science: the suppression of uncertainty," *The Journal of Post-Keynesian Economics* 17(2), pp. 165–184.

(1997a). *Integrated Environmental Assessment Forum: Developing Guidelines for 'Good Practice'.* ULYSSES WP-97-1. Center for Interdisciplinary Studies in Technology, Darmstadt University of Technology, Darmstadt.

(1997b). "A leap into the unknown," *The Times Higher,* 28 May. London.

(1999). "Developing principles of good practice in Integrated Environmental Assessment," *International Journal of Environment and Pollution* 11(3), pp. 1–23.

Rayner, S. (1984). "Disagreeing about risk: the institutional cultures of risk management and planning for future generations," in S. G. Hadden (ed.), *Risk Analysis, Institution and Public Policy.* Associated Faculty Press, Port Washington, WI, pp. 150–168.

(1991). "A cultural perspective on the structure and implementation of global environmental agreements," *Evaluation Review* 15(1), pp. 75–102.

(1992). "Cultural theory and risk analysis," in S. Krimsky and D. Golding (eds.). *Social Theories of Risk,* Praeger Publishers, Westport, CT, pp. 83–115.

Read, D., A. Bostrom, G. M. Morgan, B. Fischhoff, and T. Smuts (1994). "What do people know about global climate change? Part 2: Survey Studies of Educated Laypeople," *Risk Analysis* 14(6), pp. 971–982.

Renn, O., T. Webler, and P. Wiedemann (eds.) (1995). *Fairness and Competence in Citizen Participation – Evaluating Models for Environmental Discourse.* Kluwer Academic Publishers, London.

Riesco Chueca, P. (1999). *The Challenge of Climate Change for Water Technologies: An Institutional Perspective.* Institute for Prospective Technological Studies, Seville.

Risbey, J., M. Kandlikar, and A. Patwardhan (1996). "Assessing Integrated Assessments," *Climatic Change* 34(3–4), pp. 369–395.

RIVM (2000). *Baby-LOV (Leef Omgevings verkenner (English: "Environment Explorer")),* RIVM, Maastricht.

Rosa, E. A. (1999). "The quest to understand society and nature: looking back, but mostly forward," *Society and Natural Resources* 12, pp. 371–376.

Rosa, E. A., and T. Dietz (1998). "Climate change and society. Speculation, construction and scientific investigation," *International Sociology* 13, pp. 421–455.

Rosen, R. (1977). "Complexity as a system property," *International Journal of General Systems* 3, pp. 227–232.

Rosenau, J. N. (1992). "Governance, order and change in world politics," in J. N. Rosenau and E.-O. Czenpiel (eds.). *Governance without Government: Order and Change in World Politics.* Cambridge University Press, Cambridge, pp. 1–30.

Rothman, D. S., and J. B. Robinson (1997). "Growing pains: a conceptual framework for considering Integrated Assessment," *Environmental Monitoring and Assessment* 46(1/2), pp. 23–43.

Rotmans, J. (1990). *IMAGE: An Integrated Model to Assess the Greenhouse Effect.* Kluwer, Dordrecht.

(1998). "Methods for IA: the challenges and opportunities ahead," *Environmental Modelling & Assessment* 3, pp. 155–180.

Rotmans, J., and B. de Vries (eds.) (1997). *Perspectives on Global Change: The TARGETS Approach.* Cambridge University Press, Cambridge.

Rotmans, J., and M. B. A. van Asselt (1996). "Integrated Assessment: a growing child on its way to maturity. An editorial essay," *Climatic Change* 34(3–4), pp. 327–336.

(1999). "Perspectives on a sustainable future," *International Journal of Sustainable Development* 2(2), pp. 201–230.

(2002). "Integrated Assessment: current practices and challenges for the future," in H. Abaza and A. Baranzini (eds.), *Implementing Sustainable Development: Integrated Assessment and Participatory Decision-Making Processes.* Edward Elgar, Cheltenham (in press).

Rotmans, J., M. B. A. van Asselt, C. Anastasi, S. Greeuw, J. Mellors, S. Peteres, D. Rothman, and N. Rijkens (2000). "Visions for a sustainable Europe," *Futures* 32, pp. 809–831.

Rotmans, J., M. B. A. van Asselt, C. Anastasi, D. Rothman, S. Greeuw, and C. van Bers (2001). "Integrated visions for a sustainable Europe: VISIONS Final Report." ICIS, Maastricht University, the Netherlands.

Rotmans, J., et al. (1994). *Global Change and Sustainable Development: A Modelling Perspective for the Next Decade.* RIVM, Bilthoven.

Rutherford, P. (1999). "The entry of life into history," in É. Darier (ed.), *Discourses of the Environment.* Blackwell, Oxford, pp. 37–62.

Schellnhuber, H.-J., and V. Wenzel (1998). *Earth System Analysis: Integrating Science for Sustainability.* Springer Verlag, New York.

Schlumpf, C., J. Behringer, G. Dürrenberger, and C. Pahl-Wostl (1999). "The personal CO_2 calculator: a modeling tool for participatory Integrated Assessment methods," *Environmental Modeling and Assessment* 4, pp. 1–12.

Schlumpf, C., C. Pahl-Wostl, A. Schönborn, C. C. Jaeger, and D. M. Imboden (forthcoming). "IMPACTS: an information tool for citizens to assess climate change from a regional perspective."

Schmidheiny, S., and F. Zorraquín (1996). *Financing Change.* MIT Press, Cambridge, MA.

Schneider, S. H. (1997). "Integrated assessment modeling of global climate change: transparent rational tool for policy making or opaque screen hiding value-laden assumptions?" *Environmental Modeling and Assessment* 2(4), pp. 229–249.

Schneider, S. H., and L. H. Goulder (1997). "Achieving low-cost emissions targets," *Nature* 389, pp. 13–14.

Schüle, R. (2001). *Public Perceptions of Global Climate Change – A Case Study from the Frankfurt Area.* Peter Lang, Frankfurt.

Schüle, R., Y. Haffner, and A. Jordan (1998). *The Presentation of IA-Models in Focus Groups: Draft Report.* Technical University Darmstadt, Darmstadt.

Schwarz, M., and M. Thompson (1990). *Divided We Stand: Redefining Politics, Technology and Social Choice.* Harvester Wheatsheaf, New York.

Selman, P., and J. Parker (1997). "Citizenship, civicness and social capital in Local Agenda 21," *Local Environment* 2(2), pp. 171–184.

Senge, P. (1990). *The Fifth Discipline: The Art and Practice of the Learning Organization.* Doubleday, New York.

Shackley, S., and É. Darier (1998). "Seduction of the sirens: global climate change and modelling," *Science and Public Policy* 25(5), pp. 313–325.

Shackley, S., and T. Skodvin (1995). "IPCC Gazing and the interpretative social science. A comment on Sonja Boehmer-Christiansen's 'Global climate protection policy: the limits of scientific advice'," *Global Environmental Change* 5(3), pp. 175–180.

Shackley, S., and B. Wynne (1995). "Integrating knowledges for climate change. Pyramids, nets and uncertainties," *Global Environmental Change* 5(2), pp. 113–126.

Shackley, S., É. Darier, and B. Wynne (1999). "Towards a 'Folk Integrated Assessment' of climate change?" *International Journal of Environment and Pollution* 11(3), pp. 351–372.

Shackley, S., J. Risbey, and M. Kandlikar (1998). "Science and the contested problem of climate change: a tale of two models," *Energy and Environment* 9(1), pp. 61–82.

Shackley, S., B. Wynne, and C. Waterton (1996). "Imagine complexity: the past, present and future potential of complex thinking," *Futures* 28(3), pp. 201–255.

Smelser, N. J. (1998). "The rational and the ambivalent in the Social Science," *American Sociological Review* 63, pp. 1–16.

Social Learning Group (ed.) (2001). *Learning to Manage Global Environmental Risks, vol. 1: A Comparative History of Social Responses to Climate Change, Ozone Depletion and Acid Rain.* MIT Press, Cambridge, MA.

Stern, P. C. (1993). "A second environmental science: human–environment interactions," *Science* 260, pp. 1897–1899.

Stern, P. C., O. R. Young, and D. Druckman (1992). *Global Environmental Change. Understanding the Human Dimensions.* National Academy Press, Washington, DC.

Stewart, D. W., and P. N. Shamdasani (1990). *Focus Groups: Theory and Practice.* Sage, Newbury Park, CA.

Stockholm Environment Institute (1993). *Towards a Fossil Fuel Energy Future: The Next Transition. A Technical Analysis for Greenpeace International.* Greenpeace International.

Stocks, J. (1998). *Citizen Discussions of Computer Models in Global Climate Change Focus Groups.* Working Paper. Carnegie Mellon University, Pittsburgh, PA.

Stoll-Kleemann, S., T. O'Riordan, and C. C. Jaeger (2001). "The psychology of denial concerning climate mitigation measures: evidence from Swiss focus groups," *Global Environmental Change* 11 (2), pp. 107–117.

Susskind, L., and P. Field (1996). *Dealing with an Angry Public: The Mutual Gains Approach to Resolving Disputes.* The Free Press, New York.

Tàbara, D. (1998)."Citizen Participation and Equity in Global Environmental Change: The IA-Focus Group Process". Paper presented to the fourth session on Lifestyles and Environment-Participation and Equity, "Lifestyles, Participation and Environment, Brussels, 16–17 March. European Commission.

Tarnas, R. (1993). *The Passion of the Western Mind: Understanding the Ideas that Have Shaped Our World View.* Ballantine Books, New York.

Thompson, M. (1998). "Three Visions of the Future". Paper presented at the kick-off workshop of the VISION project, 6–7 May, Maastricht.

Thompson, M., R. Ellis, and A. Wildavsky (1990). *Cultural Theory.* Westview Press, Boulder, CO.

Thompson, M., and S. Rayner (1998). "Cultural discourses," in S. Rayner and E.L. Malone (eds.), *Human Choice and Climate Change: The Societal Framework.* Battelle Press, Columbus, OH, pp. 265–343.

Tol, R. S. J., N. van der Grijp, A. Olsthoorn, and P. van der Werff (1999). *Adapting to Climate Change: A Case Study of Riverine Flood Risks in the Netherlands.* Institute for Environmental Studies, Free University of Amsterdam.

Tol, R. S. J., and P. Vellinga (1998). "The European Forum on Integrated Environmental Assessment," *Environmental Modeling and Assessment* 3, pp. 181–191.

Toth, F., and E. Hizsnyik (1998). "Integrated Environmental Assessment methods: evolution and applications," *Environmental Modeling and Assessment* 3(3), pp. 193–207.

Toth, F., B. Kasemir, and V. Masing (1998). *Climate Policy as a Business Opportunity for Venture Capital in Europe.* ULYSSES WP-98-2. Center for Interdisciplinary Studies in Technology, Darmstadt University of Technology, Darmstadt.

Toth, F. L. (1986). *Practicing the Future: Implementing "The Policy Exercise Concept."* WP-86-23, May. International Institute for Applied Systems Analysis.

    (1988a). "Policy exercises: objectives and design elements," *Simulation & Gaming* 19(3), pp. 235–255.

    (1988b). "Policy exercises: procedures and implementation," *Simulation & Gaming* 19(3), pp. 256–276.

    (1995). "Simulation/gaming for long-term policy problems," in D. Crookall and K. Arai (eds.), *Simulation and Gaming across Disciplines and Cultures: ISAGA at a Watershed.* SAGE Publications, Thousand Oaks, CA, pp. 134–142.

Tucker, M. (1997). "Climate change and the insurance industry: the cost of increased risk and the impetus for action," *Ecological Economics* 22, pp. 85–96.

Tuxworth, B. (1996). "From environment to sustainability: surveys and analysis of Local Agenda 21 process development in UK local authorities," *Local Environment* 1(3), pp. 277–297.

UNDP (1997). *Synergies in National Implementation: The Rio Agreements.* Sustainable Energy and Environment Division, United Nations Development Programme, Geneva.

Union of International Associations (ed.) (2001). *Yearbook of International Organizations 2001/2002*. K. G. Saur Verlag, Munich.

UNEP (1997). "GEO 2 Regional Meeting of Collaborating Centers from Latin America and the Caribbean, Mexico City, Mexico, 6–9 May 1997." UNEP/DEIA.MR/97.01, UNEP, Nairobi.

UNEP, US NASA and The World Bank (1998). *Protecting Our Planet – Securing Our Future. Linkages Among Global Environmental Issues and Human Needs.* United Nations Environment Program, US National Aeronautics and Space Administration.

UNITAR, and Consortium for North–South Dialogue on Climate Change (2001). *Who Needs What to implement the Kyoto Protocol? An Assessment of Capacity Building Needs in 33 Developing Countries* Report, Geneva.

UNU, GEIC, and IAS (1998). *Global Climate Governance: Interlinkages between the Kyoto Protocol and other Multilateral Regimes.* United Nations University (UNU), UNU Institute of Advanced Studies (UNU/IAS), and the Global Environment Information Centre (GEIC). Global Environment Information Centre,Tokyo.

UNU, MOFA Japan, MOE Japan, and GLOBE (2001). *Inter-linkages: Strategies for Bridging Problems and Solutions to Work Towards Sustainable Development.* World Summit for Sustainable Development International Eminent Persons Meeting, 3–4 September, United Nations University Centre, Tokyo, Japan (2001). United Nations University, Tokyo.

van Asselt, M. B. A. (2000). *Perspectives on Uncertainty and Risk: The PRIMA Approach to Decision Support.* Kluwer Academic Publishers, Dordrecht.

van Asselt, M. B. A., A. H. W. Beusen, and H. B. M. Hilderink (1996). "Uncertainty in Integrated Assessment: a social scientific approach," *Environmental Modeling and Assessment* 1(1,2), pp. 71–90.

van Asselt, M. B. A., and S. C. H. Greeuw (1999). "VISIONS for the Green Heart," Interim Report. ICIS, Maastricht University, The Netherlands.

van Asselt, M. B. A., and N. Rijkens-Klomp (2002), "A look in the mirror: reflection on participation in Integrated Assessment from a methodological perspective." *Global Environmental Change* 12(3), pp. 167–184.

van Asselt, M. B. A., and J. Rotmans (1996). "Uncertainty in perspective," *Global Environmental Change* 6(2), pp. 121–157.

(1997). "Uncertainties in perspective," in J. Rotmans and B. de Vries (eds.), *Perspectives on Global Change: The TARGETS Approach.* Cambridge University Press, Cambridge, pp. 105–222.

van Asselt, M. B. A., and J. Rotmans (2002). "Uncertainty in integrated assessment modelling: from positivism to pluralism," *Climatic Change* 54, pp. 75–105.

van der Sluijs, J., and J. Jäger (1998). "Towards a Typology for Computer Tools for Participatory Integrated Assessment." Working Paper. University of Utrecht, Utrecht.

van 't Klooster, S. A., M. B. A. van Asselt, and S. P. Koenis (2002). "Beyond the essential contestation: construction and deconstruction of regional identity." *Ethics, Place and Environment* 5(5), in press.

Viguier, L. (2001). "Fair trade and harmonization of climate change policies in Europe," *Energy Policy* 29(10), pp. 749–753.

Voisey, H., C. Beuermann, A. L. Sverdrup, and T. O'Riordan (1996). "The political significance of Local Agenda 21: the early stages of some European experience," *Local Environment* 1(1), pp. 33–50.

von Weizsäcker, E., A. B. Lovins, and H. L. Lovins (1997). *Factor Four: Doubling Wealth – Halving Resource Use: The New Report to the Club of Rome*. Earthscan, London.

Webb, J. W., and L. L. Sigal (1996). "SEA of an environmental restoration and waste management program, United States," in R. Thérivel and M. R. Partidario (eds.), *The Practice of Strategic Environmental Assessment*. Earthscan, London, pp. 62–72.

Webler, T., and O. Renn (1995). "A brief primer on participation: philosophy and practice," in O. Renn, T. Webler, and P. Wiedemann (eds.), *Fairness and Competence in Citizen Participation – Evaluating Models for Environmental Discourse*. Kluwer Academic Publishers, London.

Welford, R. (2000). "Deep change or slow death: what future for business?," in R. Welford, (ed.), *Corporate Environmental Management 3: Towards Sustainable Development*. Earthscan, London, pp. 148–173.

Welsch, H. (1996). "Recycling of carbon/energy taxes and the labor market." *Environmental and Resource Economics* 8, pp. 141–155.

Wenzler, R. W., and A. M. van't Noordende (1995). "A policy exercise for the Dutch power industry," in D. Crookall and K. Arai (eds.), *Simulation and Gaming across Disciplines and Cultures: ISAGA at a Watershed*. Sage, Thousand Oaks, CA, pp. 143–150.

Weyant, J., O. Davidson, H. Dowlatabadi, J. Edmonds, M. Grubb, E. A. Parson, R. Richels, J. Rotmans, P. R. Shukla, R. S. J. Tol, W. Cline, and S. Fankhauser (1996). "Integrated Assessment of climate change: an overview and comparison of approaches and results," in J. Bruce, H. Lee, and E. Haites (eds.), *Economic and Social Dimensions of Climate Change: Contribution of Working Group III to the Second Assessment Report of the Intergovernmental Panel on Climate Change*. Cambridge University Press, Cambridge, pp. 367–396.

Wigley, T. M. L., R. Richels, and J. A. Edmonds (1996). "Economic and environmental choices in the stabilization of atmospheric CO_2 concentrations," *Nature* 379, pp. 240–243.

Wilbanks, T. J., and R. W. Kates (1999). "Global change in local places: how scale matters," *Climatic Change* 43, pp. 601–628.

Wittgenstein, L. (1958). *Philosophical Investigations*. Basil Blackwell, Oxford.

World Energy Council (1993). *Energy for Tomorrow's World*. St. Martin's Press, New York.

Wynne, B. (1984). "The institutional context of science, models, and policy: the IIASA Energy Study," *Policy Sciences* 17(3), pp. 277–319.

   (1992a). "Risk and social learning: reification to engagement," in S. Krimsky and D. Golding (eds.), *Social Theories of Risk*. Praeger Publishers, Westport, CT, pp. 275–297.

   (1992b). "Uncertainty and environmental learning. Reconceiving science and policy in the preventive paradigm," *Global Environmental Change* 2, pp. 111–127.

(1995). "Public understanding of science," in S. Jasanoff, G. Markle, J. Petersen, and T. Pinch (eds.), *Handbook of Science and Technology Studies*. Sage, Thousand Oaks, CA, pp. 361–388.

Yin, Y., and S. J. Cohen (1994). "Identifiying regional goals and policy concerns associated with global climate change," *Global Environmental Change* 4(3), pp. 246–260.

Young, S. C. (1996). *Promoting Participation and Community-Based Partnerships in the Context of Local Agenda 21: A Report for Practitioners*. Government Department and Manchester University, Manchester.

(1997). "Local Agenda 21: the renewal of local democracy?" in M. Jacobs (ed.), *Greening the Millennium? The New Politics of the Environment*. Blackwell, Oxford, pp. 138–147.

Zacharakis, A. L., and G. D. Meyer (1998). "A lack of insight: do venture capitalists really understand their own decision process?" *Journal of Business Venturing* 13, pp. 57–76.

Index